29.95

STOCK
INDEX
FUTURES

STOCK

INDEX

FUTURES

Buying and Selling the Market Averages

Allan M. Loosigian

Addison-Wesley Publishing Company, Inc.

Reading, Massachusetts · Menlo Park, California · Don Mills, Ontario
Wokingham, England · Amsterdam · Sydney · Singapore · Tokyo
Mexico City · Bogotá · Santiago · San Juan

Library of Congress Cataloging in Publication Data

Loosigian, Allan M., 1938–
  Stock index futures.

  Includes index.
  1. Stock index futures. I. Title.
  HG6043.L665   1985   332.63'222   84-24473
  ISBN 0-201-10267-6

Cover design by Mike Fender
Text Design by Kenneth J. Wilson
Set in 10 point Optima by Compset, Inc.

ISBN 0-201-10267-6

ABCDEFGHIJ-AL-898765

First printing, July 1985

CONTENTS

FOREWORD

In his two previous books—*Interest Rate Futures* and then *Foreign Exchange Futures*—Allan M. Loosigian delineated the practical applications of those novel financial instruments. Now, he has turned his attention to yet another investment innovation.

Since their debut, stock index futures have been promoted in a somewhat ambivalent fashion. They have been billed by their sponsors as "exciting," and the markets' early participants have indeed fomented much excitement. At the same time, the exchanges have emphasized in their educational literature the role of stock index futures in reducing market risk in common stock portfolios as well as their usefulness in improving investment performance.

As has been the case with listed stock options, the development of proven risk-reducing and other strategies involving stock index futures—and the acceptance of such strategies by conservative investors—may require an extended period of time. Meanwhile, even conservative entrants may exploit the price disparities that typically occur during the early stages of a new market.

Regardless of one's risk tolerance—whether disposed toward "exciting" speculation or hewing to "conservative" investing—there is a place in the financial arena for stock index futures. Allan Loosigian provides worthwhile instruction and guidance for their use in either direction. Traders and investors alike will profit from this book.

RICHARD N. STILLMAN
Managing Partner
Stillman Partners

INTRODUCTION

When I set forth from the family homestead to carve out a career for myself on Wall Street a number of years ago, my grandfather cautioned me to avoid two pitfalls: drinking during market hours and speculation.

Though I cheerfully confess to a few happy transgressions, I've never had much trouble heeding Granddad's first bit of advice. But speculation—well, that's another story. In fact, after some twenty-odd years in and around the stock exchange, I've yet to hear a satisfactory definition of *speculation*. Where does "investing" leave off and "playing the market" begin? I may eventually find the answer, but I'm not counting on it. Like beauty, it probably lies in the eye of the beholder.

Prudence and patience are not necessarily rewarded in the stock market. Sticking with the tried and true blue chips does not guarantee you a profit. Even those issues universally regarded as the soundest are vulnerable in a general sell-off. On the other hand, blatant and uninformed speculation—what traders unceremoniously refer to as "crapshooting"—may pay off often enough to keep alive the dream of quick and easy gains.

If he or she endures for any length of time, a stock trader learns that the imponderables of the market—expectations, sentiment, confidence, call them what you will—are just as decisive in determining the outcome of an investment as are such finite variables as earnings per share, price-earnings ratios, and dividend rates. Indeed, these imponderables provoke much of the continuing fascination with the stock market and cause entire libraries to be filled with books about how to "beat" it.

Now we have stock index futures, which my grandfather would no doubt have considered more reprehensible than imbibing during business hours, and yet another book. This one, I hasten to add, does not aspire to explain how to beat anything. It will have served its purpose if it explains to the reader's satisfaction what stock index futures are, how they work, and some of the uses to which they might be put by investors and traders.

This book is divided into three parts. Part 1 is chiefly narrative in nature. The first two chapters trace the development of common stock indexes since 1884, when Charles Dow published his list of eleven representative stocks that evolved into today's Dow Jones Averages, the formation of the commodity futures markets in the United States, and the recent introduction of stock index futures trading on commodity exchanges in Chicago, New York and Kansas City. Chapter 3 explains the procedures and arithmetic of index futures trading.

Part 2 takes an analytical approach in appraising the principal forces that influence stock prices in the aggregate and consequently determine the behavior of stock index futures prices. Chapter 4 investigates the numerical relationships among the various indexes and their related futures contracts and the effect of these relationships on futures trading. The so-called "macroeconomic" factors that are reflective of the overall economy are considered in chapter 5, while chapter 6 deals with the "microeconomic" elements affecting various industry groups and individual companies. Chapter 7 examines the consequences of government policies and measures, particularly those in the monetary and fiscal spheres. Insofar as they can be identified, the effects of prevailing market psychology—those imponderables mentioned above—are treated in chapter 8.

The third and final part of the book, headed "The Professionals," is devoted to the actual use of stock index futures by individuals and institutions. Chapter 9 views the market from the perspectives of an exchange floor trader and an equity portfolio manager. Chapter 10 describes various trading and investment techniques involving index futures and options employed by a second professional manager and relates the protracted and sometimes frustrating course encountered by the officials of one exchange in introducing a stock index futures contract.

Stock index futures are still in their infancy. Only time and experience will establish their proper place and role in the investment/trading nexus. Their detractors allege that a futures contract on what is after all merely a statistic is little more than a lottery ticket and can only serve to incite the dubious speculation Granddad deplored. Their proponents claim that stock index futures are legitimate portfolio management tools that afford investors an added means of securing protection and profitability.

Like the blurring of investment and speculation that has distracted me since my arrival on Wall Street, I suspect that stock index futures contain an element of both, and that they will do different things for different people—which is as it should be. In any case, one bit of Wall Street lore that is beyond dispute is that it's a good idea to look before you leap. This book aims to afford stock market denizens of every stripe—as well as their opposite numbers in the commodity futures markets—an opportunity to do precisely that.

PART 1

History and Evolution of Stock Indexes and Futures

CHAPTER 1

Leading Stock Market Indexes

Walk into a stockbroker's office—though some such offices prefer to be known as financial services companies these days—and its identifying features are immediately apparent. Rows of customer representatives sit at their desks with telephone receivers affixed to their ears while their eyes follow the green illuminated figures that glide across the electronic stock ticker. If the office happens to be at street level, there will likely be a sign in the front window that announces what may, to some passersby, be a cryptic message:

DJIA
+3.57

But most people, whether they are themselves investors or not, know that the letters stand for the Dow Jones Industrial Average and that the trend of stock prices is momentarily up.

The telephone, ticker, and market averages are the principal tools of the stockbroker's trade, the medium and message with which they display their wares to the buying and selling public. It is probably not a coincidence that all three originated during the same decade a century ago.

The Stock Exchange Grows

Wall Street and the New York Stock Exchange trace their common history as the country's premier securities market back to 1792, when the stock and bond dealers who congregated there formed what amounted to a cartel by agreeing to adhere to a compulsory and uniform schedule of brokerage fees.

The exchange itself was not formally organized until 1817, and its volume of trading did not reach 1,000 shares a day until the railroad boom of the 1830s. The *New York Evening Post* in 1835 listed stock prices for 22 New York City banks; 14 banks outside New York; 21 railroads; 32 insurance companies; and 7 gas, coal, or canal companies.[1] There were at that time no manufacturing, or industrial, shares listed. Within forty years, the list had expanded to 163 stock and 334 bond issues, the railroads by then having supplanted the banks as the most numerous and actively traded group of securities.

The speculative fever among New York City residents incited by the Civil War prompted the establishment of more than two dozen self-styled stock exchanges throughout Lower Manhattan. Trading at some of these exchanges continued through the night, while at least one of them shifted its locale daily, much like a floating crap game. The New York Stock Exchange remained the preeminent stock trading institution in the city, however, and by 1880 had prevailed upon the municipal government to suppress the majority of what it alleged were nothing more than gambling dens. If there was to be any gambling in securities, the governors of the exchange may have reasoned, it had damned well better be done on their premises and to their profit.

The building that housed the exchange, situated then as now at the corner of Broad and Wall streets, was a splendid edifice designed by the architect who was later responsible for St. Patrick's Cathedral. To be an exchange member in those years was to be counted among the social as well as the commercial elite of New York. In 1882 there were eleven hundred exchange members. Those members who had purchased their seats five years earlier for forty-five hundred dollars were gratified to observe new applicants paying nearly eight times that amount for the privilege of membership. Business was booming, and the New York Stock Exchange was the place to be in business.[2]

The Advent of Stock Tickers

The introduction of the stock ticker and the western thrust of railroad expansion, with its attendant flotation of new railroad securities, were the principal causes of booming times on the stock exchange.

Although Samuel Morse had invented the telegraph in 1832 and the Western Union Company was established before the Civil War, the new technology did not immediately create much in the way of new business for New York City brokers. Out-of-town investors needed price information on which to make a decision to buy or sell a stock, and if there happened to be a local exchange nearby, they might not go to the trouble and expense of sending a wire to New York. Well aware of this constraint, Western Union and the other telegraph companies worked to develop a "continuous telegraph" that could print current stock prices throughout the country.

Independently, a vice-president of the New York Gold Exchange produced a device for printing gold quotations, and by 1867 fifty such tickers were installed throughout New York City. In the same year, E.A. Calahan of the American Telegraph Company improved upon the gold ticker so that it could print quotations on a number of stocks as well. Calahan eventually organized the Gold and Stock Telegraph Company and began installing his machine in New York brokerage offices for a fee of twenty-five dollars a month. He then formed an alliance with Western Union to extend his operation farther afield and in the process purchased for forty thousand dollars the rights to Thomas Edison's superior design.

While welcoming the increased business that the telegraphic ticker brought to it from the hinterland, the New York Stock Exchange nevertheless viewed these developments with some disquiet. Western Union and Gold and Stock Telegraph were transmitting what the exchange believed was proprietary information without paying it a fee. What could over time prove to be more harmful was the possibility, so long as the new ticker technology remained outside its control, that the private operators would sell price information to nonexchange members, who might use it to undercut New York's prices and commission rates.

By threatening to eject the Western Union operators from the trading floor and organize its own telegraph company, the stock exchange in 1885 coerced the private companies into paying it a franchise fee and accepting its supervision in the dissemination of price quotations. Still not satisfied, the exchange carried out its threat five years later by organizing the New York Telegraph Company and compelling Western Union to agree, as the price of retaining its franchise, to install tickers only in members' brokerage offices and in other locations approved by the exchange.

During the years that the New York Stock Exchange was exercising its political clout to suppress or absorb rival markets and tightening its control over access to the stock ticker, telephones were introduced to Wall Street. The first phone lines were installed at the exchange in 1878 and went hand in glove with the ticker in facilitating the transmission of orders to buy and sell securities listed there. By the close of the 1880s, most urban areas throughout the country had at least local service. It would require several more decades, however, and the completion of AT&T's long-distance lines for this new technology to match the importance of the ticker in fostering the public's participation in the securities markets and in channeling this participation onto the New York Stock Exchange floor.

Dow and Jones Come to Town

Directly adjacent to the scene of this commercial and technological ferment, the third element was taking form. In November 1882 two newspapermen from Providence, Rhode Island, Charles H. Dow and Edward D. Jones, rented office space at 15 Wall Street, a ramshackle building next to the stock exchange. From a small, second-floor room down the hall from a soda fountain, the newly established Dow Jones & Company hand-delivered news bulletins to its subscribers in the financial district.[3]

Charles Dow served his newspaper apprenticeship at the *Springfield* (Mass.) *Daily Republican* and pursued his career at the *Providence Journal,* where he wrote articles on such topics as the development of steamboat navigation between Boston and New York and a history of Newport, Rhode Island, from its exploration by Leif Ericson in the tenth century. In the summer of 1879, Dow traveled to Leadville, Colorado, where he reported on the "frenzied finance" and other goings-on in that mining boomtown and hobnobbed with overnight silver tycoons and eastern financiers out for their share of the riches. Following the Leadville interlude, Dow moved to New York City, where he spent the rest of his life on, and writing about, Wall Street.[4]

In New York, Dow worked as a reporter for the Kiernan News Agency, an organization that prepared and delivered by messenger to subscribing banks and brokerage firms styloed or hand-impressed tissue sheets that contained London stock quotations, railroad and bank earnings, and other financial news. While at the Kiernan Agency, Dow teamed up with Edward Jones, a native of Worcester, Massachusetts, and a Brown University dropout, whom he had first met when they both worked on Providence newspapers.

The journalist-entrepreneurs went into competition with their former employer, the two of them taking turns collecting news items and supervising their reproduction and delivery several times daily to the fledgling company's Wall Street subscribers. As the business grew, the staff of messenger boys doubled as the reporters and subscription salesmen during their frequent rounds among the banks and brokers.

The Dow Average Takes Shape

In 1883 Dow Jones & Company added to its service a printed summary of the day's principal news that was included with the final hand delivery of the day. This *Customer's Afternoon Letter* has receded into the mists of journalistic history. Its successor publication, the *Wall Street Journal,* which first appeared on July 8, 1889, with Dow as its editor, has not.

Among his duties as editor, Dow wrote many of the *Journal*'s editorials until shortly before his death on December 4, 1902. Although it was not then the custom for editorial writers to sign their work, many of the early *Journal* editorials pertaining to the stock market and to the behavior of stock prices are generally accepted as bearing Dow's stamp. In one of his later editorials, "Watching the Tide," on January 31, 1901, he wrote:

A person watching the tide coming in and who wishes to know the spot which marks the high tide, sets a stick in the sand at the points reached by the incoming waves until the stick reaches a position where the waves do not come up to it and finally recede enough to show that the tide has turned.

This method holds good in watching and determining the flood tide of the stock market, the average of 20 stocks is the peg which marks the height of the waves. The prices-waves, like those of the sea, do not recede all at once from the top. The force which moves them checks the inflow gradually and time elapses before it can be told with certainty whether high tide has been set or not.[5]

The "average of 20 stocks" to which Dow referred in his editorial was not the first such measurement of stock price movement he had undertaken. He had published in the July 3, 1884, issue of his *Customer's Afternoon Letter* the average closing price of eleven active "representative stocks," a figure that he believed expressed the overall behavior of the market—that is, an "index." Dow's initial eleven-stock list, consisting of nine railroad issues and two industrials, appeared irregularly thereafter in the *Afternoon Letter* and is regarded as the first attempt to compile a statistical index of American stock prices.[6]

In choosing eleven active, representative stocks, Dow did not enjoy a wide selection in 1884. Though steadily rising, the average daily volume on the New York Stock Exchange was still only a quarter-million shares, and most of that was in railroad issues. The few industrials that had begun to attract attention were held to be unseasoned and speculative, offering no record against which traders could measure current performance. It was only after a dozen years of additions, deletions, and substitutions that Dow was able to publish a list consisting entirely of industrial stocks.

Averages, Medians, and Means

Dow's method of computing his eleven-stock average was the simplest possible. He added the closing prices of the stocks on his list and divided the total by eleven. But even at that early stage, individuals who would later become known as statisticians were aware that there were several methods of deriving averages, or "means," and debated the alleged merits and drawbacks of the various approaches.

Let us come back to today's stock market to illustrate the various means (the pun is by all means intended) of averaging the same list of prices. The fifteen most active New York Stock Exchange Composite stocks for June 10, 1982 (see table 1.1) will do as well as any other.[7]

The total of the fifteen closing prices on the June 10 most active list is 415.25. Dividing that sum by 15—Dow's original method—we arrive at what

Table 1.1 Most Active Stocks, June 10, 1982

	Open	High	Low	Close	Change	Volume
Mesa Petroleum	17¾	18¼	17⅝	18	+ ¼	1,245,900
Halliburton	29⅝	29¾	28¼	28⅞	− ½	857,800
Exxon	27¾	28⅛	27⅝	28	+ ⅛	785,300
IBM	58	59	58	58¾	+ ⅝	684,200
Atlantic Richfield	41⅞	42⅛	41¾	42	+ ⅜	646,600
Central Louisiana Energy	17⅝	17⅝	16½	17½	− ¼	627,900
Schlumberger	39	39½	38⅝	39½	−1⅛	602,100
Tandy	27½	27¾	27	27½	+ ¼	538,500
Ralston Purina	13½	13½	13⅜	13½	0	525,300
Cities Service	35	35½	34¼	34¾	+ ¼	511,600
Sony Corp.	12⅞	13⅛	12⅞	13	0	479,300
Commonwealth Edison	22	22	21¾	21¾	− ¼	414,900
Western Company of North America	9¾	9¾	9	9¼	− ½	410,300
Standard Oil of Indiana	44½	44¾	43⅝	44	− ⅜	403,800
Sears, Roebuck	18⅝	18⅞	18½	18⅞	+ ⅛	396,900

SOURCE: *Wall Street Journal,* June 11, 1982, 48.

is known as the *arithmetic mean* for that particular series of prices, or 27 3/4. This is the method of averaging that is familiar to most people and the one that is easiest to use. Another advantage claimed for the arithmetic mean is that it can itself be averaged and be put to other statistical uses. A purported shortcoming of the arithmetic mean is the distortion that results when a few extremely high prices are included in the list. If, for example, the June 10 list had included Merck & Company at 72 3/8 and General Electric at 61, instead of Western Company of North America at 9 1/4 and Ralston Purina at 13 1/2, the arithmetic mean would have been 35 instead of 27 3/4, a figure that might not have been representative of the majority of stocks traded that day.

A second kind of average, the *median,* is the middle point that divides the list into two equal parts. The median of the June 10 list was Tandy, the eighth most active stock, which at 27 1/2 was nearly identical to the list's arithmetic mean. Interestingly enough, if the fifteen most active stocks had been ranked. according to their prices rather than by the number of shares traded that day, their median would still have been Tandy Corp. at 27 1/2.

Medians are the easiest kind of average to obtain when an odd number of prices is involved since they can be arrived at by observation, avoiding the chore of adding the individual prices and dividing by the number of prices on the list. Where there is an even number, the midpoint cannot be so easily determined, even though it lies within a determinate range. Unlike arithmetic means, medians cannot be combined, averaged, or otherwise statistically manipulated. Moreover, when a particular list is short, medians tend to be erratic in their behavior.

And third, the *geometric mean* is derived by multiplying together all of the prices on a given list and taking the nth root of the resulting product, n being the number of prices in the series. In the case of the June 10 most active list, the product of the fifteen closing prices is 69,558,480,992,517, and

$$\sqrt[15]{69{,}558{,}480{,}992{,}517} = 24 \ 1/2$$

This is yet a different result from the arithmetic mean or the median. Statisticians maintain that in spite of how cumbersome this method of calculation is, the geometric mean provides, for their purposes, a more meaningful average.

The geometric mean is not distorted by an asymmetrical distribution of prices and, unlike the arithmetic mean, can be shifted from one base period to another without producing inconsistent results. This latter quality allows direct comparisons between price levels at different dates under investigation. In addition to the laborious method of computation, geometric means are unfamiliar to many, if not most, laypersons and are therefore more susceptible to misinterpretation than are arithmetic means.[8]

Base Periods and Weighting

Whatever method of averaging is employed to compile a series of index numbers, the resulting figures are expressed in relation to a base figure that is usually assigned a value of 100. All preceding and subsequent numbers are divided by the base prices, and the quotients are multiplied by 100. These products are, in the case of an arithmetic mean, added and then divided by the number of prices in the series to obtain the final index number.

The base period may be as short as a single day or as long as ten years. The longer the period, the less likelihood there is of distortion in the index due to exceptionally high or low prices. The distortion of scattered prices is to some extent avoided by the use of "chain" indexes, which compute a year's average rise or fall in relation to the preceding year's prices instead of a distant base period. One difficulty with a chain index is that, although year-to-year variations are comparatively easy to measure with relative accuracy, the prices used as divisors change every year.

Statisticians also realized early on that some prices in a given series are more significant than others, a situation that gives rise to weighting. In many price series the weight assigned to each of the component figures is determined subjectively according to the statistician's own bias. In the June 10 most active list cited above, the weighting is determined according to the number of shares of each stock that was traded on that day. As an actual index, the most active list has the drawback of consisting of different stocks each day, with oil shares attracting traders' attention during one trading session airline stocks being affected by an adverse government ruling the next, and so on.

The "Industrials" Appear

Charles Dow weighted his original representative list heavily in favor of railroad stocks because the rails were the predominantly active issues in 1884. By then, however, the balance was already beginning to tilt to industrial stocks. Up to and during the Civil War, most manufacturing enterprises in the United States remained local in their scope of operation. They grew in number but not necessarily in size during the postwar decade, as many newly established companies followed the long-standing example of the railroads and formed pools to limit the production or sale of individual units. It was not until the widespread adoption of the voting trust form of organization that nineteenth-century corporations began to approach their modern shape and size. The Standard Oil Trust, organized in 1879, served as the model for similar tie-ups in many industries.

Although the term *trust* continued in popular usage, a revision of the New Jersey incorporation law that allowed one corporation to own the stock of another soon prompted the combination of individual companies through mergers rather than by the device of a voting trust. The merged corporations enjoyed economies of scale, standardization, and specialization and rapidly overtook the railroads in size. The industrials' capital structure and financial requirements increased proportionately, a development that in turn stimulated the flotation and trading of corporate securities. The years that saw the formation of U.S. Steel, American Tobacco, General Electric, and International Harvester witnessed a tenfold increase in the number of industrial shares listed on the New York Stock Exchange and a corresponding rise in their volume of trading.[9]

Dow's Industrial Average

Dow's efforts during those years to develop a list of representative stocks reflected these changes. He revised his initial list repeatedly during the 1880s and early 1890s until, on May 26, 1896, he had settled upon a list consisting entirely of industrial stocks. This twelve-issue list, computed on that first day at 40.94, is recognized as the original Dow Jones Industrial Average.[10]

In 1916, fourteen years following Dow's death, the industrial list was expanded to twenty issues and in 1928 was increased again to thirty stocks, its present size. Over the ensuing years the Dow Jones thirty-stock industrial average has attained prominence as the most widely quoted and extensively used American stock price average. The only two stocks that have remained on the list since its inception are American Tobacco, renamed American Brands in 1969, and General Electric. Only about one-half of the present thirty stocks go back as far as 1928.[11]

After establishing a separate list of industrial stocks, Dow continued to tabulate a twenty-stock rail average. In 1970 that list was broadened to include other types of transportation companies and renamed the Transportation Average. In 1929 Dow Jones & Company introduced a utility average. The three lists—industrials, transportation, and utilities—together comprise today's Dow Jones Averages (see figure 1.1). But it is the industrial list (see table 1.2) to which people refer when they ask the question "What did the Dow do today?"

One of the ostensible problems with the Dow Jones Averages is that they are no longer averages as we have defined that term. They are not arithmetic or geometric means, nor medians. Dow originally computed them as arithmetic means. But as the various constituent stocks were split and stock dividends were paid and substitutions were made over the years, simple averaging no longer sufficed. What, for example, should Dow have done when one of his original twelve issues—or today, one of the thirty industrials—was split two-for-one? Should he thereafter have divided the total of prices by 13—or by 11?

If no adjustment was made for splits and stock dividends, the average would be distorted. To use a simple example, the arithmetic mean of three stocks, each priced at 10, is 10:

$$\frac{10 + 10 + 10}{3} = 10$$

If one of the stocks was split two-for-one and no recognition was made of the split, the next day's average, assuming there was no market price movement, would be:

$$\frac{5 + 10 + 10}{3} = 8.33$$

Dow dealt with this complication by multiplying the price of each split share by the amount of the split, which, in the above example, would mean counting the $5 stock twice. As such splits became more frequent, however, and some stocks were split repeatedly, this technique became cumbersome and another solution was sought.

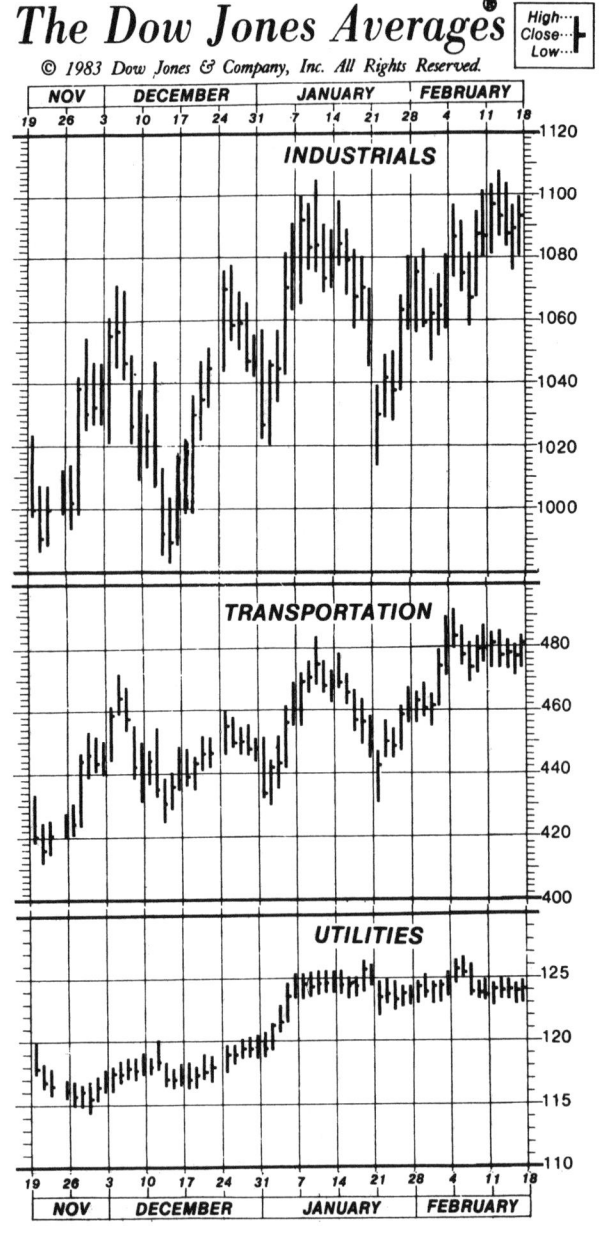

Figure 1.1   The Dow Jones Averages—Industrials,
Transportation, Utilities. (*Wall Street
Journal*, 45. February 22, 1983.
Reproduced by permission.)

Table 1.2   Dow Jones 30 Industrials, as of December 31, 1982

Stock	Closing Price
Alcoa	32¾
Allied Corp.[a]	45⅜
American Brands[a]	51
American Can[a]	35¾
American Express	70¾
AT&T	64⅝
Bethlehem Steel[a]	23½
Du Pont	44⅜
Eastman Kodak	98⅛
Exxon[a]	32¼
General Electric[a]	100
General Foods	47¾
General Motors[a]	64½
Goodyear	36⅞
IBM	98
Inco[a]	14¾
International Harvester[a]	8½
International Paper	51⅝
Merck	88¼
Minnesota Mining and Manufacturing	79⅜
Owens Illinois	29⅝
Procter & Gamble	123
Sears, Roebuck[a]	32
Standard Oil (Calif.)	42⅞
Texaco[a]	34⅞
Union Carbide[a]	61
U.S. Steel[a]	30⅛
United Technologies	58⅞
Westinghouse[a]	40½
Woolworth[a]	29⅛

[a]Included in the original list of thirty industrials, first published October 1, 1928.

In 1928, long after the founder had passed from the scene, Dow Jones & Company adopted the present method of changing the price divisor. Applying this method to our simple example, the divisor would be reduced from 3 to 2.50 to provide for the two-for-one split. If the division was then carried out, we would have:

$$\frac{5 + 10 + 10}{2.50} = 10$$

leaving the average unchanged after the split. The divisor for the Dow Jones Industrial Average is no longer the number of stocks in the average—and has not been since 1928. When the industrial list was increased from 20 to 30 stocks in that year, the divisor became 16.67. By 1950 it had been reduced in stages to 8.92. At the end of 1970 it was 1.826, and in December 1982 it was 1.359.[12]

Turning to an actual example, table 1.2 shows the closing prices of the 30 Dow Jones industrial stocks on December 31, 1982. Dividing their total of 1422.24 by the divisor of 1.359 then in effect, we arrive at 1,046.54, which was .83 points below the previous day's closing average.

The Dow Jones Averages are unweighted, meaning that prices of the constituent stocks are the only factors taken into account in computing them. As a consequence, individual stocks exert a greater or less than one-thirtieth influence on the industrial average, according to their respective prices. Thus, General Motors, at 64 1/2 a share on December 31, 1982, had nearly twice the impact on that day's average as Texaco, at 34 7/8 a share. Expressing the relative effect of prices another way, a 10 percent rise or fall in Procter & Gamble (123) would cause the industrial average to move up or down by 9.05 points (12.3/1.359), while a 10 percent change in U.S. Steel (30 1/8) would move it by 2.21 points (3.0/1.359). Dow Jones & Company cautions investors who may refer to the industrial, rail, or utility averages that a movement of a certain number of points should not be confused with the gain or loss of so many dollars and cents per share of stock. A ten-point drop in the industrial average from a level of 800—a decline of about 1.2 percent—is comparable to a depreciation of sixty cents a share, or less than five-eighths, on a fifty-dollar stock. Dow Jones stresses that its averages, like the other leading stock indexes, are statistical compilations and should not be taken as a measure of the performance of individual stocks.[13]

Standard & Poor's 500 Index

Next to the Dow Jones Industrial Average, the most widely known and quoted stock market index is the Standard & Poor's 500. The "S&P 500," as this indicator is popularly called, does not enjoy the longevity and public recognition that the Dow Jones Averages do, but it does claim some advantages that the Dow Jones cannot.

Henry Varnum Poor began publication of his annual *Poor's Manual* of corporate statistics in 1860, twenty-two years before the founding of Dow Jones & Company. *Poor's Directory of American Officials* first appeared in 1886, and his *Handbook of Investment Securities* followed four years later. In 1941 Poor's Financial Services were merged with the Standard Statistics Company, another leading publisher of financial data, to form the present company. In 1966 Standard & Poor's Corporation became a subsidiary of McGraw-Hill and remains the world's largest publisher of financial statistics and other information services.

Standard & Poor's is best known for its *Corporate Records*, a set of loose-leaf volumes that contain frequently updated information on companies whose shares are listed on the major stock exchanges or are traded in the over-the-counter market. The company's other publications include the *Bond Record, The Outlook,* and a number of *Industry Surveys.*

The company began computing stock price indexes in 1946, compiling separate averages for 425 industrial, 20 rail, and 55 utility issues. The present S&P 500-stock index is a statistical composite of 400 industrial, 40 financial, 20 transportation, and 40 utility stocks. The four subgroups are in turn broken down into 97 separate industry groups. The financial group, for example, includes bank, insurance, and consumer finance companies, while the transportation group consists of rails, airlines, trucking, and air freight companies. S&P also compiles four supplementary group indexes: capital goods, consumer goods, high-grade common stocks, and low-priced common stocks.

The group indexes and the composite index were, until 1976, restricted to stocks listed on the New York Stock Exchange. A small number of American Stock Exchange and over-the-counter issues were then added to include leading bank and insurance company stocks and otherwise make the list more representative of today's stock market.

Standard & Poor's describes the criteria the company employs in selecting stocks for its group and composite indexes in the following way:

> Each stock added to the index must represent a viable enterprise and be representative of the industry group to which it is assigned. Its market price movements must in general be responsive to changes in industry affairs. Aggregate market value of the stock and its trading activity are important considerations in the selection process. There is no judgement as to investment appeal of stocks in the selection process.[14]

Because some industries are typically comprised of companies with small capitalization, the composite index does not consist of the 500 largest companies with shares traded on the New York and American stock exchanges and in the over-the-counter market. The total market value (share prices times the number of outstanding shares) of stocks contained in the S&P 500 does, however, exceed 75 percent of the aggregate market value of all NYSE-traded stocks. The purpose of the index is, according to Standard & Poor's, "To portray the pattern of common stock price movement."[15]

Unlike the Dow Jones Averages, the S&P 500 is a capitalization-weighted index, meaning that the total market value and not simply the share price of each stock is considered in the computation of the index. This aggregate market value is then expressed as a percentage of the average market value of the 500 stocks during the 1941–43 base period. The percentage figure is in turn divided by 10 to produce the actual index number. It is not necessary to change the divisor, since the multiplication of share prices by the number of outstanding shares automatically adjusts for stock splits.[16]

Standard & Poor's describes its index as a "base-weighted aggregative" and claims for it the advantages of flexibility in adjusting for stock dividends and splits and of accuracy due to its method of calculation. The company believes that the selection of outstanding shares as its weighting factor ensures that each constituent stock influences the index in proportion to its actual market importance and that by employing a base period when market value was relatively constant, the index reflects only fluctuations in current market prices.[17]

To assist users in interpreting its indexes, Standard & Poor's publishes supplementary per-share data organized by the various industry groups. This information includes earnings, dividends, sales, depreciation, working capital, and other significant ratios published annually in the *Analyst's Handbook*. In table 1.3 are listed the ten most heavily weighted groups in the 500-stock composite index as of May 1982.

The NYSE Composite Index

In 1966 the New York Stock Exchange and the American Stock Exchange introduced their own stock price indexes based upon the issues traded on each exchange. The American Stock Exchange index is computed by adding the advances and subtracting the declines from the previous trading day's closing prices. The net figure is then divided by the number of issues listed on the Amex, and that quotient is added (if positive) or subtracted (if negative) from the previous day's index figure.

The New York Stock Exchange Composite Index is, like the S&P 500, comprised of industrial, financial, transportation, and utility subgroups. It also

Table 1.3 Ten Most Heavily Weighted Groups in S&P 500

Group	% of S&P 500
1. Oil (integrated international)	8.43
2. Oil (integrated domestic)	7.34
3. Office and business equipment	6.49
4. Drugs	4.73
5. Electric companies	4.54
6. Foods	3.19
7. Oil well equipment and services	3.05
8. Chemicals	2.49
9. Electronic companies (major)	2.28
10. Hospital supplies	2.01

SOURCE: Standard & Poor's Corporation, *Information Bulletin, S&P 500*, May 1982, 2.

is weighted according to the number of outstanding shares of each stock but is a broader index than Standard & Poor's, in that it encompasses all of the nearly 1,300 common stocks listed on the NYSE.

As with the computation of the S&P 500, the products of prices and outstanding shares of each stock are added to determine the total market value of a given day's trading. The NYSE Composite Index is a figure that expresses the relationship between current market value and a base market value as of December 31, 1965, after certain adjustments have been made.[18] A value of 50 was selected as the base value rather than the customary figure of 100 to allow the index to approximate more closely the actual fifty-three dollar average price of all listed stocks on the December 31, 1965, base date. The industrial, financial, transportation, and utility subgroup indexes are also measured against a value of 50 as of the base period.

As a simple illustration of the method of calculation, assume that the total market value of all NYSE-listed common stocks (preferred stocks are not included in the index) as of a given day was $600 billion and that the comparable figure as of the base date was $500 billion, expressed as 50. The current index would therefore be computed in the following manner:[19]

$$\frac{\$600 \text{ billion}}{\$500 \text{ billion}} = 1.2$$

$$1.2 \times 50 = 60$$

If the current market value increases to, say, $625 billion and the base market value remains unchanged, the index changes as follows:

$$\frac{\$625 \text{ billion}}{\$500 \text{ billion}} = 1.25$$

$$1.25 \times 50 = 62.50$$

As is the case with the other indexes, the base market value must be adjusted to reflect changes in capitalization, new listings, and the occasional delisting of stocks that fail to meet the exchange's requirements. The prevailing principle is that the adjusted base market value must bear the same relationship to the new market value as the old base value had to the market value before the capitalization change; that is:

$$\frac{\text{New market value (after change)}}{\text{New base value}} = \frac{\text{Old market value (before change)}[20]}{\text{Old base value}}$$

As with the S&P 500, stock dividends and splits do not compel an adjustment of the base since the aggregate market value of a stock is not thereby changed. New listings and delistings do require an adjustment in direct proportion to any change in the exchange's aggregate market value, as described in note 21. No adjustment is necessary if a merger between two listed companies is accomplished by means of a share-for-share exchange, in which event the combined market value of the merging companies' shares does not change. If a company whose shares are listed acquires an unlisted company, or if there is a rights offering where stockholders are invited to subscribe to newly issued shares, the base market value must be adjusted to account for any increase in the current value of the increased number of outstanding shares.

The Value Line Composite Index

The fourth leading stock price index is the Value Line Composite Index, which was devised, and is computed by, Arnold Bernhard & Company on the basis of the approximately 1,700 stocks reviewed by that company's Value Line Investment Survey. Value Line, like S&P and Dow Jones, computes separate industrial, rail, and utility averages to supplement its composite index.

The distinguishing feature of this index is that it is the only one of the leading stock averages that is derived from the geometric mean of its constituent stocks—that is, by the application of the following formula:

$$\sqrt[n]{\text{the product of } n \text{ stock prices}}$$

where n is the number of stocks in the designated list.

The closing price of each stock in the Value Line list is divided by the prior day's closing price. If, for example, one of the 1,700-odd stocks in the composite index climbs from 40 to 40 3/4 during the course of a trading session, that day's price increase would be expressed as:

$$40\ 3/4 \div 40 = 1.01875$$

Should that stock, on the other hand, drop in price from 40 to 39 1/4, the decline would be computed as:

$$39\ 1/4 \div 40 = 0.98125$$

The price changes of all the stocks on the list are then averaged geometrically, and the resulting figure is multiplied by the preceding day's closing Value Line Composite Index. June 30, 1961, is the base period selected for this index, with the market value on that date expressed as 100. If, for example, the geometric mean of Tuesday's price changes was computed at 1.015, and the composite index at the close of Monday's trading stood at 118.75, the index at Tuesday's close would be:[21]

$$1.015 \times 118.75 = 120.53 \text{ (up 1.78)}$$

The Value Line index is not weighted according to the number of outstanding shares of each stock on the list. Stock dividends and splits are accounted for by adjusting the preceding day's prices of those issues that are affected in that manner. The composite list is expanded from time to time to include stocks that have recently been added to the Value Line Survey. Value Line maintains that the addition of stocks to, or their deletion from, the list does not distort the composite index because of the large number of stocks in its base.

Which Index Is Best?

Investment analysts and portfolio managers continually debate the relative merits and shortcomings of the various indexes as accurate measures of overall stock market performance.

It has become fashionable to belittle the Dow Jones Industrial Average for failing to keep up with the times. The continuity of its average that Dow Jones & Company prizes is taken by critics to be proof positive that the DJIA is out of date and consequently is a poor barometer of today's market behavior. The days when the broadly capitalized blue chips—such as AT&T, Eastman Kodak, and General Electric—were representative issues are long over, they argue, and Dow Jones has failed to expand and change the composition of the 30 industrials accordingly. In fact, they remonstrate, American Telephone & Telegraph is not even what is generally considered an industrial company.

Supporters of the Dow average rebut this criticism by pointing out that the thirty stocks comprise nearly one-fourth of the total market value of all common stocks listed on the New York Stock Exchange and account for 7 percent to 10 percent of each day's trading volume. Moreover, the pro-Dows contend that the size of these thirty companies and the economic impact they exert on the operations—and, thus, on the stock prices—of other companies imbue them with an influence far greater than their number alone might suggest.

As was noted earlier in the chapter, the Dow Jones Industrials are also criticized for being too "high" because their divisor, instead of their base value, is reduced to adjust for splits. As a consequence, it is argued, movement of the average in points exaggerates underlying dollar changes in share prices. The proposal is frequently made to "split" the average itself, perhaps twenty-to-one, to make it more closely approximate the price of an average share. Dow Jones retorts that to do so would mean starting what would in effect be a new average and thereby giving up the advantage of nearly a century of price continuity.

Wall Street professionals are prone to praise the S&P 500 for being what they claim the Dow Jones Industrials are not—a broadly based, and hence representative, indicator of general market trends. The S&P 500 is in fact one of the U.S. Commerce Department's twelve leading economic indicators and is regarded by economists as a significant barometer of conditions well beyond the trading activity on the stock exchange floor.

The worst that one can say about the New York Stock Exchange and the Value Line composite indexes is that they are unhallowed by time and therefore lack tradition. Despite their statistical refinement, their ebbs and flows are rarely reported on the television evening news.

What he evidently regarded as slavish adherence of the investing public to the Dow average incited one pro-NYSE Composite Index commentator to remark that:

> Everyone with the possible exception of the general public knows that the Dow is fundamentally a poor index. But everyone looks to it anyway for reasons right out of Catch-22. Everyone looks at the Dow because it's prominently displayed. It's displayed because everyone looks at it.[22]

This critic chooses to ignore what the television news directors do not. Namely, that each of the several indexes is as much a medium as it is a message and that—for a broad sector of the public, at least—familiarity is as great a virtue as statistical purity.

There probably is no single "best" stock market indicator. The big, blue-chip stocks dominate the Dow Jones Industrial Average through deliberate selection and the S&P 500 and NYSE composite indexes through their large capitalization and the method of weighting that is employed in computing the latter indexes. At certain stages of a stock market cycle, when Exxon, GM, GE, and others of their ilk catch and hold for a time the trading public's fancy, they will be the best indexes. When the attention and, what is more important, the capital of investors are drawn to the shares of smaller and presumably more speculative companies, Value Line may become the truest barometer of investor sentiment.

The trends and fads that materialize in the investment world, only to fade and be displaced by new fashions, and the variety of attitudes and objectives pursued by different investor groups make it likely that there will remain a place for several stock market indexes.

A commodity that is always in short supply on Wall Street is certainty. The fact that no one, neither professional portfolio manager nor private investor, can say with certainty which of the stock indexes is the best one, let alone how any of them will behave tomorrow and the day after, is the condition that prompts us to shift our historical survey from the lower tip of Manhattan Island to the Chicago lake shore.

CHAPTER 2

Development of Index Futures Contracts

Chicago is about a thousand miles from New York. But to most upper-crust New Yorkers in Charles Dow's time—including his fellow stock exchange members—it might as well have been on the far side of the moon. To be sure, they acknowledged Chicago as the hub of the country's rapidly expanding agricultural sector. And investors were becoming familiar with the shares of such dynamic young Chicago-based corporations as International Harvester in farm machinery (included in the Dow Jones Industrial Average in 1925) and Swift & Company, the largest meat packer (added to the average in 1959 and included as Esmark until acquisition of the latter by Beatrice Foods in 1984).

But in terms of being a financial center, most Wall Street denizens probably regarded Chicago in the 1880s as an overblown version of the Colorado boomtown Dow visited before he moved to New York. So far as they took notice of the commodity exchanges that were beginning to flourish there, Dow's stock exchange colleagues very likely considered them a manifestation of the sort of "frenzied finance" Dow had reported on from Leadville. To suggest that Wall Street would one day try to imitate the financial cowboys in Chicago—and, in some instances, fail—would have evoked hoots of derision. Yet that is what happened.

How Futures Markets Evolved

Like the stock market, what we today refer to as the commodity, or futures, market did not suddenly materialize in its present form. It evolved over a number of years as individuals and businesses that were engaged in the production, processing, and distribution of various commodities encountered vexatious—and in some instances, disastrous—pricing and financing problems that stemmed in large part from the seasonal nature of most farm crops.

Chicago in the mid–nineteenth century had little to recommend it apart from its location. Incorporated as late as 1833, it was regarded—insofar as it was known at all—as "an ugly little town cuddled on the shore of the lake."[1] But its aesthetic shortcomings were more than compensated for by its strategic position, abutting both the lower end of the Great Lakes and the rich farmland of northern Illinois. Within a decade, Chicago became a major transshipment point for foodstuffs, supplying grain, beef, and pork to the eastern population of the United States and to the export markets abroad.

The primitive state of overland transportation was an early obstacle to the smooth flow of these products eastward. Horse-drawn wagons and oxcarts were the primary freight carriers before the arrival of the railroad, and the farther away from the city farmers settled, the more difficult and costly it became to haul crops and livestock in to the Chicago market. In the 1840s, the cost of transporting a shipment of wheat sixty miles by oxcart was equal to the market value of that wheat.[2]

Conditions improved with the opening of the Illinois-Michigan Canal in 1848 and the laying of the early railroad lines. World events also accrued to Chicago's commercial benefit. The city shipped grain to both sides in the Crimean War and supplied the Union armies throughout the American Civil War. It was not only for the purpose of reshipment but also to provide for the growing human and livestock population of the city itself that the demand for grain increased. But as demand grew, so did the transportation, storage, and financing problems that an increasing volume of traffic created for both producers and dealers.

The fertility of the Illinois soil is enhanced by its moisture. But wet soil brings with it muddy roads, which in the case of the fall corn crop, meant that farmers had to store the corn over the winter in their own cribs or else haul it by sled or oxcart over frozen roads to be stored by country merchants at the river's edge. Following the spring thaw, the corn could be barged to Chicago (see figure 2.1). The winter storage of corn created substantial financing problems for the farmers or merchants who were carrying it. Corn held in inventory is not earning money for its owner. On the contrary, someone has to bear the storage costs. In those early years the costs were often financed by the Chicago merchants who were awaiting delivery in the spring, or else by bankers in the city. Both the city merchants and the bankers made such inventory loans with reluctance, since the ability of the borrowers to repay them depended upon the price they obtained for the corn when it ultimately reached the Chicago market.

Chicago

Figure 2.1 Canals, Rivers, and Storage
Points in Nineteenth-Century
Illinois

The seasonal cycle for wheat created a different set of storage and financing
problems. Wheat harvested in the spring and summer could be shipped to
Chicago immediately. It was in the city itself that wheat was stored, often to
overflowing, as loaded wagons stood in congested streets awaiting the arrival
of incoming ships to haul it to the eastern markets and abroad. In the face of
this annual glut, merchants soon reached their capacity and were unable to
accept additional consignments. On their part, bankers were unwilling to
finance further inventory expansion, forcing farmers to sell their crops for what
amounted to giveaway prices. Having done so poorly with their current crop,
many had to sell their horse teams and wagons to raise enough cash to plant
the next year's crop.

The eastern buyers, who had their agents on the scene, knew all they had to
do was wait during the glut period and prices would drop even further as laden
wagons arrived daily. Price swings became extremely erratic, reflecting supply-

Table 2.1 Wheat and Corn Prices at Chicago (in Cents per Bushel)

Year	Wheat		Corn	
	High	Low	High	Low
1863	115	80	98	42
1864	226	107	140	76
1865	155	85	88	38
1866	203	78	100	33¾
1867	285	155	112	56¾
1868	220	104½	102½	52
1869	147	76½	97½	44
1870	131½	73¼	94½	45
1871	132	99½	56½	39½
1872	161	101	48⅝	29½

SOURCE: Commodity Research Bureau, Commodity Yearbook, 1940, 179 & 667.

demand imbalances that changed hourly, and the risk of raising or storing a wheat crop became greater than many farmers and merchants could or would tolerate (see table 2.1).

It was to alleviate such price risks that a system of forward contracting evolved among farmers, merchants, and buyers. Country merchants traveled to Chicago in the fall and winter, where they entered into contracts with the larger grain dealers there to deliver in the spring at a firm price a specified quantity and grade of corn. The first such "time" contract for which a record remains was made on March 13, 1851, for the delivery of three thousand bushels of corn the following June at a price one cent per bushel below the March 13 price.[3]

These time, or forward, contracts served to ameliorate the pricing and financing problems of the country merchants. The Chicago merchants to whom they sold felt more secure about advancing funds with which the country dealers could pay the farmers when time contracts were used. Bankers also were more forthcoming with loans where time contracts could be offered as collateral. In either instance, country merchants were able to make more rational bids for corn, and farmers generally received a better price than they did when time contracts were not used.

In the case of wheat, the Chicago merchants were sellers rather than buyers of time contracts. They, not the growers or country merchants, bore the price risks and attendant financing problems, which they endeavored to circumvent by selling forward to their customers, the eastern millers and exporters.

Commodity Exchanges Appear

The commodity exchanges predated the widespread practice of forward contracting in Chicago. Like the early stockbrokers in New York, the Chicago grain merchants initially gathered to transact their business on street corners, often moving to different locations at various times of the day. As the volume of business increased, these roving outdoor markets became impractical—as well as extremely uncomfortable during the intemperate Chicago winters—prompting the dealers to seek an indoor site. The Board of Trade of the City of Chicago (which is still its formal name) was organized in 1848, with 82 members, for the purpose of promoting commerce in the city. To this end, the Board of Trade offered the grain merchants the use of its premises and a sideboard of cheese, crackers, and ale to encourage them to conduct their business under its auspices.

In addition to laying out a free lunch—though it has become a byword in the financial world and elsewhere that there is no such thing—the Chicago Board was instrumental in developing a system of inspecting and weighing grain. This was an important step toward making grain stocks "fungible"—that is, interchangeable—and facilitated the use of warehouse receipts to prove ownership and to post as collateral in financing arrangements.

The use of forward contracts to buy and sell wheat and corn developed more or less spontaneously, usually off the exchange floor, rather than as a practice purposefully designed and promoted by the Board of Trade. It was generally to resolve disputes among the members that the board's governors gradually adopted regulations covering forward trading. They passed a rule in 1863 directing the suspension of members who failed to meet the terms of their contracts. Later rules provided for the deposit of margin money, the standardization of contract terms and delivery procedures, and an arbitration procedure to settle disputes among members.

Enter the Speculators

Though a fairly active market in forward contracts had evolved by the mid-1870s, one further step had to be taken before the Board of Trade could qualify as what we today consider a futures exchange. All of the forward contracts for corn or wheat had until that time been settled by an exchange of title to the physical commodities. Since the underlying motive for forward contracting was to transfer price risk, such dealing presupposes the availability of individuals who are disposed to assume that risk. As Professor Thomas A. Hieronymus points out, little was accomplished by passing risks from people who did not want and could not carry them to other people who didn't want or couldn't carry them either.[4] That is a fair description of the farmers, country and city merchants, and eastern buyers—all of whom were endeavoring to reduce their business risks. Forward contracting between any of these parties would only be acceptable if the contract prices included substantial risk premiums that allowed them to share the risk. These risk premiums would then require that lower prices be paid to farmers or higher prices charged to end-users of those commodities.

Thus entered the much-maligned speculators, willing embracers of such risks. To quote Hieronymus:

> Speculators did not step nobly forward to assume their necessary place. They rushed in with enthusiasm and abandon to participate in an exciting game that held out the promise of huge profits. They cared not at all about their place in the economic world but were motivated by avarice and excitement. In large measure, they took the play away from the commercial trade. Speculation, then, is an activity in itself.[5]

Speculators could be anyone with the money and desire to get into the "exciting game." They were people with available capital from every trade and profession who simply wanted to make a buck—indeed, many bucks—and saw in the emerging market for wheat and corn contracts an opportune place to do just that. For the most part, they had no grain to sell, nor did they have the slightest wish to own any.

Self-appointed guardians of the public morality were quick to denounce speculation then, as they are now. But of the farmers who lost their crops, teams, wagons, and everything else because there was no efficient market in 1850, they seemed to have little if anything to say. Certainly, forward pricing and speculation are all of a piece, and their intertwined past is a colorful, not to say a checkered one. The history of the Chicago Board—and other commodity and stock exchanges—is replete with tales of corners, rigging, and manipulation. Numerous legislative attempts were made to outlaw all kinds of forward contracting as gambling, and in 1867 ten Board of Trade members were arrested on the exchange floor on that charge. Warehouse receipts were issued for which no grain was found to exist. Several Board of Trade presidents went belly-up during those early years, suggesting that the most prominent, if not the most accomplished, insiders were just as susceptible to the vagaries of the market as the most naive outsiders.

Chains of "bucket shops" opened and flourished. These were sham brokerage firms that accepted, but did not execute, their customers' purchase and sale orders on the exchange on the supposition—probably correct in view of the bucket shops' success—that the customers would guess wrong most of the time. The majority of brokerage houses that operated above board howled with outrage and demanded that the bucket shops be suppressed, as did the stockbrokers associated with the New York Stock Exchange during the same era. It would appear from newspaper accounts of the day that most customers were not aware of any difference between bucket shops and legitimate brokers, and if they were, they didn't seem to care. So long as the bucket-shop brokers made good on their customers' winnings, the latter weren't concerned with what transpired in the back office.

Mercantile Exchange's Roots

Other exchanges were organized in Chicago and elsewhere to enable market participants to trade and eventually to engage in forward contracting for their particular commodities. The egg business was a typical example. Poultry and egg production was initially a farm sideline, something for the farmer's wife to earn "egg money" for her household needs. As some farmers began to specialize in egg and poultry production and volume grew, distribution became concentrated in the hands of a few wholesale egg dealers. The business was affected by its own problems of seasonal variation, storage, and financing. Spring was the peak period for egg production, followed by a decline in summer and a slack fall and winter. Eggs were first pickled and then stored in ice houses to spread the spring production over the balance of the year. Egg prices were quoted according to the order of their desirability, with the highest prices charged for fresh eggs, next for iced, and lowest for pickled.

Dealers in the Illinois countryside and their opposite numbers in Chicago constantly faced the decisions of what portion of the spring egg production to put into storage and the rate at which eggs should be withdrawn from storage to obtain optimum prices. These decisions made the difference between business success and failure. Large amounts of money, most of which was borrowed from banks, were tied up in the financing of inventories.

Financing costs and price risks increased along with the volume of business. To spread some of those costs and risks, dealers sold eggs to those of their friends and acquaintances who were interested in taking a flyer, thereby transferring from the banks some of the financing burdens. When an accommodating friend wished to realize the profit or loss, he or she sold the eggs back to the dealer at the prevailing price, and the dealer would in turn sell them to someone else.

This clubby system was limited by the size of a dealer's network of friends and acquaintances—in this case it often literally paid to be a likable person. To put the trade on a more businesslike footing, the egg dealers combined with other produce merchants in 1874 to establish the Chicago Produce Exchange. In 1895 the Butter and Egg Board was organized as a subdivision of the Produce Exchange. Like the Chicago Board of Trade, it paid little attention to forward contracts at first, allowing those dealings to take place on such congenial off-floor premises as neighboring saloons. Eventually, however, the board, reorganized in 1919 as the Chicago Mercantile Exchange, determined that this barroom market was not in its best interest and drafted rules to bring futures trading onto its floor and under its supervision.

The markets continued to evolve during the next century, but growth generally followed the pattern established in the mid-1800s. New exchanges were organized in various cities, including New York, to trade contracts for cotton, wool, coffee, sugar, cocoa, potatoes, copper, gold, and silver. Other wheat exchanges were opened in Kansas City and Minneapolis to supplement the principal market in Chicago.

Trading practices were refined over the years. The quantities, grades, and delivery locations specified by the various contracts became standardized (although a Kansas City wheat contract could not be traded in Chicago, and vice versa). Exchange rules and hours of trading were made uniform. All of these improvements made the markets an effective mechanism for setting commodity prices and facilitating the movement of basic foodstuffs and raw materials through their successive stages of production and distribution.

Innovation in Futures

The first radical departure from the established pattern occurred in the 1970s. Then, as a century earlier, the underlying motive was economic necessity. But this time the need was not that of the commercial users of a particular commodity but of the exchanges themselves. By 1970 their traditional sources of business were drying up, and they were searching for new products and concepts with which to attract new business.

The lead in innovation came from the junior mart in Chicago, the Mercantile Exchange that succeeded the old Butter and Egg Board, and was due in large part to the persistent efforts of one man. In 1967 Leo Melamed, a lawyer turned highly successful futures trader, was elected chairman of the CME with a mandate to create new products. Looking back years later, Melamed said that he "realized that it was imperative to expand if we were going to survive. I just didn't know into what."[6]

In 1970, Melamed's attention was drawn to the world currency market at a time when the British pound was undergoing one of its recurrent crises. He thought that a profit could be made selling the pound short and was surprised to discover there was no ready means of doing so. The big banks that run the international market in foreign exchange didn't like to have private speculators, least of all egg and pork-belly traders, dabbling in it, and they politely told Melamed that he could take his business elsewhere.[7]

He never sold the pounds—the British eventually devalued, and had he been able to do so, he'd have made a bundle—but Melamed smelled an opportunity for his exchange. All of the requisite elements were there: price risk, a need for protection, and speculative potential. Why not a futures market for foreign currencies? If the bank turned him down, how many other people would they turn away?

Melamed went to New York to sound out the international bankers. Predictably, they were not thrilled by his proposal. "They treated me like I had snakebite," he remembers. "Everyone said I hadn't a ghost of a chance." Not easily put off, he continued on to Washington, where his reception was hardly more encouraging. The economic movers and shakers of the administration—Arthur Burns, George Shultz, Paul Volcker, and Herbert Stein—listened and were lukewarm. The strongest commitment Melamed could get was their agreement not to oppose his project.

Returning to Chicago, he was able to enlist a valuable ally. Professor Milton Friedman, the noted University of Chicago economist and future Nobel Prize winner, believed that the idea had merit and drafted for the CME a position paper on the feasibility of a currency futures market. The timing was propitious. As plans were underway to submit for regulatory approval applications to trade futures contracts on eight foreign currencies and to establish a separate division of the Mercantile Exchange to accommodate trading once the approval was obtained, the Bretton Woods system, which had stabilized exchange rates since the end of World War II, fell apart. In May 1972 the International Monetary Market division of the CME opened its doors. The initial volume of trading for the currency contracts was disappointing. But after a two- to three-year break-in period, business increased steadily, and Leo Melamed's "child" became enormously successful.

Other Forms of Diversification

Faced with a similar need to develop new sources of business in those years, the Chicago Board of Trade took a different approach and established a novel market in listed stock options—that is, puts and calls. The Chicago Board Options Exchange, or CBOE, became as successful in its area as the International Monetary Market was with financial futures contracts and eventually split off from the Board of Trade to operate as an independent entity.

The next wave of innovation came with the introduction of interest rate futures, once again spearheaded by the two Chicago exchanges. The rationale behind these new instruments was that, just as floating exchange rates subjected companies and individuals with foreign currency exposure to increased monetary risk, volatile interest rates had a similarly adverse effect on credit market participants. That conclusion was borne out during the 1973–74 credit crunch, when real estate, construction, and mortgage financing were among the economic sectors most severely affected by high interest rates. The 1973–74 experience turned out to be a precursor of greater troubles as interest rates climbed yet higher in the early 1980s.

Staff economists at the Chicago Board of Trade had by 1973 discussed with officials of the Federal Home Loan Mortgage Corporation and faculty members at the University of California's Center for Real Estate and Urban Economics a proposal to create a futures contract based on the market value and interest yield of residential mortgages. The credit crunch gave this idea more immediacy, and the final proposal called for a contract based on mortgage-backed securities guaranteed by the Government National Mortgage Association, or GNMA (also popularly referred to as "Ginnie Mae"). This new "interest rate futures" contract, so named because the price of its underlying security fluctuates in inverse relation to its interest rate, commenced trading at the Chicago Board of Trade in October 1975. It was the first of many such contracts based on fixed-income securities.

The International Monetary Market introduced its first interest rate contract in January 1976, based on 90-day U.S. Treasury bills. While the Board of Trade's Ginnie Mae contract was specifically designed to facilitate mortgage financing and investment, the Treasury-bill yield is a barometer of all short-term interest rates, and the "T-bill" contract was intended for use by money market participants.

New York Tries to Catch Up

A profusion of similar contracts, some of them carbon copies of the originals, soon followed: Treasury bonds, commercial paper, one-year Treasury bills and notes, and eventually certificates of deposit and Eurodollar time deposits. Some of the new contracts caught on; others were discontinued due to lack of trading interest. As the number and types of interest rate futures contracts proliferated, more exchanges rushed to share in the potential bonanza. Every exchange was eager to launch its own interest rate futures market, even those where commodity futures had never before been traded.

The American Stock Exchange, which had successfully followed the CBOE into trading listed put and call options, announced the opening of the American Commodity Exchange, promptly dubbed "ACE." This hastily-conceived creation aspired to trade its own version of a Ginnie Mae futures contract, but ACE and its contract were folded by the parent exchange after six months' disappointing performance. Also in New York, the Commodity Exchange, Inc., or Comex, proposed an instrument virtually identical to the IMM's Treasury-bill contract. Comex at least enjoyed the advantage of being an established futures exchange and was at that time a leading market for gold futures.

But the biggest splash was made by the New York Stock Exchange itself. Having turned its collective nose up at listed options while the CBOE was struggling to establish that new market, and then looked on with envy when it flourished, the leadership at the Big Board was determined not to miss the boat with financial futures. Amid a barrage of publicity and an opening-day ceremony attended by the mayor of New York (who, while cutting the ribbon, said, "I don't know what you do here, but I hope you make a lot of money at it"), the New York Futures Exchange commenced operation on August 7, 1980. The roster of NYFE (pronounced "knife") contracts included those for Treasury bills and bonds and six foreign currencies. Asked what they were offering that was not already available in the seasoned Chicago markets, NYFE officials replied that this was *New York* and hinted broadly that what the financial futures market really needed was the Big Board's sanction and participation to give it legitimacy.

Since their respective beginnings, the securities and commodity markets in the United States had developed separately, functionally as well as geographically. They were comprised of, and served, different participants. But with the advent of futures contracts, first on foreign currencies then on government securities and various types of money market instruments, the distinctions became blurred, and the two markets began to overlap. That the innovation kept coming from Chicago was a blow to the prestige as well as to the profits of the New York group. New York had been an also-ran with both listed options and financial futures, two of the most significant financial developments of the period. As stock index futures loomed mightily on the investment horizon, the Wall Street crowd was determined not to be bridesmaids for the third time. Stock index futures, after all, didn't just strike too close to home. They *were* home, and Wall Streeters were damned if they were going to cede this game to the cowboys in Chicago.

The Beginnings of Index Futures

Yet, as it transpired, the initial impetus behind stock index futures came neither from Chicago nor from New York. It was the Kansas City Board of Trade, a regional wheat market, that successfully waged a long and dogged campaign to translate the concept of index futures into reality.

Being able to point to the success of contracts tied to bonds and other fixed-income securities, it was not difficult to claim an economic justification—in theory, at least—for similar instruments based on common stock. Every type of investor—individuals, portfolio managers, investment bankers, and stock exchange specialists, to name the most obvious—is exposed to market risk that he or she might at certain times wish to avoid. Stock index futures could be used to offset the loss suffered in an investment portfolio or trading account during periods of general market decline, protect a dealer or underwriter against inventory losses during such periods, and facilitate the purchase or sale of large blocks of stock. These were in general terms the kind of uses to which the early wheat and corn contracts were put more than a century before.

A major stumbling block in the case of common stock, as contrasted with wheat or even Treasury bonds, was the difficulty in finding a common denominator to which all categories of investors could relate. One of the first accomplishments of the Chicago Board in its early years was to classify wheat according to its various types and quality grades, a precondition to the drafting of a standard contract. All U.S. Treasury bonds are the same except for their coupon rates and maturities, variables that can be reduced to comparable prices and yields. But how do you grade common stocks and establish a yardstick that applies equally to Exxon, say, and Digital Equipment, not to mention the thousands of other issues listed on the various stock exchanges and traded over the counter?

Planners at the Kansas City Board of Trade thought that the answer lay in a contract based on one of the popular stock market averages. The averages, after all, were intended to be representative indicators of the entire stock market, and a contract based on one or the other of them, the planners argued, could serve stock investors as well as the successful Treasury bond and Ginnie Mae contracts were serving the holders of those securities. At the same time, people who thought of themselves as traders rather than investors might use such a contract as a vehicle for stock speculation.

The Kansas City exchange specializes in trading futures contracts on hard winter wheat, as contrasted with the soft winter variety traded in the larger Chicago market. Business boomed in Kansas City during the 1970s as a consequence of the huge export orders placed by the Soviet Union for that type of grain. The local traders savored this taste of prosperity and craved more. Stock index futures were to be their bid to enter the new age of futures trading.

Following a script that resembled the one written by Leo Melamed in bringing to fruition his foreign currency contracts ten years earlier, the chief executive officer of the Kansas City Board, Walter N. Vernon III, who also happened to be a lawyer, set out to obtain the necessary authorization and support to begin trading an index contract. Vernon hoped to receive the green light within a matter of months. It took instead more than four years for the light to change.

The Commodity Futures Trading Commission, the federal agency responsible for regulating the futures industry, must approve all new contract applications. Vernon accordingly submitted to the commission in early 1977 an application to undertake trading of a contract based on "an average of thirty industrial stocks"—obviously a reference to the Dow Jones Industrial Average. He then approached Dow Jones & Company for its authorization to use the average for that purpose. Dow Jones would not hear of it. Citing its "proprietary rights" and the damage to its name such an association would cause, the company threatened to take Vernon and the Kansas City Board to court if they persisted with their proposal.

Vernon, lawyer that he was, wasn't inclined to fight. He instead turned to Standard & Poor's but was rebuffed again. S&P was at that time being wooed by the Chicago exchanges to the same purpose and could afford to play a waiting game. He finally received a welcome at Arnold Bernhard & Company. The Bernhard organization had no objection to lending its Value Line name to a novel trading instrument. It rather liked the idea, in fact. A bargain was struck, and the Kansas City Board filed with the federal regulators an amended application specifying the Value Line Composite Average as the basis for its proposed contract. Even so, a great deal of time would elapse before the commission felt disposed to approve the application.

Getting Into the Act

While the hard-wheat traders from Kansas City awaited the commission's decision, the other exchanges directed their planning staffs to come up with index proposals of their own. The New York Futures Exchange had an obvious claim on the composite index of its parent. "For the first time you're going to see a bunch of pros trading futures on the NYFE," declared one senior stock exchange member. "We are not going to miss the boat on stock index futures."[8]

But the Chicago exchanges weren't about to surrender their leadership in contract innovation, either to the junior futures exchange in Kansas City or to their New York rivals. Melamed & Company at the Chicago Mercantile Exchange were not the sort to rest on their laurels. The CME obtained from Standard & Poor's the exclusive rights to introduce a contract based on the S&P 500 index. It thereupon organized a new division, the Index and Option Market, or IOM, to accommodate trading as soon as regulatory approval was received. Said Leo Melamed with assurance, "The index we have [S&P 500] is definitely the one investment managers use to measure their portfolios. It's only logical to assume that this will be the dominant market."[9]

The Chicago Board of Trade was determined to contest Melamed's claim. But its choices were dwindling. With the other leading indexes already spoken for, the only option remaining was to induce—or coerce—Dow Jones to consent to its use of the Industrial Average. An offer of $2 million was reportedly made to buy that consent. The offer was refused. The Chicago Board nevertheless filed a proposal (as Kansas City had earlier done, without success) to trade what was referred to as a "portfolio futures contract based on thirty industrial stocks." Once again, there was no doubt concerning which thirty stocks the Board of Trade had in mind. In case there was anyone who didn't understand the message, two other "portfolio futures" contracts were also proposed, based on twenty transportation and fifteen utility stocks.

Dow Jones certainly got the message. It promptly responded that the "portfolio futures" were in fact based upon its copyrighted averages and that unless the Chicago Board dropped its proposal, its lawyers could argue the case before a judge. As it turned out, more than one judge heard the case. Suits and countersuits were filed in state and federal courts in New York, Washington, and Chicago. Dow Jones contended that its copyrights precluded any unauthorized use of its name or its averages and that its name and image would be harmed by being linked with a speculative trading vehicle. The company maintained that investors would take such an association as a tacit endorsement by Dow Jones and that it would suffer discredit when some of them lost money trading such contracts. Should the regulatory commission and the courts support the board's application, Dow Jones said that it would change the way in which the averages were computed and published. As a last resort to prevent their alleged exploitation, it threatened to suspend them altogether.

The Chicago Board's rejoinder was that the Dow Averages were so widely available as to be virtually in the public domain. The exchange stipulated that, in any case, the Dow Jones name would not be used in connection with the allegedly anonymous "portfolio futures," and so it wouldn't be tarnished. But, as if to contradict its own argument, the board warned that if Dow Jones should change the composition of its averages, the contracts would be modified to reflect the change.

Both sides won favorable rulings, but in the end Dow Jones prevailed. In July 1982 an Illinois appellate court barred the Chicago Board from trading a contract, whatever its nominal title, that was based on the Dow Jones Averages. That ruling reversed an earlier state court decision that the company's name would not be damaged because the board had promised not to mention it in connection with its proposed contracts.

The Chicago Board was not the only suitor that was rebuffed in the courts. Eager not to be left out of the running, the Comex in New York disputed Standard & Poor's right to grant the CME an exclusive license and went ahead with plans to introduce an index contract it baldly called the "Comex 500." S&P thereupon filed a copyright infringement suit against Comex, charging that exchange with misappropriation of proprietary information, unfair competition, and dilution of S&P's trademarks, The court supported S&P's claim, ruling that "Comex intended improperly to link S&P with Comex as a commercial prop" and was "misappropriating the skill, expenditures, labor and reputation of S&P in generating and producing the S&P index."[10] A Comex spokesman voiced the usual expressions of surprise and disappointment and announced the intention to consider another index if court rulings in the case continued to be unfavorable to the exchange.

Other would-be players expressed their desire to get into the game. The American Stock Exchange, its foray into futures having foundered with the demise of ACE, petitioned the SEC for approval to trade options based on the Amex market value index.[11] The CBOE touched all bases in applying to both the SEC and CFTC for permission to create a contract pegged to an unnamed index of 100 stocks, as well as options based on individual industry groups. Not to be overlooked, the NASD—National Association of Securities Dealers—announced its interest in creating a vehicle based on the NASDAQ composite index of approximately three thousand stocks.

Negative Reviews

While the exchanges, index makers, courts, and regulatory agencies debated who would tie up with whom, both elected and self-appointed guardians of the public good began decrying the whole idea. Stock index futures were nothing more than gambling, they said.

It could scarcely have been coincidental that while Dow Jones was resisting the Chicago Board's embrace, the *Wall Street Journal* printed a column that began, "Drop those dice, tear up those football-betting cards. A new gambling game is coming. . ."[12] Without troubling to mention his publisher's involvement in litigation concerning the contracts, the *Journal's* correspondent pooh-poohed the idea that investors would actually use them to reduce risk— that is, to hedge. He worried that neophytes would be hoodwinked by unscrupulous brokers and that the nation's economy might be undermined by more volatile stock prices and higher equity financing costs if such dealings were allowed. The would-be art critic was of the opinion that, "[The] stock index contract is an abstraction of traditional futures trading—sort of what Picasso might have dreamed up if let loose in a futures pit."[13]

The fact that the *Journal's* reporter—and, to be sure, many other people— found so troubling was that, unlike all previous futures contracts, nothing but money was to change hands when the index contracts fell due. It was hard to demonstrate an actual commercial use for them when no stock was to be delivered from sellers to buyers. The contracts' designers claimed that it was impractical to deliver one share of each stock that made up a particular index and that their proposed system of cash settlement would be much more efficient.

As a practical matter, the contracts' designers may have been correct. But the disassociation of the contracts from any underlying securities was bound to lend them a greater speculative flavor than that of physical commodity contracts or even the earlier financial futures. If you couldn't see the "commodity" or hold it in your hand, there was more credence to the argument that this was simply a new way to gamble.

With the fate of innocent investors and the nation's economy at stake, it was inevitable that Congress would make its feelings known on the issue. The chairmen of the House Energy and Commerce Committee and the House Government Operations Subcommittee both asked the commodity commission to defer any decision on the contract applications until they could conduct committee hearings and subject the matter to closer scrutiny.

Other government agencies and departments also urged caution. The Federal Reserve Board was concerned that the disparity between stock and commodity margins—they're much lower for futures—would weaken the Fed's control over stock market credit. The IRS fretted that the lower capital gains rate on futures transactions could reduce investors' tax liability.

Troubles at the CFTC

The agency that was charged with sorting out these matters was at that time experiencing difficulties of its own, which were to a great extent exacerbated by the stock index controversy. The Commodity Futures Trading Commission, or CFTC, was established in 1974 and given the authority to regulate the futures industry as the SEC had regulated the securities markets since its founding forty years earlier. The CFTC was from its inception hampered by budget and staff deficiencies, criticized by Congress for its alleged failure to police the industry properly, and exposed to the bureaucratic incursions of older agencies that coveted its powers. The proposal was repeatedly put forth to disband the commission and to transfer its regulatory role to the SEC. A less drastic measure would have been to cut the CFTC's jurisdiction back to the traditional agricultural and natural resource commodities and divide the responsibility for the rapidly expanding financial futures markets among the SEC, Treasury Department, and Federal Reserve.

Amid this atmosphere of uncertainty and antagonism, the CFTC was called upon to determine whether stock index futures were in, or contrary to, the public interest. Hearings were held in Washington, where volumes of testimony were taken. Still, the commission could not or would not decide. The various contract applications were shelved while the five commissioners and their staff were busy skirmishing in the jurisdictional war. No action was taken regarding the index proposals until the presidential election of 1980 caused a reshuffling within the commission. The incumbent chairman stepped down but remained a commissioner, and the incoming administration placed its appointee at the head of the commission. The new chairman's previous affiliation as counsel to the Chicago Board of Trade was not thought to be an impediment to prompt action. The board and the other exchanges with applications pending were anxious to obtain the long-awaited clearance and get the index futures sweepstakes underway.

The regulatory dispute was temporarily muted as the CFTC and SEC drew up a "peace pact" recognizing the jurisdictional status quo. The new CFTC chairman brought the proposals to a vote in early 1982, nearly 4 1/2 years after the Kansas City Board submitted its original application. The commission voted, with the former chairman in solitary opposition, to approve the applications as being in the public interest and serving a valid economic purpose.

As the exchange that had waited the longest, the Kansas City Board saw its application approved first. Kansas City was not a magnanimous winner, however. Having waited over four years to enjoy its day in the sun, it sought to block approval of the other applications until it had an opportunity, it said, to recover its research and development outlays. The commission took that as a bid to steal a march on the competition and rejected it. The CME and NYFE applications were cleared within weeks, and the race was on. The unrequited suitors, the Chicago Board and Comex, were left standing on the sidelines as the winning contestants cranked up their publicity machines and set about capturing a major share of the new market.

On February 24, 1982, the Kansas City Board held its long-deferred opening-day ceremony with the usual speeches and ribbon cutting. The mayor of Kansas City, who was one of the honored guests, later told a reporter, "It was very exciting. They even let me ring the opening bell."[14]

CHAPTER 3

Mechanics and Arithmetic of Index Futures Trading

Trading index futures contracts is not the same as buying and selling shares of stock. The sooner an investor who intends to use futures appreciates that, the better off he or she will be. Most investors think in terms of buying and holding. That is what investing in the stock market is all about. People trade futures; they don't invest in them. They must be as ready to sell contracts as they are to buy them. In fact, those investors who plan to employ index futures to hedge their stock portfolios against price depreciation will sell these contracts first and buy them later.

A would-be futures trader should have little difficulty visualizing the train of events that attend the purchase or sale of a physical commodity for future delivery. It is possible to picture in the mind's eye a bushel of wheat, or even five thousand bushels, the size of a standard futures contract, as the commodity moves toward its ultimate disposition. Wheat, after all, is a tangible product, one that can be seen, held, and eventually consumed in some form.

Values of Index Futures

But how does one visualize a stock index? It is only a number. And what should be the accepted standard quantity for such a number, comparable to a

Table 3.1 1982 Price Range, Stock Index Contracts

	August 6 Low	November 9 High	Dollar Change per Contract
December 1982 Value Line	111.65	163.45	+$25,900
December 1982 S&P 500	103.00	145.80	+$21,400
December 1982 NYSE Composite	58.90	83.85	+$12,475

bushel of wheat or, for that matter, a share of stock? There was no such measure until the various index contracts were devised.

The contract designers sought a unit that would express, in dollars, movements in the particular index on which their contract was based. Their solution was to multiply the index by an arbitrary dollar figure and to regard the result as the underlying value of the futures contract. The $500 multiple upon which they settled was a compromise. Professional portfolio managers accustomed to dealing in hundreds of thousands and sometimes millions of dollars' worth of stock might have preferred a larger contract size. Average investors who typically deal in one- or two-hundred-share lots would have liked a smaller contract.

Multiplying the S&P 500 Composite Index by $500 when the index stands at, say, 120.00 creates a contract worth $60,000 (120.00 × $500). That is comparable to a $15,000 aggregate value for 5,000 bushels of wheat at $3 a bushel or to 400 shares of a $60 stock having a market value of $24,000. To continue with the illustration, if the S&P index then fell to 110.00, the futures contract would have lost $5,000 in value ([120.00 − 110.00] × $500). That, in its most basic form, is how index futures contracts work. The only mathematical difference between them and other futures contracts or even shares of stock is that the index value itself is not used as a "price;" rather, the index value is used as a "quantity," which—when multiplied by the $500 multiple—gives the dollar value of the index contract. All of the contracts—S&P 500, Value Line, and NYSE Composite—carry the same $500 multiple. Because the NYSE Composite Index stands at roughly half the level of the two other indexes, its contract value is proportionately less. But because it moves up and down in the same point increments, the dollar value of a one-point gain or loss is the same (see table 3.1).

It is therefore in terms of relative contract values, and not share prices, that index traders calculate their gains and losses. If a trader's intent is to hedge his or her stock portfolio against loss with index futures, the first task is to translate the market value of that portfolio into the equivalent number of futures contracts. If the portfolio has a value ranging between $50,000 and $60,000, the trader should sell one S&P 500 or Value Line contract. If the stock portfolio is worth twice that amount, the trader will need to sell two contracts. He or she is better off using the NYSE Composite contract if the portfolio falls within the $25,000 to $30,000 range. Index contracts cannot be divided into "odd lots," so a prospective hedger should have a portfolio equivalent at least to the value of one contract for the hedge to be effective.

Some Basic Characteristics

Traders who use index futures for speculation are only concerned with the underlying value of the contracts insofar as the changes in such values are what determine gains and losses. The index figures per se are computed to two decimal places where a point is taken to be 0.01. In terms of the contracts, each 0.01 is equal to $5 (0.01 × $500); this amount was the increment that the sponsors intended should be the minimum price fluctuation when the contracts were introduced. As trading commenced in Kansas City, however, it immediately became apparent that $5 was too narrow a range for efficient trading, and the minimum was quickly raised to the 0.05-level, or $25—the increment that floor traders had intuitively adopted as a more practical figure.

When the Kansas City Board of Trade Value Line Average (KCBT-VLA) is quoted at 122.50, the next transaction completed at another price will be at least 0.05 above or below that figure—that is, either 122.55 or 122.45. Depending upon whether he or she holds a long or a short position, an index trader in this case profits or loses by the number of contracts times $25. The other exchanges subsequently adopted the same minimum fluctuation for their contracts.

All futures contracts have a fixed expiration date, a condition that invests each contract with a limited life. There are at any time several quarterly expirations in effect—usually in a March, June, September, and December series—affording traders the option of buying or selling contracts falling due in any one or more of those months. The August 10, 1983, price listings for the Value Line, S&P 500, and NYSE Composite quarterly contracts are reproduced in table 3.2.

Although a trader may buy or sell contracts for any of the expiration dates—called "delivery months"—that are listed, he or she must close the position out by an offsetting transaction in the same maturity. The purchase of a March 1984 Value Line contract, for example, can only be offset by the sale of a March Value Line contract for the same year. That applies to all other contracts and delivery months as well. Trading in a particular contract ceases when the nearest delivery date is reached, and a new contract is then introduced at the distant end of the quarterly series.

The August 10 prices also provided a number of illustrations of how gains

Table 3.2 Stock Index Futures Prices, August 10, 1983

Expiration Date	Life-of-Contract High	Life-of-Contract Low	Daily High	Daily Low	Daily Settle	Daily Change	Open Interest
			NYSE Composite Index (NYFE)				
Sept. '83	100.80	59.65	94.25	92.55	93.70	+0.65	10,073
Dec. '83	101.45	60.88	95.00	93.25	94.40	+0.65	1,161
Mar. '84	101.65	79.25	95.60	94.20	95.10	+0.65	778
June '84	103.00	82.30	96.00	95.00	95.80	+0.65	408
			Vol. 17,076				
			S&P 500 Stock Index (CME)				
Sept. '83	173.85	121.00	163.40	160.50	162.60	+1.15	23,396
Dec. '83	175.05	143.70	164.60	161.80	163.90	+1.15	5,466
Mar. '84	177.30	153.75	165.70	164.00	165.20	+1.15	84
June '84	175.80	166.30	167.00	164.75	166.50	+1.15	30
			Vol. 39,532				
			Value Line Stock Index (KCBT)				
Sept. '83	212.10	111.50	195.75	192.05	194.50	+0.90	3,821
Dec. '83	213.35	111.40	196.30	192.95	195.45	+0.85	487
Mar. '84	214.80	161.65	—	—	198.00	+1.00	—
June '84	212.00	211.40	—	—	199.20	+1.00	—
			Vol. 3,495				

SOURCE: *New York Times,* August 11, 1983, D12.

and losses on index contracts are calculated. According to table 3.2, the December 1983 S&P 500 contract gained 115 points, from 162.75 (not reported in the table) to 163.90. The 115-point rise represented an appreciation of $575 (115 × $5) in that contract's value. Had a trader sold four December contracts at 162.75 on August 9, his or her loss by the end of the following trading day would have been $2,300. All the expirations of a particular contract do not necessarily rise or fall by the same amount on a given day. For example, while the September 1983 Value Line contract rose 90 points on August 10, the next delivery, December 1983, gained 85 points, and the following two deliveries, March and June 1984, each gained 100 points.

The Long and Short of Trading

As was noted above, most investors have a bias in favor of buying and holding stock. Selling short—that is, selling borrowed stock with the hope of making a profit by repurchasing and returning it to the lender at a lower price—is not only risky but also carries a connotation of manipulation and shady dealing. Wall Street sages like to state the obvious fact that, while the price of a stock can drop only to zero, it can rise indefinitely, creating unlimited losses for the short-seller. The admonition "Don't sell America short" implies that it is somehow unpatriotic to be pessimistic about the stock market.

Such attitudes have no place in the futures market. It is precisely because stocks do drop in price that index futures were created. Anyone who enters this market with an economic or moral prejudice against selling short will be going in with one hand tied behind his or her back. And that can be—and usually is—a grave handicap in an arena where one needs to have the dexterity of a juggler.

Index contracts aren't conventional investments because one cannot "own" them in the sense that he or she owns stocks or bonds. A contract is a commitment to perform rather than an asset to be acquired and held. You either "go long" futures (that is, you buy them) with the expectation that their price will rise, or you "go short" (sell them) with the expectation that the price will fall. In the case of physical commodities, a seller assumes an obligation to deliver the commodity in question at some point unless the contract is otherwise terminated. A contract buyer, on the other hand, is obliged to accept delivery of that commodity and at the time of delivery to pay for it in full. The unique cash settlement terms of index futures render the delivery aspect of the contracts somewhat nebulous. As was noted in the previous chapter, the absence of any provision for the delivery of securities at the contract's expiration date has provoked criticism that they are more gambling tokens than legitimate financial instruments.

In the August 10, 1983, example, the rising prices denoted profits for long contract holders. They could as well have meant losses for short holders. If prices had the following day reversed direction and gone down, short position holders would have enjoyed gains, and long holders would have suffered losses.

If, on August 10 or any other day, a trader felt that the stock market was about to advance, he or she would be disposed to buy index futures. The trader would have to decide which of the three index futures to buy, the number of contracts, the specific delivery month—the term persists even though no delivery is involved—and the price he or she wishes to pay. If that analysis leads the trader to buy three June 1984 Value Line contracts at 199.20 and, by way of illustration, the price of that contract advanced to 213.40 in three weeks' time, he or she might then sell the contracts and realize a profit, disregarding brokerage commissions for the moment, of $21,300, computed as follows:

$$(213.40 - 199.20) \times \$500 \times 3 = \$21,300$$

When it comes time for the trader to realize the resulting profit, it is the June 1984 Value Line contracts he or she must sell, and they can be sold only where they were initially bought, on the Kansas City Exchange.

To demonstrate the reverse side of the futures coin, another trader may have held a bearish view of the stock market on August 10 and decided to sell short four December 1983 NYSE Composite contracts at 94.40. If, during the same three-week period cited above, those contracts had risen in price to 99.60, that trader would have been a loser to the tune of $10,400—that is:

$$(99.60 - 94.40) \times \$500 \times 4 = -\$10,400$$

The disappointed trader might have taken some consolation in the fact that the loss was less than half what it would have been had he or she sold four Value Line contracts instead of the NYSE Composites.

Trading on Expectations

With all due respect to the Bard of Stratford upon Avon, to buy or to sell is the question that can make or break you in the futures market. Whether you are long or short determines your market exposure. That is your "position," in futures-market lingo. The subsidiary issues of which index futures, the delivery month, and the number of contracts you buy or sell will determine how much you make or lose. These are by all means important questions, and ones that will be discussed at length throughout the remainder of this book. But whether to buy or to sell—aye, there's the rub.

Index futures are claimed to be effective hedging instruments on account of the close connection between contract prices and the market value of well-diversified stock portfolios. When stocks go down, contract values are supposed to go down by a comparable amount. Yet, as we quoted Professor Hieronymus in the last chapter, when speculators enter the futures game, they tend to take it over.[1] The consequence is that, as their mood swings from bullish to bearish and back to bullish, futures prices perform somewhat independently of stock prices, and the connection between them can at times become rather tenuous.

This phenomenon is evident in table 3.2. On August 10, 1983, each successive delivery of the S&P 500 and the NYSE Composite contracts was quoted at a higher price than the one preceding it: 162.60 for September 1983, 163.90 for December 1983, 165.20 for March 1984, and so on for the S&P 500 contract; 93.70, 94.40, 95.10, and so on for the NYSE Composite. The most distant S&P 500 delivery, June 1984, was priced at 166.50, slightly less than 500 points, or $2,500 per contract, above the actual August 10 closing S&P index of 161.54. The most distant NYSE Composite contract, also June 1984, was quoted at 95.80, 250 points, or $1,250 per contract, above that day's closing NYSE index of 93.30.

Such a pattern is known as a premium price structure. It occurs when successive deliveries are quoted at increasingly higher prices over the actual index number; in futures terminology, the current, "real" price is referred to as the "cash" price. Conversely, a series of consecutively descending contract prices in an expiration series is termed a discount price structure.[2]

The primary causes of these variations are traders' changing *expectations* regarding the future course of stock prices as reflected in the indexes. Futures market participants expected the Value Line S&P 500, and NYSE Composite indexes to rise to higher levels in early 1984 than the point at which they stood in mid-August 1983. They accordingly bid the prices of distant contract delivery months up to levels that matched those expectations. An answer to why expectations regarding the several indexes should vary on any given date, here August 10, should be sought in the mix of stocks that comprise each index. It might be reasoned that the variation among the contracts on August 10 had to do with the outlook for the smaller, and presumably more speculative, issues that the Value Line index incorporates but that the other two indexes ignore.

Relationships and Differences

Whatever the differences may be between a particular index and its related futures contracts, they tend to vanish as each contract approaches its expiration date. This *convergence* between futures prices and the actual index occurs because the two values, according to the terms of the contract, become identical on the final settlement day. As that date nears, the linkage between futures price and index becomes more binding, and expectations play a less consequential role.

The convergence factor lends a favorable bias to a short position in distant expiration dates when there is a premium price structure. If, as is theoretically possible but unlikely, an index stays at the same level over an extended period, the erosion of the premium over time works to a short contract holder's advantage. This advantage is only relative, however, since the index might advance during that period, in which case the disappearance of the premium may only serve to reduce a potential loss. By the same token, the convergence of a discounted contract is beneficial to a long position holder but does not in itself guarantee him or her a profit.

In addition to the daily settlement price, table 3.2 shows the daily high and low prices for each contract, the life-of-contract highs and lows, daily volume, and the current open interest for each delivery month. The volume is the number of contracts that are traded each day. There is a seller for every buyer, though it may require, say, five individuals selling two contracts each to satisfy a single buyer of ten contracts. Open interest is the number of contracts currently in force for each delivery date. That is a variable figure, which typically expands over the life of a contract and finally shrinks to nearly zero by its final settlement day as the majority of long and short contract holders close their positions out. Both volume and open interest are heaviest for the two nearest delivery dates of each contract, witness the September and December 1983 contracts in table 3.2. They then fall off sharply for the more distant deliveries.

There are other important differences between trading futures and buying stocks that individuals who are moving from one market to the other for the first time should consider. There is of course no such thing as "holding for the long pull"—often the credo of a disappointed speculator—a futures contract that has a limited life. You cannot put off a decision to sell or to buy back a contract beyond its expiration date because, by that time, the contract no longer exists.

Notes on Margins

All futures transactions are made on margin. Whatever category they happen to fall into—private investor, portfolio manager, dealer, underwriter, stock specialist, and so on—index futures traders never put up the full value of the contracts they buy or sell. To make matters even more confusing, futures margins are not the same as margins on stocks. An investor who buys stock on margin pays part of the total purchase price, typically 50 percent to 75 percent of it, and borrows the remainder from his or her broker so that the seller of the stock is paid in full. Futures margin, on the other hand, is "good-faith money"—a performance bond that both the buyer and seller of a contract deposit with their respective brokers to guarantee the timely fulfillment of their contractual obligations. If the contract price drops, the buyer's margin deposit is used to pay the corresponding profits that are due the seller. If the contract price goes up, the payment flow is reversed, with the appropriate portion of the seller's margin deposit going into the buyer's account.

Such performance margins are usually extremely low in relation to the underlying value of a contract and are a great deal less than the margin that would be required to buy an equivalent amount of stock. The margin on 90-

day U.S. Treasury-bill futures, for example, has been as low as $1,000. That is about .1 percent of the contract's $850,000 to $900,000 underlying value. Normally, futures margins range from 2 percent to 5 percent of a contract's value.

As was noted in the preceding chapter, the Federal Reserve Board, which sets the margin rates on stock purchases, expressed its concerns before stock index futures were approved for trading that this wide disparity between securities and futures margins would undermine the Fed's control over stock market credit. To assuage the Fed's fears and to forestall any further delay in the approval process, the exchanges took it upon themselves to propose that margins on index futures be set substantially higher than the norm. The figure the concerned parties eventually agreed to was $6,500 per contract, or somewhat more than 8 percent of the underlying value of $500 times the Value Line or S&P 500 index at, say, 150.00.

That $6,500 is called *initial margin*. It is the amount a trader must deposit with his or her broker to buy or sell an index contract. After this deposit is made and the contract(s) are bought or sold, adverse market action may render the trader liable to deposit additional money—called *maintenance margin*—if the initial deposit is impaired by a predetermined amount. As long as the market price moves against the trader—down if he or she is long or up if short—the trader will be required to make repeated margin deposits to maintain that position. Futures gains and losses are computed daily, a procedure known as "marking to the market." If the computation discloses that the margin funds that were deposited in a trader's account have been impaired by as much as 40 percent, the shortfall must be replaced, or else the broker carrying the account is compelled to liquidate the position to prevent further loss.[3]

Lower margin rates are applied to those traders who qualify as bona fide hedgers, inasmuch as they use index contracts to reduce the risk of owning stock. The rationale behind preferential rates for hedgers is that their market exposure—and hence, their risk—is a great deal less than that of speculators who carry outright long or short positions.

Commissions and Limits

Brokerage commissions on futures transactions are charged only on the second trade, when a position is closed out; the two trades constitute a "round-turn." A single "round-turn" commission covers both a purchase and sale—or a sale and purchase in the case of a short position—in contrast to the commission charged for the purchase of a stock, followed by a second commission charge when that stock is sold. Like stock commissions, futures commission rates are negotiable, depending upon the amount and type of service a broker provides and the size and activity of the customer's account.

Pandemonium in the Pits

There are differences in the way in which futures and stock exchanges are organized and the means by which orders are executed there. The New York Stock Exchange operates on the specialist system. These "brokers' brokers" perform the dual—and sometimes contradictory—functions of maintaining orderly markets in particular stocks that are assigned to them and of executing orders that are placed with them by other exchange members. Futures exchanges do not have specialists or market makers. There, all members are of equal rank, although each has his or her distinctive technique of trading. Prices are established by open outcry among all the members present rather than through two members' withdrawing to a corner and striking their private deal.

A hundred shares of stock—say, General Motors—that is purchased on one stock exchange can without much trouble be sold on another exchange where GM is traded. The same does not hold true of index futures or any other kind of futures contracts. It is not possible, for example, to buy or sell a Kansas City Value Line contract at the Chicago Mercantile Exchange's Index and Option Market or at the New York Futures Exchange. Moreover, positions usually must be liquidated through the same broker that initiates them, although there are exceptions to that practice.

If a visitor to a futures exchange were asked to describe in one word a first impression of the scene around him or her, the visitor might well respond: Pandemonium! Men—and, recently, a few women—attired in outfits resembling beige mess jackets with large identification badges pinned to the lapels stand either around a waist-high railing or on the steps of a miniamphitheater shouting and waving their arms at one another. Some of them appear to be shaking their fists. A second glance reveals that they are making hand signals.

On the periphery, clerks are seated at banks of telephone stations. Runners carry messages between them and the people who are engaging in this bizarre ceremony. It is hard to believe there is order underlying all this commotion; yet that is very much the case.

The people in the mess jackets are exchange members trading by open, competitive outcry. And outcry it literally is. Prospective buyers are shouting their best bids. Would-be sellers are as vociferously responding with their lowest offers. The result is a highly liquid and efficient marketplace. As was noted above, there are no specialists on a futures exchange. The membership performs the specialist function collectively—and loudly. New members soon learn that it's more practical (and less costly) to be manhandled wearing a drab mess jacket amid the arm waving and jostling than an elegant Brooks Brothers or Yves St. Laurent suit coat. Futures trading is very physical work.

Brokers and Traders

Exchange members fall into one of two primary categories. There are those members who, either as principals or as employees, exercise the memberships owned by their firms. They concentrate on handling the orders of their firms' customers, what the trade refers to as "outside paper." Nearly all of the major brokerages—including Merrill Lynch, Shearson Lehman Brothers, Paine Webber, Prudential-Bache, and Dean Witter Reynolds—own at least one seat on each of the major commodity exchanges in the United States and abroad. These investment firms compete for customer accounts with companies that are exclusively commodity-oriented, such as Cargill and Geldermann Peavey, Inc. In recent years firms that had traditionally conducted either an exclusively securities or an exclusively commodity brokerage have combined through acquisition or merger with a company on the other side to develop an integrated service, reflecting trends within the markets themselves.

The second group of exchange members consists of traders who have their own seats and make their living buying and selling for themselves. These so-called locals are solo operators who occupy a pivotal but sometimes controversial role within the trading structure. They are for the most part rugged individualists who wield substantial power inside the membership councils of their exchanges, as do stock exchange specialists. The locals maintain, with justification, that it is chiefly their capital, and their willingness to put that capital at risk, that provide the futures markets with the liquidity that is essential to their efficient operation.[4] On the other hand, locals are often criticized for having an unfair advantage over nonmember traders who must buy and sell through the big brokerage firms.

There is no question that being at the center of the action is an advantage. But it can also be argued that the lofty price of an exchange seat—recently ranging as high as $250,000—makes that advantage a very expensive one to acquire. People would not pay such prices for the privilege of doing business on the exchange floor—usually buying their seats with borrowed money—unless they expected to earn a handsome return on their investment. Members themselves complain that they are so restricted by exchange rules intended to prevent them from exploiting their favored position that they are hampered in fulfilling their legitimate risk-taking function. Besides, some of the more outspoken among them might add—and, as we've just mentioned, being outspoken is a major job qualification in this instance—they're risking not just money but strained vocal chords and fallen arches, and they do so to make more money, not to provide a public service.

Three Kinds of Locals

The locals are further divided into three loose groupings, which reflect a member's individual approach to trading. There is first a group that carries the colorful label of "scalpers," each of whom may make as many as several hundred transactions during a single trading session. A scalper seeks to make only one or two "ticks"—minimum price fluctuations—each time he or she buys and sells, often within a matter of seconds, and counts on many such rapid-fire trades to provide a worthwhile profit by the end of the day.

A scalper in Kansas City may look to his or her right and accept a neighboring trader's offer to sell one December Value Line contract at 184.50, then immediately turn to the left and sell the just-purchased contract at 184.60. Net profit: $50. His or her counterpart at the CME's Index and Option Market in Chicago might sell two March S&P 500 contracts at 155.80, only to close out that short position a moment later when the price moves up to 155.95. Net loss: $150. If scalpers can guess right 50 times more often than they guess wrong each day, they can make a good living at this fast-paced game. The trick is to recognize immediately when you're on the wrong side of a momentary swing in the market and not to wait for it to swing back before getting out. Scalpers who cannot master that knack will be looking for a different line of work when their starting capital is depleted.

It is because they pay no brokerage fees and are literally in the thick of things that scalpers are able to trade profitably in this fashion. It is in large part their particular brand of trading that creates the action on the exchange. The scalpers' repeated buying and selling provide the futures market with the liquidity that is necessary to attract outside participants. A mutual fund manager would not choose to use index futures as hedging instruments if a single order to sell one hundred contracts drove the price down forty points. That is what might happen if the scalpers were not there, waiting to make their quick turns. Rather than being antagonists, the one side attempting to gain at the other side's expense, the local traders and the outside participants are actually dependent upon each other to maintain a market in which all have a chance to operate successfully.

The second group of locals, the day traders, take a somewhat longer view. Their targets are the twenty- to fifty-point moves that occur one or more times during the course of a trading session. Day traders may buy or go short at the market's opening and carry that position until the closing bell. Or they may reverse their position, as scalpers do, several times daily according to the prevailing drift of the market. True to their tag, however, day traders seldom carry open positions overnight, preferring to wipe their slate clean by the close of each session and to start afresh the following day.

The locals who have the longest perspective are the position traders. They are prepared to stick with a position for weeks, or perhaps months, to capture a major move in the market. In terms of the various indexes, a major swing may run anywhere from ten to thirty points. A position trader who carries, say ten contracts for a profitable move of two thousand points on the Value Line or S&P 500 index will amass a gain of about $100,000, disregarding brokers' commissions (2,000 points × $5 × 10 contracts). If he or she can duplicate that performance several times a year, a position trader's profits can surpass those of scalpers and day traders. The former's pace of trading may be slower, but on the other hand the risk of carrying large positions over relatively long periods is greater than the risk level most short-term traders normally care to accept. To repeat our oft-quoted maxim yet one more time: There is no such thing as a free lunch.

Types of Orders

Prospective portfolio hedgers and off-floor speculators must learn to deal with the exchange professionals on the latter group's terms. It is, after all, their market. Those terms include the proper drafting and transmission of buy and sell orders. If they do not express their intentions to the floor brokers in the prescribed fashion, the efforts of the most astute analysts and forecasters will go unrewarded. To put it bluntly, they will most likely lose money.

It is usually the broker's responsibility to advise his or her clients concerning the different types of orders that are available to them and to recommend the one that is best suited to the situation at hand. For their part, the customers should be aware of the advantages and shortcomings of each type of order and what it is meant to accomplish. Figure 3.1 illustrates the placement and execution of various types of orders.

The simplest and most expeditious type of order is the *market order*. It directs a firm's floor broker to execute the order at the best price available the moment he or she receives it. If the order is to buy two June NYSE Composite contracts, and the lowest offer to sell that contract is then 85.30, that is the price at which the contracts will be purchased. If the order is instead to buy ten June contracts, and only three contracts are offered for sale at 85.30, the remaining seven contracts would be bought at the next lowest offers—say, two at 85.35 and five at 85.40. Because futures prices are much more volatile than stock prices, the use of market orders may provoke some unpleasant surprises, as when they are executed at unexpectedly high prices on buy orders and at low ones on sell orders.

One means of avoiding such unpleasant surprises is through the use of a

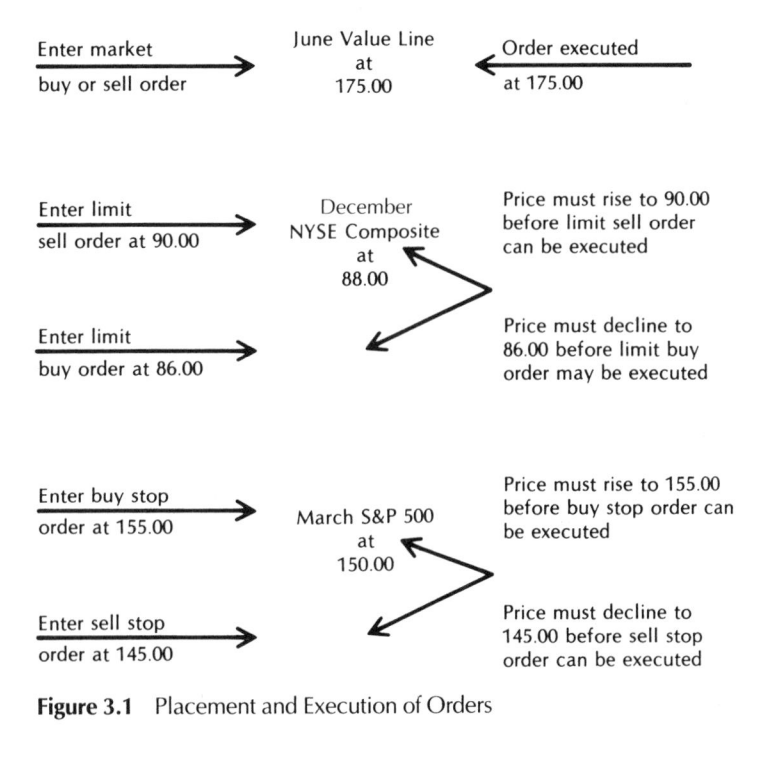

Figure 3.1 Placement and Execution of Orders

limit order. If a trader wants to sell five March Value Line contracts at 177.50 and will not accept a lower price, he or she should instruct the broker to specify that price on the order, as follows:

Sell 5 March 198X KCBT-VLA 177.50

There is, however, no guarantee that all or any of the contracts will in fact be sold at that price. If there are no bids to buy March VLA contracts at 177.50 or higher when the exchange clerk hands that order to his or her floor broker, the latter can only hold the order and hope that the market price will rally to the specified price. Sometimes it does, and sometimes it doesn't. Thus, one unpleasant surprise may be exchanged for another—namely, that the order is never executed at all. The trader must therefore decide beforehand which of the potential evils will be the least damaging to him or her: to get an unfavorable price or to get no price at all.

Orders may be limited in terms of time as well as price. If an order includes a price limit but not a time limit, it will automatically expire if it is not executed by the end of the trading day. Otherwise, it may be made "good through week" or "good through month" if the trader wants it to remain in force for so long a time, or good until a specified hour if the intended time span is less than one day.

An order may be left in force indefinitely, until it is either executed or the trader and his or her broker decide to cancel it. It is, logically enough, called an "open" or "good till cancelled (GTC)" order. As a general rule, it's not a good idea to leave an open order in force for an extended length of time. Despite automatic reminders from the brokers holding such orders, people tend to forget them and suddenly find themselves saddled with positions they no longer wanted.

Stop orders—commonly referred to as "stop-loss" orders, although there are other uses to which they may be put—are the only type that is entered to buy at a price above the prevailing market price or to sell below the current price. Traders who use stop orders aren't willing to pay more than they have to or to receive less than the market is offering. Their purpose is to establish (and to act at) a price where they've decided to "bail out" of a losing position—hence, the term *stop loss*. Fixing such an escape price is a discipline to which futures traders *must* rigidly adhere, but it's one that many, to their ultimate sorrow, fail to follow.[5]

Stop orders can take some of the doubt and anguish out of realizing a loss because the decision is made before that loss occurs. For example, a trader buys two September S&P 500 contracts at 141.80 because he or she feels bullish about the stock market. But the September S&Ps start to fall in price. At what point does the trader admit that his or her timing was wrong—141.30, 140.00, 135.00, or lower? Anyone who has traded futures or stocks can recite by heart the thousand and one reasons why he or she should wait another week—or another month—before taking a loss. Something might happen. Yes, something usually does happen. The loss becomes bigger, and the trader becomes more tormented and irrational. It is a story as old as the history of markets.

Preparing Escape Routes

Having passed that way too many times, a trader finally says to himself or herself, "I'm confident that the market is going up (or down). But *if* I'm wrong, let me get out before the loss kills me." That is the beginning of wisdom, and the only salvation for a futures trader. If the trader decides to buy futures and determines that a thousand dollars per contract is as much of a loss as he or she is willing to incur, the trader also knows that the contracts must be sold no more than 200 points below his or her purchase price. This is where a stop order comes into the picture. If the trader had *gone long* September S&Ps at

141.80, he or she needs to bail out if and when those contracts drop to 139.80. The order is accordingly written as follows:

Sell 2 September S&P 500 − 139.80 stop

If the September contracts only fell 150 points or, better still, went up in price, the stop order would not be activated. It would, in the latter instance, be canceled as a matter of course when the contracts were sold at a profit. An alternate approach would be to keep raising the stop price as the contract price climbs, thereby preserving most of the accruing profits. That is the type of situation futures traders dream about, and the closest to having their cake and eating it—not to mention the fabled free lunch—that they're ever likely to get.

The reverse applies to a short position. If our intrepid trader had instead been bearish about the market and *sold* two September S&Ps at 141.80, he or she would need protection against the contract price's going up. Such protection could be obtained by placing a stop order to *buy* two contracts at 143.80, if a thousand dollars per contract was once again his or her loss limit. As in the case of a sell stop order, this order wouldn't be activated unless the stop price was touched.

Stop orders are also employed by traders who follow price charts and believe that a contract should only be bought or sold after a "breakout" above or below what is to them a significant price level. To waste no time establishing a long or short position after this purported breakout occurs, chart traders may instruct their brokers to enter a stop order at or close to the indicated price.

An unqualified stop order automatically becomes a market order when the stop price is touched. This may create the same sort of unpleasant surprise that a regular market order can. Traders may try to avoid that by specifying a *stop limit* price. When a stop limit order is "triggered," it becomes a straight limit order. But again, the risk exists that the order may be activated but not executed at the limit price, in which case the trader is deprived of the loss limitation he or she sought. If, as sometimes happens, a daily limit move carries the contract price through the trader's stipulated stop limit price—the term *limit* is here used in two different senses—the order is of no use whatsoever.

Role of the Clearinghouse

Once a trade is made between two floor members who are either acting for their own accounts or executing customer orders, the two traders part company so far as that particular transaction is concerned. Each becomes responsible to the exchange clearinghouse rather than to his or her opposite number for the timely fulfillment of the contractual obligation. The clearinghouse, a separate entity from the exchange itself, in this manner becomes a contracting party to each and every contract created on the exchange. It exercises the authority of the combined membership in enforcing the individual members' compliance with contract terms. By providing what amounts to a guarantee that every contract will be honored, the clearinghouse protects the integrity of the contract market and facilitates the transfer of settlement funds among its members. Because of their greater financial responsibility, the membership list of the clearinghouse is distinct from that of the exchange proper. Clearinghouse members are usually the largest and most financially secure firms among the exchange membership. All clearinghouse members are members of the exchange, but not all exchange members are members of the affiliated clearinghouse.

The clearinghouse oversees the daily "mark to the market" procedure, whereby members compute the aggregate value of their customers' positions on the basis of that day's final prices, pay to the clearinghouse the net amount of funds that are owed, or collect what is owed to their customers. By means of the mark-to-market system, all futures traders, through the intermediation of the clearinghouse and its clearing members, settle up their gains and losses on a daily basis.

The margin deposits each trader makes with his or her brokerage firm when buying or selling index contracts, or any other commodity futures, are for the purpose of covering these daily settlements. When market action favors the trader's position, his or her account is credited by the amount of the gain. When the action is adverse, the losses are charged against that account. If the customer doesn't have sufficient funds on deposit to cover those charges, plus a margin of safety to protect the broker against loss, the broker issues a maintenance margin call for fresh funds.

After all of its customer gains and losses are netted out—if there are $500,000 in gains and $500,000 in losses, admittedly an unlikely happenstance, there is no net balance—each member broker pays to the clearinghouse a check for whatever amount is owed on balance or obtains from it a check for any balance in its favor. Exchange members who are not themselves clearinghouse members must perform the same settlement through an affiliated clearing member. With this settlement procedure occurring each day before the market opening, the exchange and its combined membership are at any time at risk only to the extent of the current day's price fluctuation.

The same kind of settlement is made when each contract reaches its final expiration. In the case of nearly every other type of futures contract, there is a provision for the actual delivery of a commodity from a contract seller to a buyer. Index futures contracts are unique insofar as the final settlement is made through a transfer of cash.[6] The only difference between the daily mark-to-market procedure described above and the final settlement is that the value on which the closing gains and losses are calculated is the index itself rather than the last contract price.

Account Accounting

Finally, futures traders should have a working knowledge of the way in which the status of their accounts is figured, including an understanding of the various entries that appear on an account statement. By examining his or her statement, a trader should be able to anticipate broker calls for maintenance margin or know what funds are available for assuming additional positions. A misunderstanding of these items can easily lead to trading losses.

Every purchase and sale is reported in a *trade confirmation*, which is mailed to the holder of the account on the day of the transaction. A sample confirmation is reproduced in figure 3.2, showing the date of the trade, the number and delivery months of the contracts that were bought or sold, the transaction price, and the current money balance in the account. The confirmation advises that on October 17, Richard Rivers sold two March 198X NYSE Composite contracts at 75.50 and, following the transaction, the excess cash balance in his account was $30,000. Rivers would not have been called to deposit additional funds into the account since his starting balance was greater than the $7,000 initial margin ($3,500 per contract) required for the sale (or purchase) of two contracts.

In carrying a short position, Rivers would benefit from a drop in the March 198X NYSE contract price. Such a drop would generate an unrealized gain in his account. A price rise would create an unrealized loss. Gains and losses aren't realized until a position is closed out—that is, a long contract is sold or a short one is bought back. If, in the case of the sample Rivers account, the two short March 198X NYSE contracts were eventually "bought in" at 80.20, the account would show a realized loss of $4,700 [(80.20 − 75.50) × $500 × 2 contracts]. Another trade confirmation reporting the liquidating transaction would be mailed to Rivers, and the $4,700 realized loss plus the round-turn commission would be deducted from his current balance, bringing it to $32,200.

A *purchase and sale statement* is also mailed when each position is closed out, recording the initial price, the liquidation price, the commission charge, and the net gain or loss realized on that completed transaction.

If all of the positions held in an account were closed out at the same time and the consequent net gain or loss were added to or subtracted from the current balance, the resulting figure is the account *equity*. The equity changes as prices change. If, in the Rivers illustration, the March 198X contracts fell

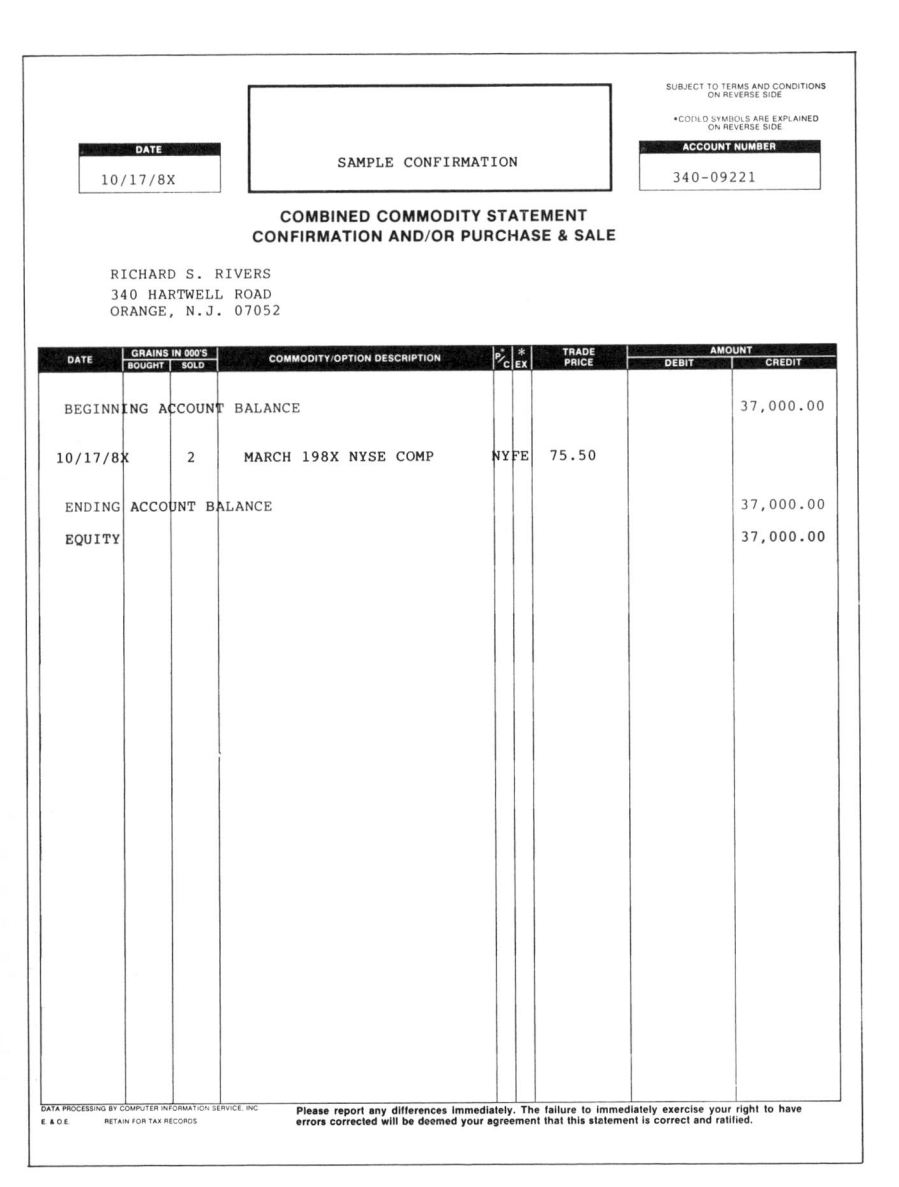

Figure 3.2 Sample Confirmation

back to 78.80 before they were liquidated, the account equity would have recovered in part, from $32,200 to $33,600.

The *excess* in an account is equal to the equity minus the initial margin required to carry each position. Excess is the amount that is available to buy or sell additional contracts or to meet maintenance margin calls in the event of unrealized losses. A trader may withdraw all or part of the excess from an account. But if he or she takes it all out, it must be restored if adverse price action causes fresh maintenance calls. The excess moves up and down with the equity in an account as contract prices fluctuate.

A customer's monthly statement itemizes all of the activity that has taken place in his or her account during the past month and lists the open contracts and cash balance in the account. The entry at the upper right-hand corner of the statement records the balance brought forward from the previous month, and below it are all of the subsequent deposits to and withdrawals from the account, credits from profitable trades, and debits as a result of losing ones. The net figure is the current ledger balance, which is carried forward into the next accounting period.

The lower half of the monthly statement lists open positions by contract and records the settlement price for each one as of the month's end. This information is sufficient to determine the required margin, equity, and excess in an account. For example, the sample monthly statement in figure 3.3 shows positions of four September Value Line and two December S&P 500 contracts. Deducting the $39,000 required on those positions from the equity of $84,000—that is, the current cash balance plus unrealized gains—there remains an excess of $45,000.

The major brokerage firms update the information daily on their computerized account records. It is therefore, not necessary for a customer to wait for a monthly statement and make these calculations on his or her own when a telephone call to the broker will provide the information instantly. Nevertheless, brokers have been known to make mistakes, so it's a good idea to compute the figures manually periodically as a spot check. Performing the calculations also helps a trader to understand better the consequences of past and prospective trading decisions.

Getting Information

Information on index futures is available from a variety of sources. The easiest to come by are the daily commodity price reports carried by the *New York Times,* the *Wall Street Journal,* and other newspapers that print comprehensive price listings. Naturally, the Value Line *Survey* and various Standard & Poor's publications such as the *Corporation Records* and the *Outlook* contain an

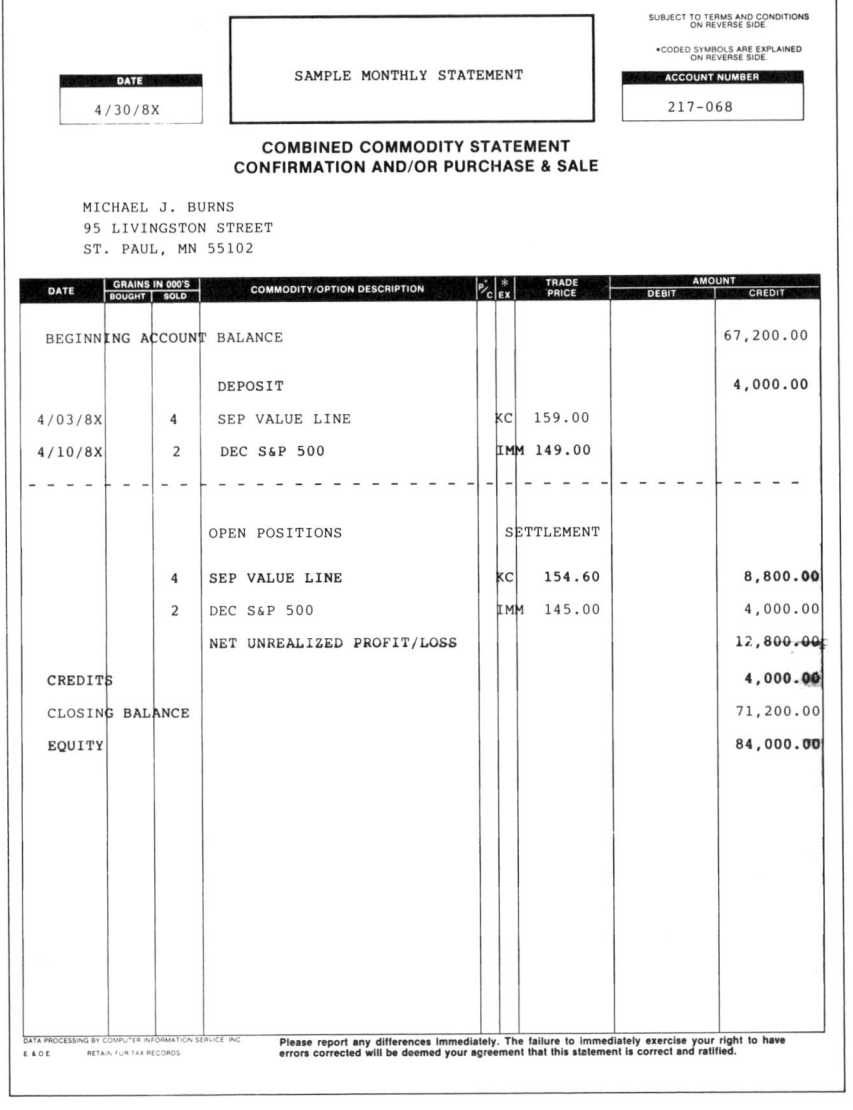

SUBJECT TO TERMS AND CONDITIONS
ON REVERSE SIDE

•CODED SYMBOLS ARE EXPLAINED
ON REVERSE SIDE

DATE

4/30/8X

SAMPLE MONTHLY STATEMENT

ACCOUNT NUMBER

217-068

**COMBINED COMMODITY STATEMENT
CONFIRMATION AND/OR PURCHASE & SALE**

MICHAEL J. BURNS
95 LIVINGSTON STREET
ST. PAUL, MN 55102

DATE	GRAINS IN 000'S		COMMODITY/OPTION DESCRIPTION	P/C	* EX	TRADE PRICE	AMOUNT	
	BOUGHT	SOLD					DEBIT	CREDIT
BEGINNING ACCOUNT BALANCE								67,200.00
			DEPOSIT					4,000.00
4/03/8X		4	SEP VALUE LINE	KC		159.00		
4/10/8X		2	DEC S&P 500	IMM		149.00		
- - - -	- -	- -	- - - - - - - - - - - - - - -	-	-	- - - -	- - - - -	- - - -
			OPEN POSITIONS		SETTLEMENT			
		4	SEP VALUE LINE	KC		154.60		8,800.00
		2	DEC S&P 500	IMM		145.00		4,000.00
			NET UNREALIZED PROFIT/LOSS					12,800.00
CREDITS								4,000.00
CLOSING BALANCE								71,200.00
EQUITY								84,000.00

DATA PROCESSING BY COMPUTER INFORMATION SERVICE INC
E & O E   RETAIN FOR TAX RECORDS

Please report any differences immediately. The failure to immediately exercise your right to have errors corrected will be deemed your agreement that this statement is correct and ratified.

Figure 3.3 Sample Monthly Statement

abundance of facts and figures pertaining to the stocks that comprise the Value Line and S&P indexes.[7]

Stock and commodity brokers distribute to their customers a great deal of research material covering the stock market in general. Some firms perform detailed analyses of index futures. Sample copies of this information will be sent upon request to people who are not clients of a particular firm. Such requests will usually prompt a solicitation call from a sales representative, inasmuch as free information is one of the means by which brokerage firms attract new customers. In any event, prospective clients should examine and evaluate the material put out by several firms before selecting the one that they wish to handle their account.

Business Week, Barron's, and *Fortune* often contain articles that are at least indirectly related to stock trends and index futures. *Futures* magazine and the *Journal of Futures Markets* print articles dealing with stock index futures from time to time, as do the *Financial Analysts Journal* and the *Journal of Portfolio Management.*

The exchanges on which stock index futures are traded make available without charge instructive brochures that describe the specifications of their particular contracts and contain basic information on how they may be used by various categories of traders and portfolio managers.

These brochures may be obtained by writing or calling the exchanges:

Index and Option Market (S&P 500 Index)
c/o Chicago Mercantile Exchange
30 South Wacker Drive
Chicago, Illinois 60606
(312) 648-1000
or
67 Wall Street
New York, New York 10005
(212) 363-7000

Kansas City Board of Trade (Value Line Average)
4800 Main Street, Suite 274
Kansas City, Missouri 64112
(816) 753-7500

New York Futures Exchange (NYSE Composite Index)
20 Broad Street
New York, New York 10005
(212) 623-4949

PART 2

Trading Techniques and Tactics

CHAPTER 4

Spreading and Hedging with Index Futures: The Key Variables

Statistics don't rank very high on most readers' lists of favorite topics. To my knowledge, no book titled *The Joy of Statistics* has ever been published. But those readers who plan to trade stock index futures should have at least a working knowledge of the statistical concepts underlying their price behavior before committing hard-earned dollars to this market.

Statistical analysis might appear the farthest thing possible from the minds of Kansas City, Chicago, or New York floor traders as they shout and gesticulate their bids and offers. Yet it should come as no surprise that the most successful floor traders make calculations in their heads while buying and selling contracts that many of us would need a minicomputer or a pocket calculator to perform.

As was related in chapter 1, each of the stock indexes under consideration is computed in a somewhat different fashion. And each of them obviously has a different makeup, ranging from the thirty Dow Jones Industrials to the nearly seventeen hundred issues that comprise the Value Line Composite Average. Therefore, even though each index is regarded as an indicator of overall market trends, it is to be expected that their performance will vary, from one day to the next and over a more extended period.

How Stocks Affect an Index

Although, owing to Dow Jones & Company's unyielding opposition, there was in 1984 no futures contract based on its Industrial Average, the company may at some time relent and sanction such a contract. Whether or not that ever happens, it is instructive to examine how the behavior of the thirty industrial issues affects the performance of the average itself. Similar factors are at work within the broader indexes, but the impact of individual stocks is in their case harder to isolate.

To reiterate an earlier point, the Dow Jones Industrial Average is computed solely on the basis of each stock's market price, disregarding its capitalization. Each of the thirty issues therefore influences the numerical average in proportion to its current share price. Table 4.1 illustrates this effect. The thirty industrials are ranked in the right-hand column according to their price on December 27, 1982, when the average reached a high for that year of 1070.55. Procter & Gamble at 123 was the highest-priced stock on December 27, exerting an influence on the average about fifteen times that of International Harvester, which at 8 1/2 was the lowest-priced stock.

But when the stock market was at its prior cyclical low, on August 12, 1982, the price rankings were somewhat different. That ranking is listed in the left-hand column of table 4.1. At a price of 77 3/4, Procter & Gamble remained the highest-priced stock on the list. But in rising from 55 to 100, General Electric climbed during the August 12 to December 27 period from fifth place to second on the list of thirty stocks, surpassing Eastman Kodak, IBM, and Merck. As other stocks moved up and down in rank, reacting to the overall market advance in different degrees, their relative weightings in the industrial average also changed. At both high and low levels, the price total was divided, as it is every day, by the then-current divisor to compute that day's average.

One often hears sweeping predictions of the Dow Industrials soaring to some lofty level like 1,500 or else crashing down to, say, 300. An analysis of the sort outlined above is useful in evaluating such extreme projections. The high and low prices of the thirty stocks for the eleven-year period from 1972 to 1982 are listed in table 4.2. Both the high and low prices are totaled and then divided by the divisor in effect at the end of 1982 to show the levels at which the DJIA would have stood in the unlikely event all of the indicated highs and lows had been achieved on the same days. Such a price-by-price comparison helps to put into better perspective the exaggerated predictions, whether of Golconda or doomsday, that some market pundits are prone to make, and to assess the likelihood of their being realized.[1]

Table 4.1 Price Ranking of Dow Jones Thirty Industrials at 1982 Lows and Highs

August 12, 1982, Lows		December 27, 1982, Highs	
1. Procter & Gamble	77¾	1. Procter & Gamble	123
2. Eastman Kodak	65⅜	2. General Electric	100
3. Merck	64	3. Eastman Kodak	98⅛
4. IBM	55⅝	4. IBM	98
5. General Electric	55	5. Merck	88¼
6. AT&T	49⅞	6. Minnesota Mining and Manufacturing	79⅜
7. Minnesota Mining and Manufacturing	48¾	7. American Express	70¾
8. Union Carbide	40⅛	8. AT&T	64⅝
9. American Brands	35⅜	9. General Motors	64½
10. American Express	35¼	10. Union Carbide	61
11. General Motors	34	11. United Technologies	58⅞
12. International Paper	32¾	12. International Paper	51⅝
13. United Technologies	31¼	13. American Brands	51
14. Du Pont	30	14. General Foods	47¾
15. General Foods	29	15. Allied Corp.	45⅜
16. Allied Corp.	28¾	16. Du Pont	44⅜
17. Texaco	26	17. Standard Oil (Calif.)	42⅞
18. American Can	25¾	18. Westinghouse	40½
19. Exxon	24⅞	19. Goodyear	36⅞
20. Standard Oil (Calif.)	23½	20. American Can	35¾
21. Westinghouse	21⅞	21. Texaco	34⅞
22. Alcoa	21⅞	22. Alcoa	32¾
23. Owens Illinois	20⅞	23. Exxon	32¼
24. Goodyear	17⅞	24. Sears, Roebuck	32
25. U.S. Steel	16	25. U.S. Steel	30⅛
26. Woolworth	15⅞	26. Owens Illinois	29⅝
27. Sears, Roebuck	15¾	27. Woolworth	29⅛
28. Bethlehem Steel	14½	28. Bethlehem Steel	23½
29. INCO	7⅞	29. INCO	14¾
30. International Harvester	2¾	30. International Harvester	8½
DJIA: 776.92		DJIA: 1,070.55	

Table 4.2   Eleven-Year Highs and Lows, Dow Jones Industrials, 1972–82

	High	Low
Alcoa	37½	12⅞
Allied Corp.	61¾	23
American Brands	51	13⅞
American Can	45¼	22½
American Express	70¾	17¾
AT&T	65⅝	39⅝
Bethlehem Steel	32	14½
Du Pont	56	28¼
Eastman Kodak	151¾	41⅛
Exxon	44½	13¾
General Electric	100	30
General Foods	47¾	16
General Motors	84¾	31¼
Goodyear	36⅞	10¾
IBM	98	37⅝
INCO	40⅛	7⅞
International Harvester	45½	2¾
International Paper	79¾	30½
Merck	103	46⅝
Minnesota Mining and Manufacturing	91⅝	43
Owens Illinois	33	13¾
Procter & Gamble	123	62¾
Sears, Roebuck	61⅝	14⅜
Standard Oil (Calif.)	58¾	10⅛
Texaco	54⅜	20
Union Carbide	76¾	29¼
United Technologies	65¾	10⅜
U.S. Steel	59⅜	16
Westinghouse	54⅞	8
Woolworth	47¼	8
TOTAL	1,978.25	676.25
Divisor as of December 31, 1982: 1.359		
Hypothetical DJIA	1,455.67	497.61

Observations About Relationships

It would be impossible to conduct such a detailed analysis of the broad-based indexes without the aid of a computer. Nevertheless, it is useful to make some general observations. On a purely numerical basis, the S&P 500 Composite Index usually stands at about one-eighth the level of the Dow Jones Industrial Average. When the closing DJIA on July 30, 1982, was 808.60, for example, the S&P 500 finished the day at 107.09. That relationship has not always held, however. When an earlier S&P industrial index was superceded by the present composite in 1957, the old index stood at about 370, relative to a 1935–39 base equal to 100. The current composite index was made relative to a 1941–43 base equal to 10, which in effect split the index ten-for-one. When it was first computed in relation to its reduced base, the index stood at about 47, nearly equal to the average price at that time for all common stocks listed on the New York Stock Exchange.

When the New York Stock Exchange Composite Index was created in 1966, a base of 50 was selected to allow the index to approximate the fifty-three-dollar price of an average NYSE share. If a conventional base of 100 had been chosen, the NYSE Composite would today stand quite near on an absolute basis to both the S&P 500 and the Value Line Composite Average. To compare them again at their July 30, 1982, levels, the NYSE Composite stood on that date at 61.51, while the Value Line was 118.40, and the S&P 500, as noted above, was 107.09. Because its base and its absolute level are about one-half those of the S&P 500 and Value Line indexes, the NYSE Composite is likely to fluctuate from day to day in the same proportion relative to the other two indexes.

The distinctive method of computing the Value Line Composite Average—taking the geometric mean of nearly seventeen hundred daily price changes—has a decisive bearing on its performance. A price change in a forty-dollar stock has twice the effect on the DJIA as the same percentage change in a twenty-dollar stock. A given price change in a stock with 25 million outstanding shares has five times the effect on the S&P and NYSE indexes as the same price change in a 5-million share stock. In the case of the Value Line Average, a 3 percent price fluctuation of one stock is accorded the same weight in the computation of the average as a 3 percent fluctuation of any other stock, regardless of their relative prices and number of outstanding shares.

Differing Performances

According to Arnold Bernhard & Company, the originator of the Value Line Index, its method of computation provides an investor with a better yardstick against which to measure the performance of the stocks he or she is likely to own than do the capitalization-weighted S&P 500 and NYSE Composite Indexes or the relatively few large-capitalization, blue-chip Dow Jones Industrials.[2]

The ostensible advantages and shortcomings of the various averages aside, the fact remains that they perform differently. (See figure 4.1 for a comparison of the performance of three major indexes during 1978–83.) These differences provide index futures traders with profit opportunities—although, where opportunities exist, risks cannot be far behind.

The leadership in signaling turnarounds in market trends appears to alternate among the indexes. When the S&P 500 and NYSE Composite Indexes were setting new highs in late 1968, for example, the DJIA lagged behind them. But when stocks moved into a bear trend, it was the Dow that led the way down. The Dow Industrials were the first to reach a major low in 1970. They turned upward in May, two months ahead of the other averages. Analysts attributed the Dow's more precipitous fall to the shrinking profit margins experienced by the major automobile, steel, chemical, and other manufacturing companies that form the core of that particular average.

Yet those were the very companies that attracted investors' buying in the spring and early summer of 1970, when, in the wake of the Penn Central Company bankruptcy, corporate liquidity rather than profit margins was their primary concern. This temporary shift of sentiment in favor of the blue-chip stocks served to reverse for a time the divergence between the Dow and the other indexes. But when their anxieties regarding corporate liquidity and further bankruptcies abated, investors' attention was drawn back to more speculative stocks, and the Dow Industrials lagged once again.[3]

But even as the Dow fell behind, the other indexes began to diverge from each other. Because of the way it is computed, the Value Line Average tends to be more volatile than both the S&P 500 and the NYSE Composite, moving farther and faster in the direction the market is going. During the major downturn from 1972 to 1974, for example, the Value Line fell from 114.05 to 48.97, a drop of 65.08 points, or 57 percent. The S&P 500 declined over the same period from 118.05 to 68.06, a 49.99-point, or 42 percent, depreciation.[4]

Stock index futures had not by then seen the light of day. But for the sake of comparison, a series of hypothetical short Value Line contracts during 1972–74 would have yielded profits totaling $32,540 (65.08 × $500), while a similar short position in a string of S&P 500 contracts would have generated gains of $24,995 (49.99 × $500).

The Value Line average displayed greater volatility during the subsequent upturn as well. Between 1974 and 1976 Value Line climbed from its 48.97 low back to 93.47, for a 44.50-point, or 91 percent, advance. S&P 500 again

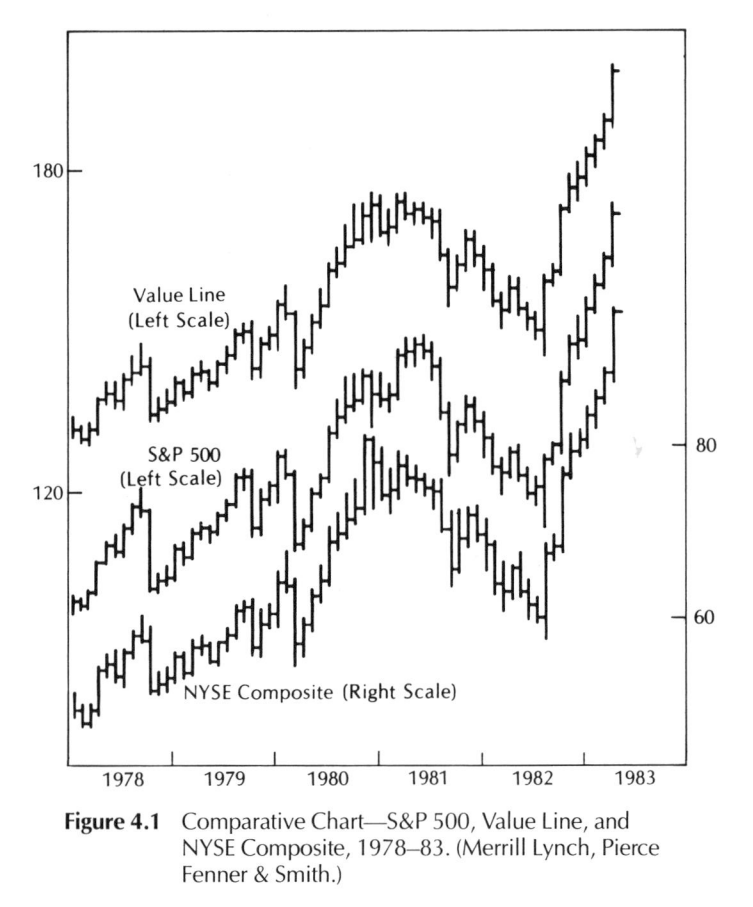

Figure 4.1 Comparative Chart—S&P 500, Value Line, and NYSE Composite, 1978–83. (Merrill Lynch, Pierce Fenner & Smith.)

lagged somewhat on the upside, rising 38.89 points, or 57 percent, from 68.56 to 107.45 points. The relationship between Value Line and S&P has not been one-sided, however. From 1971 to 1982 the Value Line index outpaced the S&P 500 up and down in six of the eleven years. During the other five years, S&P led Value Line.

Figure 4.2 displays the relationship between the Value Line and S&P 500 indexes graphically from January 1980 to April 1982. The S&P 500 (solid line) and Value Line (broken line) tracked each other closely through most of the period. But the S&P reached its peak in November 1980, seven months before the Value Line established its top. The chart has obvious implications for index futures traders. If a trader had observed the parallel movement between the two indexes, he or she might in December 1980 have sold one or more Value Line contracts short (again, assuming they had then existed) with the

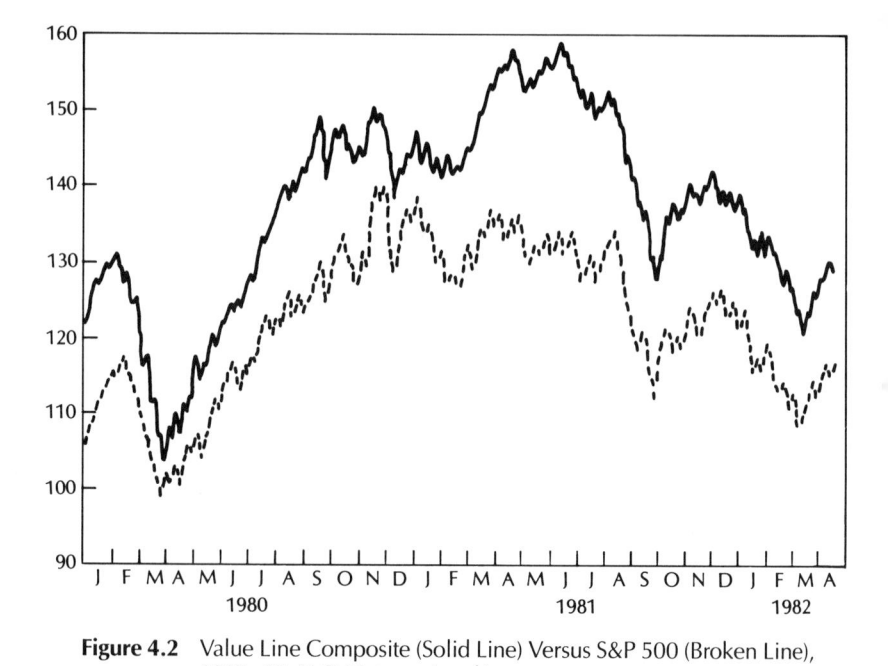

Figure 4.2 Value Line Composite (Solid Line) Versus S&P 500 (Broken Line), 1980–82. (ACLI International.)

expectation that, since the S&P 500 had just turned downward, the Value Line would shortly follow suit. Had such a transaction been made, the trader would have suffered substantial losses on that hypothetical position, especially between February and June 1981, when the Value Line moved yet higher even as the S&P was giving ground.

Spreading Index Futures

One means by which traders attempt to reduce the risk of being on the wrong side of such price movements and yet retain an opportunity to profit by the discrepancies between indexes is to engage in a technique known as *spreading*. This practice entails buying one or more contracts and simultaneously selling short an equal number of different, but related contracts. Spreads—opposite positions—may be placed between different contracts within the same group (say, Value Line and S&P index contracts) or between different expiration dates of the same contract (that is, sell March Value Line and buy September Value Line). There is nothing to prevent a trader from buying, say, a ninety-day Treasury-bill or Swiss franc contract and selling a NYSE Composite contract, assuming, of course, that he or she deposits the required margin. But those positions would not constitute a spread because there is no consistent relationship between those contracts. What is considered a bona fide spread, such as the one between two different index contracts, qualifies for reduced initial and maintenance margin rates, on the theory that the inherent risk of a spread is less than that of an outright long or short position.

A spread position is a compromise of sorts. Its defensive purpose is to avoid being caught short when the market is rising or being saddled with a long position when the contract price is falling. But if the two sides of a spread position, the long contract(s) and the short contract(s), rise or fall in price by precisely the same amount, there is no net gain or loss, since the winning and losing positions completely offset each other. The opportunity—and the risk—come when the positions diverge—that is, when one contract gains or drops in price at a faster rate than the other one. Occasionally, as is evidenced in figure 4.2, the contract prices may move in opposite directions.

Referring to the price information in figure 4.2, a spread position consisting of one long Value Line contract and one short S&P contract—there must be the same number of contracts on each side, or else there will remain a net long or short exposure—would have produced a gain on the long Value Line contract and a roughly equivalent loss on the short S&P contract between April and November 1980. While both averages were falling between June 1981 and the termination of the chart in April 1982, the relationship was reversed, with a loss accruing on the long side and a corresponding profit on the short. But during the intervening months, December 1980 through May 1981, the long Value Line–short S&P spread would have been profitable on both counts: the Value Line index was going up, spelling a gain on the long position, and the S&P 500 was retreating, for an added profit on the short side.

Timing and Position

So far, so good. But the scenario does not always unfold in such a rewarding fashion. In the situation cited above, the spread between the two indexes might have grown narrower instead of wider, or worse yet, our trader might have chosen the worst of both worlds by selling Value Line and buying S&P in December 1980. Fortunately for the trader, if that had been his or her intent, those instruments were still only gleams in Walter Vernon's and Leo Melamed's eyes at that time.

Timing and position are just as important in establishing a successful spread as they are in initiating an outright long or short position. The area between the solid and broken lines in figure 4.2 is one way—the most straightforward one—of looking at a spread relationship, in this case between the Value Line

Figure 4.3 Value Line Versus S&P Spread. (ACLI International.)

and S&P. Figure 4.3 presents the same data from a different perspective. Here, the Value Line–S&P spread is charted as a single value. A growing spread is depicted by a rising line and, conversely, a narrowing spread by a declining one. The chart shows that the spread between the Value Line and S&P indexes varied from about 5 points to about 27 points during the twenty-eight months that are covered. That range also happens to be the amount by which the spread increased between December 1980 and May 1981.

To say that during the December 1980–May 1981 period, Value Line climbed from about 140.00 to 160.00 while S&P dropped moderately from about 135.00 to 133.00 is the equivalent of saying that the spread between them opened up from 5.00 points (140.00 − 135.00) to 27.00 points (160.00 − 133.00). However it's expressed, the spread grew wider by 22 points, and a trader carrying a long one Value Line–short one S&P spread during those months might with ideal timing have realized a profit of $11,000 (22.00 × $500). If the trader had carried this hypothetical spread beyond its May 1981 high-water mark, however, it would have begun to narrow, and he or she would have surrendered some of that handsome gain.

Figure 4.4 is yet a third way of depicting a spread relationship graphically. It is a "scatter chart," in which the dots pinpoint the Value Line index on a given day along the vertical axis and the S&P 500 the same day along the horizontal

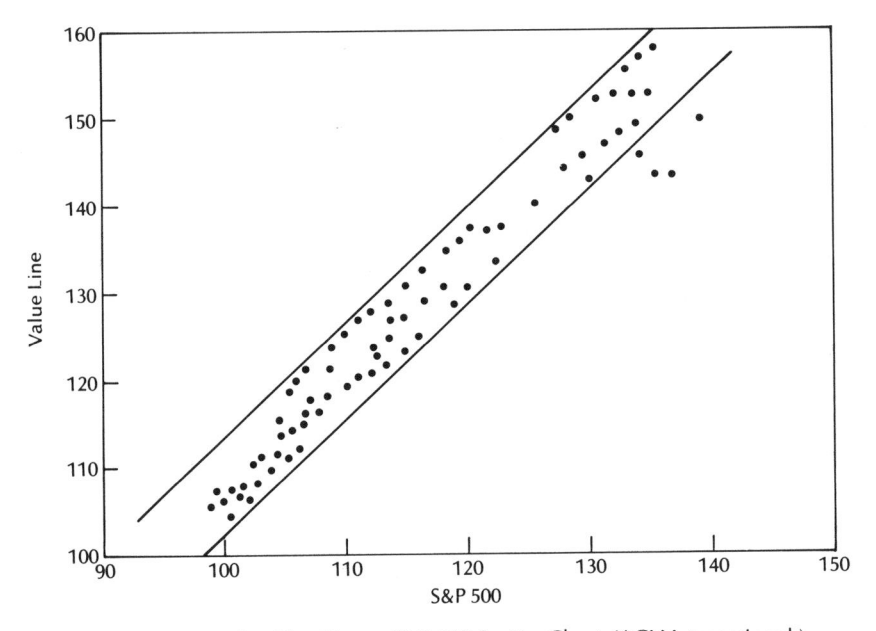

Figure 4.4 Value Line Versus S&P 500 Scatter Chart. (ACLI International.)

one. The diagonal band described by the scatter formation is a representation of the degree by which the two indexes—and presumably their futures contracts—may vary in relation to each other over time.

The data show that spreads also vary in relation to the absolute level of each index. Taking figures 4.2 and 4.3 in conjunction, we may observe that when the S&P 500 is less than 120.00, the spread between it and Value Line seldom exceeds 16 points. But when the S&P moves above 128.00, spreads greater than 20 points are not uncommon. Such information is of practical importance in timing the initiation and termination of spread positions.

Similar data should be considered in assessing the relative performance of the Value Line and NYSE Composite indexes and the S&P 500–NYSE Composite relationship. The tendency of the Value Line average to "overshoot" the S&P 500 on account of its greater volatility prevails over the NYSE Composite as well.

Why Index Futures Behave Differently

It is useful as a training exercise to hypothesize about what might have happened had index futures contracts existed in 1980–81 or some earlier date.

But we ultimately must deal with the actual prices and relationships that exist in today's markets.

We have stated earlier in this book that futures contracts to a certain degree display lives of their own and that if an index behaves in a certain manner, it does not always follow that the futures contracts tied to it will act in precisely the same way. As a matter of fact, because of traders' expectations and other forces, they usually don't.

We are now at the point where it is possible (and necessary) to define "to a certain degree" and "lives of their own" with greater clarity and precision. It is just as important—correction, it is *more* important—to gain insight into the various index-to-futures and futures-to-futures relationships as it is to understand something about the linkages between the indexes themselves. It is, after all, the contracts and not the actual indexes that are bought and sold in the futures market. A grasp of what makes the contract prices behave the way they do, and what ties them together, is what will in large part determine whether a trader walks away from the index game as a winner or a loser.

Financial analysts have long sought to define in quantitative terms a concept known as "the equity cost of capital." That is a measurement of the dividend rate on a particular stock (or on all the stocks that comprise an index), plus the prevailing premium that corporations must pay above the risk-free interest rate (typically measured by the prevailing U.S. Treasury-bill discount), to compensate investors for the risk they assume in holding the corporation's stock or, in theory, an index of such stocks. In short, the equity cost of capital is what a corporation—or the marketplace—must pay investors for the use of their money.[5]

According to one formulation, if the annualized dividend yield on a group of stocks is 6 percent and the cost of equity capital is 20 percent, a one-year contract on a particular stock or index should be priced 14 percent (20 percent − 6 percent) higher than the current price of that stock or index. Dividing that figure by four to concur with the quarterly maturities of index contracts, the price premium between successive expiration dates should be, according to the equity cost of capital theory, 3.5 percent (14 percent ÷ 4).

Applying the theory to the S&P 500 contract, we would have a hypothetical—again, that unsatisfying term—series of futures prices as follows:

S&P index (spot)	120.00
March contract	124.20
June contract	128.55
September contract	133.05
December contract	137.70

To realize the equity cost of capital, then, a trader would need to sell a one-year S&P 500 futures contract at 137.70 when the index itself stood at 120.00

for an annualized return of 14 percent plus the prevailing dividend yield. That seems straightforward enough, but the reality of the situation makes problematical a practical application of the theory. The S&P 500 is only an index, after all, and not a portfolio of stocks. No dividends are paid on the index per se. Moreover, to apply the theory properly, consideration must be given to a stock's (or index's) expected total return—that is, dividend yield plus its potential price appreciation.

The theorists have made a valiant attempt, but the price record thus far has dashed their hopes that index futures price behavior would vindicate their equity cost of capital hypothesis. In the early months of trading, futures prices have not fallen into neat and predictable slots. On the contrary, they've wandered all over the lot, often without apparent rhyme or reason. Futures prices are sometimes above the actual, or spot, index. They are at other times below it. If the equity cost of capital theory, modified to take total return into account, were to hold true, a futures contract priced at a discount below the spot index would comprise a better investment than a theoretical portfolio that duplicates the stocks in the index.

An alternate explanation of futures pricing advanced in the previous chapter is that index futures prices are in large part determined by trader and investor expectations. When traders have a bearish outlook regarding the stock market, futures contracts sell at a discount to the spot index. When sentiment turns bullish, futures quickly move to a premium over spot.

The first month's trading in the Value Line contract failed to reveal any discernible pattern. The expiration closest to the spot Value Line average, March 1982, fell 2.10 points, from 126.70 to 124.60, between the February 24 opening day and March 26. Yet the most distant expiration month, June 1983, fell 10.50 points, from 134.80 to 124.30, and in so doing moved from an 8.10-point premium over the March 1982 contract price to a 0.30-point discount below it.

Table 4.3 traces the monthly movement of the successive Value Line expiration dates in relation to the spot Value Line index. During the six months from February through July 1982, the nearby futures contracts shifted repeatedly from a premium to a discount price structure. Much of this erratic price behavior was probably due to the novelty of the contracts and the need of contracts and traders alike to undergo a "shakedown" period. With the passage of time and the accumulation of experience, it was to be expected that more rational trading patterns would emerge at all of the exchanges.

The Expiration Factor

Even at their early stage of development, however, some observations can be made regarding index futures that are consistent with observations regarding

Table 4.3 Value Line Spot Average and Futures Prices, Month's End February 1982–July 1983

	Value Line Spot Average	Change	Nearby VLA Futures Contract	Change
February 26, 1982	127.06		125.71	
March 31	125.31	− 1.75	125.31	− 0.40
April 30	131.20	+ 5.89	130.44	+ 5.13
May 28	124.88	− 6.32	122.30	− 8.14
June 30	120.57	− 4.31	120.57	− 1.73
July 25	127.06	+ 6.49	127.00	+ 6.43
August 31	129.66	+ 2.60	129.30	+ 2.30
September 30	131.95	+ 2.29	131.95	+ 2.65
October 29	148.42	+16.47	147.00	+15.05
November 30	157.82	+ 9.40	159.15	+12.15
December 31	158.94	+ 1.12	158.94	− 0.21
January 31, 1983	166.31	+ 7.37	170.10	+11.16
February 28	172.72	+ 6.41	173.95	+ 3.85
March 31	179.25	+ 6.53	179.25	+ 5.30
April 29	190.52	+11.27	190.60	+11.35
May 31	198.38	+ 7.86	197.65	+ 7.05
June 30	204.69	+ 6.31	204.69	+ 7.04
July 29	199.38	− 5.31	199.95	− 4.74

the behavior of other futures contracts. There is, for example, a close connection between the spot index and its nearby contract—that is, the earliest expiration date. As expirations become more distant, they display greater volatility, and their connection with the spot index becomes increasingly tenuous.

The variations in spreads between different expiration dates of the same contract provide trading opportunities similar to those of the Value Line–S&P 500 spread described above. As in the latter case, the risks of being long and short different expirations of a contract are usually less than the risks of an outright short or long position in that contract. On the other hand, the greater volatility of the distant expiration months creates significant profit potential if a spread trader reads the market correctly. According to table 4.4, for example, a short December 1982 and long June 1983 NYSE Composite spread position taken in July 1982 might have been terminated the following December at a $275 profit as the short December 1982 contract lost 16.30 points while the long June 1983 contract gained 16.85 points for a net gain to the trader of .55

Table 4.4   NYSE Composite Index Spot–Futures Spreads, May–December 1982

Month 1982	Spot NYSE Index—First of Month	June 1982	Sept. 1982	Dec. 1982	March 1983	June 1983	Sept. 1983	Dec. 1983	March 1984
May	68.31	(.09) 68.40	(.65) 69.05	(.70) 69.75	(.65) 70.40				
June	64.37	(−1.02) 63.35	(.10) 63.45	(.60) 64.05	(.50) 64.55				
July	62.51		(.69) 63.20	(.25) 63.45	(.30) 63.75	(.30) 64.05			
Aug.	62.49		(.71) 63.20	(.45) 63.65	(.45) 64.10	(.45) 64.55			
Sept.	67.90		(−.65) 67.25	(.20) 67.45	(.40) 67.85	(.40) 68.25			
Oct.	70.01			(−.96) 69.05	(.30) 69.35	(.35) 69.70	(.35) 70.05	(.35) 70.40	(.35) 70.75
Nov.	79.12			(.63) 79.75	(.40) 80.15	(.40) 80.55	(.40) 80.95	(.40) 81.35	(.40) 81.75
Dec.	80.13			(−.38) 79.75	(.60) 80.35	(.55) 80.90	(.55) 81.45	(.55) 82.00	(.55) 82.55

Table 4.5 Relative Volatility of Spot Value Line Index and Futures Prices

	Spot Index	March 1982 Futures	June 1982 Futures	Sept. 1982 Futures	Dec. 1982 Futures
Levels					
Mean	127.56	127.42	127.33	127.82	128.54
Std. dev.	3.67	4.32	4.56	4.65	4.77
Daily changes					
Mean	0.61	0.91	0.98	1.06	1.09
Std. dev.	0.80	1.13	1.28	1.34	1.40
Mean (+ days)[a]	0.55	0.57	0.59	0.59	0.58
Std. dev.	0.48	1.05	1.12	1.14	1.19
Mean (− days)[a]	− 0.69	− 0.75	− 0.86	− 0.91	− 0.92
Std. dev.	0.54	0.72	0.96	1.09	1.21
Daily + changes					
Mean	0.49%	0.73%	0.79%	0.85%	0.87%
Std. dev.	0.63	0.91	1.04	1.08	1.13
Mean (+ days)[a]	0.44	0.45	0.47	0.47	0.46
Std. dev.	0.38	0.84	0.91	0.92	0.95
Mean (− days)[a]	− 0.56	− 0.61	− 0.69	− 0.74	− 0.74
Std. dev.	0.43	0.58	0.78	0.88	0.97

SOURCE: ACLI International.
[a]Based upon Value Line Index changes.

points. The opposite position, long December 1982 and short June 1983, would have produced a comparable loss during the period.

As was noted above, futures contracts are more volatile than their related spot indexes, moving faster and farther over a given period of time. According to table 4.5, on days when the stock market was rising, the Value Line average rose by a daily average of 0.44 percent, the nearby March contract rose 0.45 percent, and the June contract 0.47 percent. Futures volatility was more pronounced as the stock market declined, the June contract dropping daily on average by a 24 percent greater amount than the average daily fall of the spot index.

Figure 4.5 charts the movement of the June 1982 Value Line contract relative to the spot index. The June expiration crossed the spot index, from premium to discount or vice versa, no less than eleven times during the three months from March through May 1982. When traders became bearish, they quickly drove futures prices to a discount below spot. When they turned

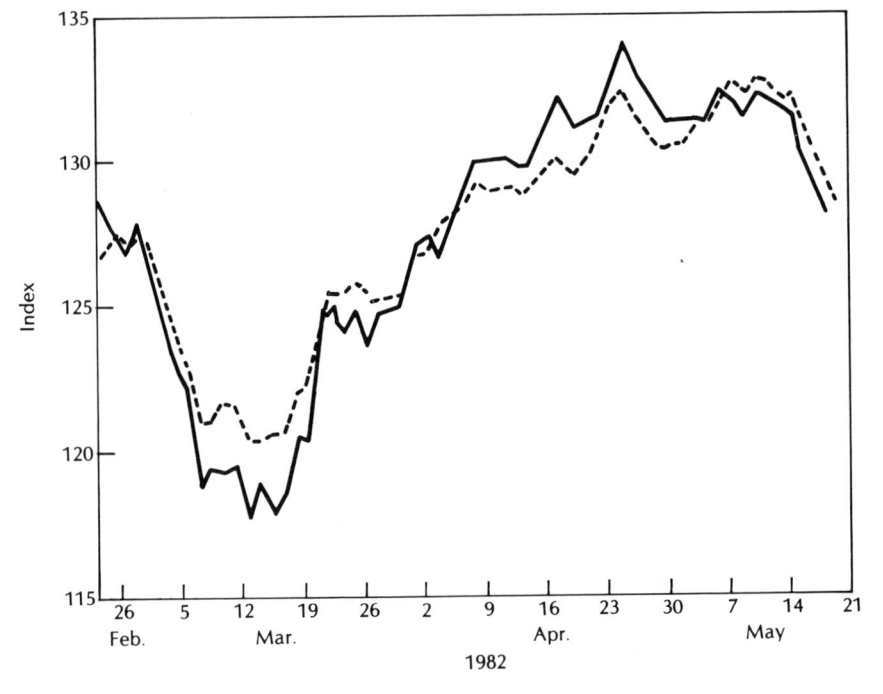

Figure 4.5   Value Line Spot Index (Broken Line) Versus June 1982 VLA
Contract (Solid Line), February–May 1982

bullish, futures immediately rose to a premium. It remains to be seen whether
time and experience will mitigate this extreme volatility.

Changes in Basis

The wide swings between futures prices and the spot index (what in futures
terminology is referred to as a change in the basis)[6] may in part be a
consequence of the system of cash settlement devised for these contracts. In
the case of physical commodities and most of the financial futures contracts—
government securities, money market instruments, and foreign currencies—
traders have the option of buying the actual commodity or instrument and
holding it for the purpose of settlement at the contract's expiration. The
possibility of physical delivery serves to hold spot and futures prices closer
together.

According to figure 4.5, the basis between the spot Value Line index and
the June expiration "weakened"—which is to say, grew wider—between late
February and mid-March as the June contract fell in price faster than the spot

index declined. From mid-March to late April, the spot Value Line–June basis became stronger as bullish sentiment pushed the contract price up ahead of the spot index. The effect of contract volatility on the basis is, as we shall see, of paramount importance in evaluating the desirability of using index futures to hedge a common stock portfolio.

The price relationships between various expirations of the same index contract are in most instances extrapolations of the relationship between the spot index and its nearest expiration. If the nearby expiration is priced higher than the index itself, traders are anticipating rising stock prices, and a premium structure among successive expirations is likely. If the nearby contract is below spot, bearish expectations are usually reflected in a discount price structure throughout the contract series.

Futures-to-futures spread charts similar to the one displayed in figure 4.6 track the changing basis between different expirations of the several index contracts. In this case it is the spread between December 1982 and December 1983 NYSE Composite contracts from October through December 1982. The chart indicates that at the beginning of the period the December 1983 NYSE contract (70.60) was priced at a 1.35-point premium over the December 1982 expiration (69.25). The spread subsequently expanded to 2.00 points on November 19, 1982 (80.85 − 78.85), narrowed to 1.60 points on December 15 (80.00 − 78.40), and again expanded to 2.65 by December 27 (84.80 − 82.15).

This series of basis changes provided opportunities for nimble traders who knew when to establish a December/December NYSE spread and at what point difference to terminate it, perhaps then taking the opposite spread position. For example, as the spread grew wider from October 4 to November 19, 1982, it paid to carry a short position in the December 1982 expiration and a long one in December 1983. As the basis opened up from 1.35 to 2.00 points, that position could have generated a $325 gain per contract for a spread trader ([2.00 − 1.35] × $500 = $325).

When the basis changed direction and began to grow narrower, a position reversal to long December 1982 and short December 1983 would have been advantageous. As the nearby expiration rose relative to the distant one over the ensuing four weeks, the reversed spread would have generated a gain of $200 per contract ([2.00 − 1.60] × $500 = $200).

It is just as important to exercise the right timing and to choose the proper position in placing a spread as it is in taking an outright long or short position. Spreading decisions are more difficult to make in some instances because there are two contract prices to consider, not just one. In the example cited above, a trader might have assumed a losing position one or both times, being long the nearby and short the distant expiration as the spread grew wider, and then

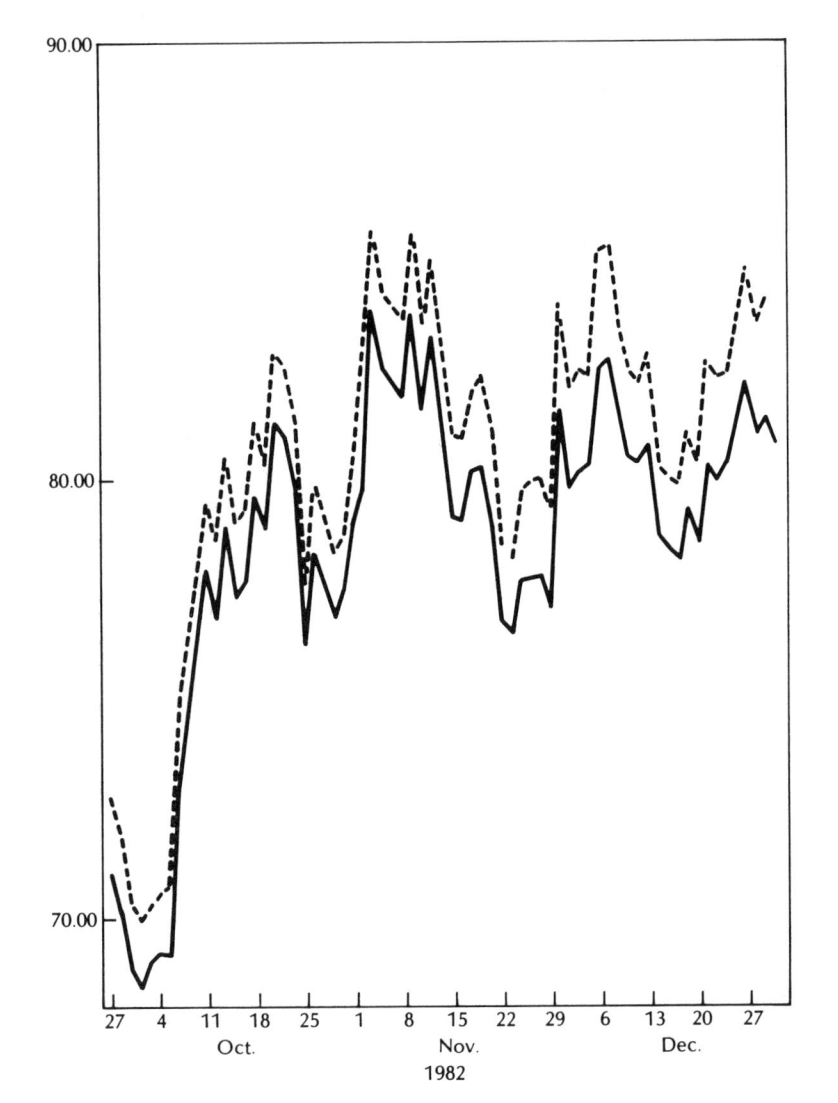

Figure 4.6 Spread Chart—December 1982 (Solid Line) Versus December 1983 (Broken Line) NYSE Composite, September–December 1982

shorting the nearby and going long the distant month just as it started to become narrower.

Table 4.4, presented earlier, lists the basis changes between the several NYSE contract expirations that were traded between May and December 1982. The table indicates, among other spread relationships, that from June of that year through September, the September 1982/December 1982 spread narrowed. But the December 1982/March 1983 spread remained relatively constant. Traders' expectations for the September to December quarter evidently were more bullish than for December to March of the following year.

Basic Analytical Tools

According to the equity cost of capital theory, the June/September and September/December NYSE spreads should have acted in a like manner. That they did not lends credence to the supposition that index futures prices, during the initial months of trading at any rate, were almost wholly determined by trader expectations. If that were the case, the prevailing expectations during the May–December 1982 period showed very little consistency. The September/December and December/March 1983 spreads crossed the actual index six times during that eight-month period, suggesting that traders had difficulty establishing a consensus concerning their stock price expectations that they were able to maintain for any extended duration.

As was the case with the Value Line contracts in Kansas City, it may be inferred that trading in the NYSE Composite contract during the opening months demonstrated more of a learning experience than a refined assessment of spread relationships. Even so, this type of analysis is highly important, not only as it affects spread trading but also because of its implications for hedging a common stock portfolio. Such a hedge is, after all, a unique type of spread in which one of the sides happens to be an actual portfolio of stocks rather than a market index or its related futures contract.

Correlation analysis is a statistical method that is used to measure the extent to which two variables—as, in a business context, air conditioner sales and temperature or housing starts and interest rates—move together. Applied to stock index futures, such measurements are important in determining how best to employ index futures to hedge common stock portfolios.

Lest readers fear that they are suddenly being transported to the esoteric reaches of higher mathematics, let me hasten to add that they've been reading about correlation all along in this chapter without the benefit—or burden—of that bit of statistical jargon. But to give the statisticians their due—I was perhaps unduly harsh in calling them "nitpickers" in an earlier treatise—there are some instances in which their sort of decimal-laden analysis can be of practical value, and futures pricing is one of them.[7]

An even more forbidding expression than correlation is *regression analysis*. Yet both terms refer to essentially the same thing: a comparison of two or more sets of statistics to determine the extent to which changes in one set are matched by changes in the other sets and the use of this information to predict the future behavior of one of those sets.

To use a simple example, take two numbers, X and Y, and assume that X is a value we know something about. In statistical jargon X is termed an "independent variable." Y is the value we wish to learn more about, particularly the effect on it that a given change in X will produce. Y is accordingly the "dependent variable."

The relative movement of the X and Y variables is often presented in the form of a scatter diagram, such as the one displayed in figure 4.4.[8] There, the Value Line Composite Average is the independent variable—that is, X—and the S&P 500 is the dependent one, Y. Each point in the diagram represents the values of the two indexes on a given day, where Value Line is measured along the vertical axis and S&P along the horizontal. The diagonal pattern of the points, or their "scattering"—there is, it seems, some sense to these profound terms after all—confirms that there is a measurable relationship between the Value Line and the S&P. That should not come as a surprise, since both indexes encompass a large number of stocks, although at about seventeen hundred issues, Value Line includes over three times the issues in the S&P 500.

If, instead of the scatter formation, all of the points in the diagram had fallen along a straight diagonal line, the line would have depicted a "perfect linear correlation," in which the two indexes move up and down in, well, perfect harmony. But in statistics, as in most human pursuits, we rarely approach, let alone achieve, perfection. We observe that the points in figure 4.4 in fact diverge, or "regress," away from this theoretical straight line. Even so, there is sufficient consistency in the path of points above and below such a line to demonstrate that a fairly predictable relationship—the correlation—between the indexes exists.

In graphic terms, the tighter the formation of points around the straight line, the higher the degree of correlation. The *correlation coefficient* is an expression of the extent to which individual points may vary from the line of perfect linear correlation and in the present context is a measure of how closely the Value Line and S&P indexes are related. A coefficient of 100 percent means a perfect match—which, to repeat, is rarely realized. In most comparisons of this kind, a coefficient above 90 percent is considered very high and those between 70 percent and 90 percent fairly high. Coefficients below 70 percent are not considered high enough to produce consistently efficient hedges. The higher the percentage, the more accurately correlation analysis may be used to predict future movement of the dependent variable.

To take our rudimentary correlation analysis of the stock indexes one step

Table 4.6 Correlation Coefficients—Value Line, S&P 500, DJIA, 1971–82

	VL/S&P 500	DJIA/S&P 500	VL/DJIA
Daily closes	.78	.54	.27
Weekly closes	.79	.54	.27
Monthly closes	.79	.54	.27
Daily changes (%)	.71	.91	.68
Weekly changes (%)	.78	.92	.74
Monthly changes (%)	.76	.89	.76

SOURCE: ACLI International.

farther, we can compare the Value Line and S&P indexes each in turn with the Dow Jones Industrials. Table 4.6 summarizes the results of such an analysis. The table lists average daily, weekly, and monthly changes in the DJIA, S&P 500, and Value Line indexes and the correlation coefficients among the indexes for each of those time spans. As might be expected, the coefficients between the broad-based Value Line and S&P 500 indexes are appreciably higher than the coefficients between Value Line and DJIA. Since, on the other hand, both the DJIA and the S&P 500 indicators are based upon large-capitalization, blue-chip stocks, the coefficients between them are also higher than those between the Value Line and Dow averages.

The Beta Factor

The expression "It's Greek to me" is doubly apt when it comes to considering the relative volatility of index and futures price movements. The standard measure of such volatility carries as its label the Greek letter b, or *beta*, a different measurement than correlation. Beta is a statistical expression of the volatility of an individual stock or portfolio of stocks relative to the overall market or of a futures price relative to its spot index. We have already noted that the Value Line average is subject to wider swings than the other indexes because of its greater complement of speculative stocks. That is a simple description of beta. On a quantitative basis, differences in volatility among the several indexes are difficult to detect from day to day or even week to week. But from month to month, the greater volatility of the Value Line becomes evident.

Beta has been adopted by analysts and portfolio managers as an important measure of price behavior. In the case of either an individual stock or a large

Table 4.7 Relative Volatility—Value Line, S&P 500, DJIA, 1971–82

	Average Change	Standard Deviation
Daily changes		
VL	0.61%	0.86%
S&P 500	0.65	0.88
DJIA	0.72	0.92
Weekly changes		
VL	1.77	2.37
S&P 500	1.66	2.30
DJIA	1.69	2.23
Monthly changes		
VL	4.57	6.04
S&P 500	3.41	4.50
DJIA	3.35	4.48

Source: ACLI International.

portfolio, beta expresses in statistical terms how that stock or portfolio is expected to act on the basis of its past performance in relation to the overall stock market. A relatively volatile stock or portfolio has a high beta value. One with low volatility is accorded a low beta. In this regard, beta has become accepted by professional portfolio managers as a standard measure of risk, as well as of expected rates of return relative to general market movement.

If, for example, the stock market advances 10 percent over the course of one year and XYZ stock also advances 10 percent during that time, the stock is said to have a beta value of 1.0. But if ABC stock had in the same year gone up 20 percent, it would have a beta of 2.0. By striking an average of the betas of its constituent stocks, the relative volatility of an entire portfolio may be measured and ranked in the same manner.

Beta values can also be computed to express the relative volatility of the indexes. If, as stated in table 4.7, the average monthly movement of the Value Line Composite was 34 percent greater than that of the S&P 500 during the period indicated, Value Line would have a beta of 1.34 relative to Standard & Poor's.

Turning to table 4.8, we see that Value Line's volatility was less than S&P's on an average daily and weekly basis and therefore had a beta of less than 1.0 for those time periods. But over an extended period (monthly), the Value Line beta increased markedly.

Table 4.8 Beta of Value Line Versus S&P 500

	Beta	Standard Error of Beta
Percentage changes		
Daily	0.83	0.01
Weekly	0.95	0.02
Monthly	1.17	0.06

SOURCE: ACLI International.

Beta's Role in Hedging

Inasmuch as stock volatility has become an accepted measure of investment risk, and since the purported economic justification of stock index futures is to reduce that risk, beta is obviously an important consideration in the use of index futures to hedge portfolio values. Most if not all of the other concepts discussed throughout this chapter—convergence, premium and discount price structures, expectations, and correlation—have a bearing on the hedging problem as well. To recapitulate, the rationale of hedging with index futures is to recoup from a short position in those contracts the dollar amount by which a common stock portfolio depreciates due to a stock market decline. All of these factors must be taken into account in determining which and how many contracts to sell, when to sell, and when to repurchase them.

Before the advent of stock index futures, portfolio managers and private investors sought to reduce their market risk through application of the time-tested adage "Don't put all your eggs in one basket"—that is, by diversifying their investments.[9] But diversification is at best a partially effective risk-reduction technique because an investor or manager is normally faced with two types of risk, only one of which is mitigated by owning a number of stocks. The first type is associated with stock selection. An investor must have a good idea of which stocks to buy and which to avoid. The second type of risk is that inherent in market timing. Once having made his or her stock picks, the investor or manager must decide when to buy them and how long to hold them.

Investment analysts refer to the risk associated with stock selection as company-related, or unsystematic, risk. In the same vein, they describe timing risks as market-related, or systematic. As the popular song about love and marriage admonished, you supposedly couldn't have one type of risk without assuming the other type. But markets change, as do social mores—indeed, that's the underlying theme of this book—and the creation of stock index futures permitted for the first time the separation and management of company-related and market-related risks. Portfolio managers and, to a lesser extent, individual investors whose forte was stock selection could use index futures to hedge the market component of their portfolio risk and concentrate on what they did best—picking stocks. Managers and other traders whose specialty was market timing could use the same contracts to fine-tune the market sensitivity of their portfolios, increasing or decreasing the market risk as they saw fit. Neither type of hedger would need to incur the commission costs of buying and selling specific securities.

As the number of stocks in a portfolio increases, market risk surpasses company-related risk as the predominant risk component. Once the number of stocks exceeds ten, nearly all of the portfolio risk is market-related and can be effectively hedged through the sale of stock index futures. The only stock portfolios from which market risk can be totally eliminated through the sale of index futures are those portfolios that contain the same stocks that make up the index. There are such "index funds." All other portfolios must be "cross-hedged."[10] The effectiveness of a cross-hedge, like that of a spread transaction, is determined by the spot and futures price variables that have been the subject of this chapter.

Basic Hedging

Textbooks on hedging usually portray, as their first example, a one-for-one hedge. In the case of index futures, that might be a situation in which a $1.2-million stock portfolio is hedged by selling twenty S&P 500 contracts when that index stands at 120.00. In reality, the number of contracts that best fits a particular portfolio is determined by the relative volatility of that portfolio—that is, its beta.

The first step in establishing the hedge is to compute the appropriate number of S&P contracts to cover the portfolio's market risk. At a level of 122.00 times the standard $500 contract size, the value of one contract is $61,000. Dividing the portfolio value of $10 million by that figure yields a quotient of 164, the proper number of contracts to place a one-for-one hedge. But a one-for-one ratio does not take the portfolio's beta value into account. The assumed beta of the portfolio is 0.80, meaning that for every 10 percent that the stock market—and, presumably, the S&P 500 index—moves up or down, the portfolio should move 8 percent. In that case, a short position of 164 contracts would be excessive, likely to fall in value by a greater amount than the portfolio depreciates. By adjusting the hedge ratio to the portfolio's beta value, multiplying 164 by 0.80, the resulting figure of 132 contracts should provide the proper match between the portfolio's movement and the total appreciation or depreciation of the contracts.

Another consideration is the eventual convergence of the futures price from a two-point premium to parity with the stock index. This particular

Table 4.9 Quarterly Summary of Hedged Portfolio

End of:	Position Short 132 Contracts	Closing Price S&P 500 Contract	Gain or (Loss) Contract Points × $500 × 132 Contracts		Value of Stock Portfolio	Portfolio Gain (Loss)
1st qtr.	122.00	115.40	6.60	$435,600	$9.56 million	($440,000)
2d qtr.	122.00	125.75	(3.75)	($247,500)	$10.25 million	$250,000
3d qtr.	122.00	113.35	8.65	$570,900	$9.42 million	($576,000)
4th qtr.	122.00	110.00	12.00	$792,000	$9.33 million	($666,666)

convergence works in the hedger's favor, reducing the loss on the short futures position in the event the stock market (and, of course, the index) rises or enhancing the prospective gain if the market and the index were to decline while the hedge was in effect. A futures discount would in this instance have worked to the hedger's detriment.

In either case, a rising market or a declining one, the manager accomplished his or her objective of insulating the portfolio from price depreciation—or, more precisely, of offsetting such depreciation with futures gains. In terms of risk and reward, the manager chose to surrender some or all of the portfolio's potential capital gains in return for what was to him or her the greater benefit of removing market risk.

A manager is often faced with the dilemma of wishing to buy stocks with high beta values to enhance a portfolio's company risk/reward component but having at the same time to increase the market-related risk of the portfolio. The option to hedge his or her market-related risk with stock index futures eases if not entirely solves the manager's dilemma.

Table 4.9 sets forth the example cited above in greater detail. It summarizes the status of the hypothetical $10-million portfolio hedge at the end of each quarter over the one-year duration of the hedge. The "bottom line" of the hedge—the net difference between portfolio gains or losses and, in opposite measure, losses or gains on the 132 index futures contracts—is in this case listed by quarter in the far-right column of the table. Although the net figure may itself be a small profit or loss, the hedger remains responsible for meeting the broker's maintenance margin calls when the market rises. According to the quarterly summary in table 4.9, the hedger would have incurred maintenance margin calls on the short futures position totaling $247,500 in the second quarter. But when the market reversed and the S&P index dropped in the third and fourth quarters, the second-quarter futures loss was recouped (while the portfolio's value was depreciating), and the equity in the hedge account increased by the amount of the futures gains.

CHAPTER 5

Business Cycles and Stock Prices

Having discussed at some length what stockbrokers mean when they inform their customers that "the market" (translation: the Dow Jones Industrial Average) went down by some value like 8.42, it's time to address the inevitable question, Why did the market go down? If a broker responds with the facetious answer that there were more sellers than buyers in the market that day, he or she is stating the obvious fact that the supply of stock exceeded the demand. But what the broker is really saying without putting it in so many words is that there is no pat answer to what determines the balance between supply and demand on any given day.[1]

It stands to reason that the forces that propel common stock prices up and down also push stock index futures in the same direction. This chapter, and the three that follow, are devoted to a consideration of these forces. Although their effect on stock prices cannot be pinpointed from day to day, futures traders as well as investors should be aware of them and appreciate their influence.

This chapter examines the macroeconomic environment within which stock prices move. That means, in less imposing language, the relationship between business cycles and stock market cycles. The subsequent chapters deal in turn with the possible effects of corporate and industry developments, government action—especially in the monetary sphere—and psychological and technical factors. The latter are those elements that emanate from within the marketplace itself, and from the successive waves of buying and selling that sweep through it, rather than reactions to events that occur outside the market.

Tracking the Indicators

It is easy to be overwhelmed by the superabundance of economic and financial statistics that are churned out by numerous government and private agencies. And it's very tempting to seek hard-and-fast answers about whether to buy or sell from such seemingly precise figures as inflation-adjusted gross national product, new housing starts, labor cost per unit of output, and earnings per share. We are already on record as saying traders and investors should pay careful heed to these measures of economic activity. But they should also be aware that these figures are not the last word. The other factors listed above are just as important, sometimes more so. To assume that stock and futures prices will respond to certain economic data in a preordained manner is simplistic. Economic statistics are better regarded as clues than as gospel. That is why they are called indicators.

Economic cycles have been observed and measured for many years. Perhaps the first recorded cycle is the one Joseph foretold from Pharaoh's dream about the fat and lean cattle and the healthy and withered ears of corn.[2] Closer to the present, there were thirty such cycles in the United States between 1854 and 1982, although, fortunately, the Great Depression of the 1930s was the only one that approached the seven years of famine recounted in the Bible. Since the end of World War II, the country has gone through eight complete cycles of expansion and contraction.

Anyone who works—not to mention people who have lost their jobs or are trying to get jobs—knows that the economy goes through recurring bouts of growth and slack. There is the sardonic saying about the definition of a recession being when the guy next door is out of a job and of a depression being when you're out of one. Although these ups and downs are familiar occurrences, there is little certainty about what causes them. The most convincing explanation—though hardly a scientific one— is that booms and busts are brought on by our own excesses. Most people, so the explanation goes, are shortsighted in an economic sense (as well as in other ways). When business conditions are good, we tend to believe that the party will continue indefinitely. We go overboard with our spending, consuming, and investing— the last of which at the end becomes rank speculation. When times are hard, we become pessimistic and behave as if there will never be a recovery. The economy is shaped by these collective swings from peaks of confidence to valleys of gloom.

The Business Cycle: Going Up

To describe the cycle in a bit more detail, well into an upswing virtually anyone who wants a job can find one (disregarding for the purposes of this discussion the so-called unemployables, who are as much of a social and political problem as they are an economic one), factories are operating at or close to full capacity, and prices and wages are climbing. Business is good, and business people, whether they're self-employed or run large corporations, are intent on making hay while the sun shines. With demand for their goods and services rising, they become convinced that it's smart business to expand plant capacity and to increase output. That's called "optimizing profits" in graduate schools of business, and it's done by borrowing a lot of money.

The tempo of business goes from brisk to frantic. Enthusiasm increasingly crowds out sound judgment, and confidence degenerates into profligacy. In the stock market, to cite but one example that is close to home, brokers are delighted to discover that their "work" increasingly consists of merely answering their telephones (at the peak of a bull market, all brokers worth their salt have at least three telephones on their desk) and writing out customers' orders as rapidly as they can. The economy overall is on a binge, and those who are swept along with it—including the three-telephone stockbrokers— start to suspect that things are getting out of hand. No one questioned rising prices and wages so long as profits were climbing faster. The pie was growing for everybody. But gradually, price and wage increases start to outstrip profit gains. Interest rates are rising as well, serving to undermine profit margins. The optimizing, hay-making executives realize they've gone too far too fast. They've expanded their means of production (steel mills, jetliner fleets, auto assembly plants, or whatever) beyond what they can realistically expect in the way of increased sales. In the process, they've incurred burdensome borrowings to pay for this excess capacity. "Optimizing profits" has turned out to be a will-o'-the-wisp, and the not-yet-paid-for new plant and equipment have become millstones.

The Business Cycle: Going Down

Now, anxiety spreads through the executive suite. Steps are taken to pull in the reins. Inventories are drawn down, or at least the rate of accumulation is reduced. That means less business for suppliers. Available cash is used to repay loans rather than being plowed back into more new plants and equipment. Once again, that results in less business for other companies. The effects are cumulative. The ax starts to fall in the personnel department. People are let go, either temporarily or for good. Those who are laid off certainly aren't disposed to spend what could turn out to be their survival funds on home video recorders or trips to Hawaii. Workers who are kept on aren't as free and easy in spending their money as before, either. They might be in the next group to get the ax. All of this comes down to consumers staying out of the stores and sales of appliances, furnishings, apparel and entertainment falling off. The level of anxiety in the executive suite rises accordingly.

By this time, everybody knows the party's over. Inventories continue to be cut, and more employees are let go. Prices and interest rates start to drop, or they at least stop climbing. The signs of business stagnation are widespread. Sales and inventories are at depressed levels, corporate profits have gone to the dogs, and factories are standing idle. Whether it's you who is out of a job (depression) or just your neighbor (recession), times are tough. If it's your neighbor who is the unfortunate one, the chances are he or she isn't coming into your place of business and contributing the accustomed share to your weekly income. If anything, your neighbor is coming in to ask for a loan to pay the kids' dental bills, so there's little comfort there.

A consoling thought for the down and out is that it's supposed to be darkest before the dawn. That may or may not be true, but when a business cycle hits rock bottom—or the "trough" as economists like to call it—a ray of hope does appear, and conditions do start to improve. Out of the blue, sales begin to rise, and the dejected inhabitants of the executive suite shake off their despondency long enough to think about increasing production. They may not have been axed along with some of the rank and file, but they most likely had to forego the hefty year-end bonuses to which they became accustomed during better times. Their other fringe benefits, common stock options, have probably dropped to the point where they are—for the time being at any rate—without realizable value.

Those workers who were lucky enough to stay on the job during the slump start putting in longer hours. Many of those who were laid off are called back. Gradually, the stores become more crowded. The home video recorders, refrigerators, and trips to Hawaii start moving once again. Wage and salary earners have money to spend. Executives conjure up fresh visions of year-end bonuses and valuable option privileges as in days gone by. They pull down off the shelf their business school texts about optimizing profits. The cycle is on the upswing. The bloom is back on the rose.

The Business Cycle: An Overview

To look at a chart that delineates these events—and I have plenty of them for you—one gets the impression that the peaks and valleys divide the business cycle into neat segments that should be easy to predict. But nothing could be further from the truth. Economists who try to forecast the duration and severity of present and future cyclical movements on the basis of past cycles fare no better as a rule than those generals who are always fighting the last war. There is enough of a variation from cycle to cycle to render this mechanical type of forecasting quite hazardous.

Business cycles don't unfold like clockwork. It's debatable whether the stretches of feast and famine Joseph foresaw each lasted seven years precisely.

Table 5.1 Business Cycle Expansions and Contractions in the United States, 1945–82 (Duration in Months)

Business Cycle		Cycle			
Low	Peak	Contraction (Low from Previous Peak)	Expansion (Low to Peak)	(Low from Previous Low)	(Peak from Previous Peak)
Oct. 1945	Nov. 1948	8	37	88	45
Oct. 1949	July 1953	11	45	48	56
Aug. 1954	July 1957	13	35	58	48
Apr. 1958	May 1960	9	25	44	34
Feb. 1961	Nov. 1969	9	105	34	114
Nov. 1970	Nov. 1973	12	36	117	48
Mar. 1975	Jan. 1980	16	58	52	74
July 1980	July 1981	7	12	64	17
Nov. 1982		16		28	

SOURCES: Geoffrey H. Moore, "Security Markets and Business Cycles," *Financial Analyst's Handbook* (Homewood, Ill.: Dow Jones–Irwin, 1975), 769–88. U.S. Department of Commerce, Bureau of Economic Analysis, *Business Conditions Digest*, December 1982, 40. Reprinted with permission.

Whether they did or not, modern cycles run their course in considerably less time. Since 1854 the growth segments of the thirty business cycles in the United States have averaged about thirty-six months, and the downswings have lasted on average about half that time. The most noteworthy feature of cycles in the post–World War II era is that the upswings have generally increased in their duration to an average of about forty-five months and the contractions have become shorter, about eleven months on average (see table 5.1). Many of the more recent so-called recessions have not been downswings at all, but simply slowdowns in the economy's rate of growth.

Business cycles embrace every facet of economic activity, including, as noted in our thumbnail sketch, production, employment, prices, wages, interest rates, and corporate profits. It should therefore, come as no surprise that stock prices are also affected. The primary purpose of our discussion is, after all, to determine whether there is a sufficiently consistent relationship between economic trends and stock prices to assist us in making trading decisions. The implications of such a relationship so far as trading stock index futures is concerned should be obvious. Keeping in mind our earlier warning against relying on an automatic replay of past movements to predict future activity, there is nevertheless a great advantage to be gained from identifying major turning points in stock and index futures prices shortly after such turns have taken place.[3]

Business Cycles and Stock Prices

Figure 5.1, a comparative chart of the S&P 500 Composite Index and the Federal Reserve Board Index of Industrial Production, clearly shows that a close relationship does in fact exist between business cycles and stock prices. Two conclusions may be drawn from this chart: (1) stock prices as measured by the S&P 500 index (solid line) repeatedly rose more steeply than the index of industrial production (broken line), and (2) in seven of the eight postwar cycles, changes in the direction of stock prices anticipated changes in production trends, in that stock prices turned down several months earlier than production did, and they recovered from their cyclical lows before production turned around.

The 1973–74 bear market and the ensuing recession are a pronounced example of the stock price–production relationship. Stock prices experienced their deepest and most protracted decline since the 1930s. It could not have been coincidental that within a matter of months the U.S.—indeed, the world—economy endured its most severe setback since then as well.

The S&P 500 index began its descent in January 1973, registering a decline of some 12 percent by the following August. After a two-month rally during most of September and October, the index turned down again and continued to fall for another year. It did not touch bottom until December 1974, a continuous decline (with the sole interruption of the September-October rally) of 44 percent.

The growth in industrial production began decelerating in July 1973, about six months after stocks had passed their peak. Even then, the index continued to rise at an annual rate of 2 percent until December, when it flattened out for the next ten months. The FRB index went into a pronounced decline from October 1974 to April 1975, by which time stock prices had been rising for four months.

Stock prices again led the production index down at the outset of the 1981–82 recession. The U.S. economy went into a contraction phase in July 1981. By then, the S&P 500 had already been moving downward for eight months, having peaked out in November 1980. The FRB index hit its high-water mark nearly twelve months later.

No recessions have occurred in this country during the post–World War II era without a decline at some point in stock prices. And there have been few periods of prosperity that haven't been accompanied by rising prices. Prosperity and bull markets go together like ice cream and apple pie; recessions and bear markets are associated like death and taxes.

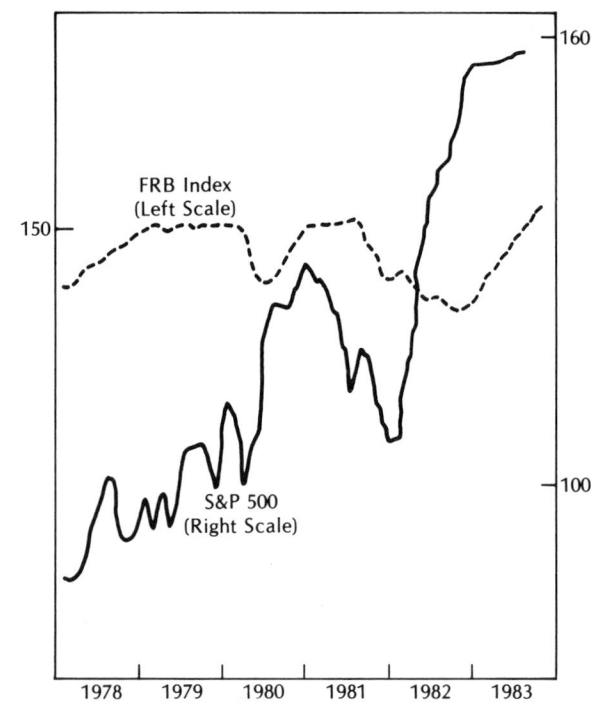

Figure 5.1 S&P 500 Versus Federal Reserve Board
Index of Industrial Production, 1978–83

Yes, But Why the Relationship?

As with the underlying causes of periodic expansion and contraction, the reasons for this consistent relationship are harder to pin down than its mere existence. It stands to reason that stocks should go up in value during periods of prosperity. Good times mean higher corporate profits, which are in turn the wherewithal for higher dividends. Even if the dividend payout on a stock isn't increased, the additional profits are available for research and development, plant and equipment outlays, an expanded work force, and other expenditures that promise still higher profits in the future. But why do stock prices lead the general economy by a number of months? Are investors clairvoyant, or are they, like Joseph, able to interpret dreams? That is not likely. If investors had the gift of prescience, they'd do a far better job of picking stocks and of timing their purchases and sales than they ordinarily do.

There are, regrettably, no definite answers. One theory holds that investors as a group base their decisions on their expectations for future business rather than on their appraisal of current conditions. Their aggregate buying and selling therefore tends to have a self-fulfilling effect. The confidence that rising stock prices instill in consumers and in corporate executives encourages them to think and act in a bullish manner, which in turn stimulates economic activity. Conversely, a bear market casts a pall over everyone in their varied roles as investors, consumers, and workers/executives that causes them to pull in their horns—an apt expression in this context—and to act in a way that depresses the stock market and the overall economy even more.[4]

Clue 1: GNP

The broadest measure of economic activity in the United States is gross national product, or GNP. This figure represents the dollar value of all goods and services produced and sold in this country and, as such, is a reflection of most of the elements mentioned thus far in this chapter. GNP statistics are prepared by the U.S. Department of Commerce and are updated quarterly in the department's *Survey of Current Business*.

Table 5.2 is a tabulation of the GNP accounts of the United States for 1982 and 1983 as reported in the *Survey*. The table divides total GNP into four sub-headings: personal consumption expenditures, gross private domestic investment, net exports of goods, and services and government purchases of goods and services. The total of these four categories represents the aggregate dollar value of the country's output of goods and services. In 1983, the most recent complete year recorded in the table, GNP totaled $3,310.5 billion.

A problem with the GNP figures as they are reported in the first section of Table 5.2 is that it's impossible to determine how much of the gain in GNP from 1982 to 1983 was due to greater output, and how much was the result of increased prices. The Department of Commerce deals with this problem by reporting each of the items under the four principal sub-headings in so-called constant dollars based on the 1972 purchasing power of the dollar. Expressed in these "real" terms, the 1983 figure for total GNP dropped to $1,535.3 billion, less than half the same year's result tabulated in current dollars.

The problem with comparing stock prices with GNP trends is the same as it is in comparing them to industrial production—namely, that stocks usually lead GNP in the business cycle. Nevertheless, the relationship is a meaningful one—what relationships aren't?—and a careful watch on GNP can provide some helpful clues concerning the future trend of stock and index futures prices.

Comparative studies have indicated that stock prices lead GNP by an average of 4.5 months at peaks of the business cycle but that there are no consistent lead times at the bottoms. The severity of recessions, as measured by a drop in GNP, has varied over the past fifty years. During the monster

Table 5.2 Gross National Product in Current and Constant Dollars

	Billions of dollars								Billions of 1972 dollars							
			Seasonally adjusted at annual rates								Seasonally adjusted at annual rates					
	1982	1983	1982 IV	1983 I	1983 II	1983 III	1983 IV	1984 I^p	1982	1983	1982 IV	1983 I	1983 II	1983 III	1983 IV	1984 I^p
Gross national product	3,073.0	3,310.5	3,109.6	3,171.5	3,272.0	3,362.2	3,436.2	3,541.2	1,485.4	1,535.3	1,480.7	1,490.1	1,525.1	1,553.4	1,572.5	1,604.3
Personal consumption expenditures	1,991.9	2,158.0	2,046.9	2,073.0	2,147.0	2,181.1	2,230.9	2,280.5	970.2	1,011.4	979.6	986.7	1,010.6	1,016.0	1,032.2	1,046.8
Durable goods	244.5	279.4	252.1	258.5	277.7	282.8	298.6	310.3	139.8	156.3	143.2	145.8	156.5	157.9	165.2	171.9
Nondurable goods	761.0	804.1	773.0	777.1	799.6	814.8	825.0	844.4	364.2	376.1	366.0	368.9	374.7	378.1	382.5	388.0
Services	986.4	1,074.5	1,021.8	1,037.4	1,069.7	1,083.5	1,107.3	1,125.8	466.2	479.0	470.4	472.0	479.4	480.1	484.4	486.9
Gross private domestic investment	414.5	471.9	377.4	404.1	450.1	501.1	532.5	595.3	194.5	219.0	178.4	190.0	210.0	230.7	245.2	272.2
Fixed investment	439.1	478.4	433.8	443.5	464.6	492.5	512.8	533.1	203.9	221.1	201.1	205.4	215.6	227.0	236.5	245.7
Nonresidential	348.3	348.4	337.0	332.1	336.3	351.0	374.0	384.2	166.1	168.4	160.5	159.9	163.0	170.1	180.7	185.9
Structures	141.9	131.1	138.6	132.9	127.4	130.9	133.0	140.3	53.4	49.7	52.2	50.3	48.3	49.6	50.0	53.4
Producers' durable equipment	206.4	217.2	198.4	199.3	208.8	220.2	240.7	243.9	112.7	118.6	108.3	109.6	114.7	120.5	130.7	132.5
Residential	90.8	130.0	96.8	111.3	128.4	141.5	138.8	148.9	37.8	52.7	40.6	45.5	52.6	56.8	55.8	59.7
Nonfarm structures	86.0	124.9	91.2	106.7	123.3	136.3	133.5	143.7	35.2	50.0	37.8	43.0	50.0	54.1	53.1	57.0
Farm structures	1.5	1.5	2.3	1.3	1.5	1.6	1.6	1.4	.6	.6	.6	.5	.6	.6	.6	.6
Producers' durable equipment	3.2	3.6	3.3	3.3	3.5	3.6	3.7	3.8	2.0	2.1	2.1	2.0	2.1	2.1	2.1	2.2
Change in business inventories	−24.5	−6.4	−56.4	−39.4	−14.5	8.5	19.6	62.2	−9.4	−2.1	−22.7	−15.4	−5.4	3.8	8.7	26.6
Nonfarm	−23.1	−5.7	−53.7	−39.0	−10.3	8.5	19.6	41.1	−8.6	−1.2	−21.1	−15.1	−3.3	3.8	8.8	8.7
Farm	−1.4	−3.7	−2.7	−.4	−4.2	−.9	−.1	21.1	−.8	−1.9	−1.6	−.3	−2.1	−5.0	−.1	8.6
Net exports of goods and services	17.4	−9.0	5.6	17.0	−8.5	−18.3	−26.1	−65.2	28.9	11.8	23.0	20.5	12.3	11.4	2.8	−6.5
Exports	347.6	335.4	321.6	326.9	327.1	341.1	346.5	357.7	147.3	138.7	136.5	137.3	136.2	140.7	140.6	143.9
Imports	330.2	344.4	316.1	309.9	335.6	359.4	372.6	402.9	118.4	126.9	113.5	116.8	123.9	129.2	137.8	150.4
Government purchases of goods and services	649.2	689.5	679.7	677.4	683.4	698.3	699.0	710.6	291.8	293.1	299.7	292.9	292.1	295.2	292.3	291.7
Federal	258.7	274.8	279.2	273.5	273.7	278.1	274.1	275.0	116.6	117.8	124.4	118.4	117.6	118.9	116.4	114.4
National defense	179.4	200.3	190.8	194.4	194.4	201.2	206.3	216.2	78.8	84.3	81.4	82.7	84.2	84.2	85.8	87.8
Nondefense	79.3	74.5	88.5	79.1	74.3	76.9	67.8	58.8	37.8	33.6	43.0	35.7	33.4	34.7	30.5	26.5
State and local	390.5	414.7	400.5	404.0	409.7	420.2	424.9	435.6	175.2	175.3	175.2	174.5	174.5	176.3	175.9	177.3

SOURCE: U.S. Department of Commerce, Survey of Current Business, April 1984, 11.

depression of the 1930s, GNP fell by nearly one-half—a disaster that, thankfully, has not been matched before or since that time. As was noted above, economic contractions have become milder and of a briefer duration during recent years. The declines in constant-dollar GNP during the eight slowdowns since 1948 have ranged between − 0.5 percent in the mildest downturn to − 2.5 percent in the severest. In three of the contractions, GNP continued to rise, though at a greatly reduced rate. During the eight upswings, GNP grew 4 percent to 12 percent in each expansion, amounting to an average annual rate of 6 percent.

Interaction of Cycles and Stocks

As in the case of industrial production, stock prices have usually been higher at the peak of a business cycle as measured by GNP than they have been at the bottom (see figure 5.2). The 1953–54 and 1960–61 recessions were the exceptions that proved the rule. In those cycles the S&P 500 Composite Index stood at a higher level at the bottom of the recession than when the downturn began.

During the eight expansion phases since 1948, the S&P 500 rose by as much as 54 percent and by as little as 34 percent. The average gain in the stock index during those upswings was 48 percent—that is, a rise, say, from 100.00 to 148.00. Its average annual gain during growth periods was 12 percent. During recession periods, the index twice declined about 10 percent but still managed on average to rise at a 4 percent annual rate.

The lesson to be drawn from these figures is that an investor who can correctly identify turns in the business cycle as measured by industrial production, GNP, or some other primary indicator will have a leg up in recognizing turns in the stock market. Needless to say, for a stock index trader as well as for a traditional investor, such a gift would be as good as gold. Calling a cyclical turn doesn't guarantee a profit in the stock market, but when taken in conjunction with the other tools and techniques that are at a trader's disposal, it can more times than not give him or her a winning edge.

To be sure, stocks suffered severe declines in 1962 and 1966, when, according to figure 5.2, there was no downturn in GNP. There was, however, a slowdown in both instances. With the sole exception of 1951–52, when the Korean War may have disrupted the normal relationship, the stock market has declined in the face of every economic contraction or slowdown since 1948. Conversely, sustained market declines have not occurred at any other time. Clearly, where there is smoke, there's fire.

That stock prices have on occasion been lower at the peak of a business cycle than at the bottom does not contradict this conclusion, because in those instances stocks began to fall earlier and to revive sooner than the economy in

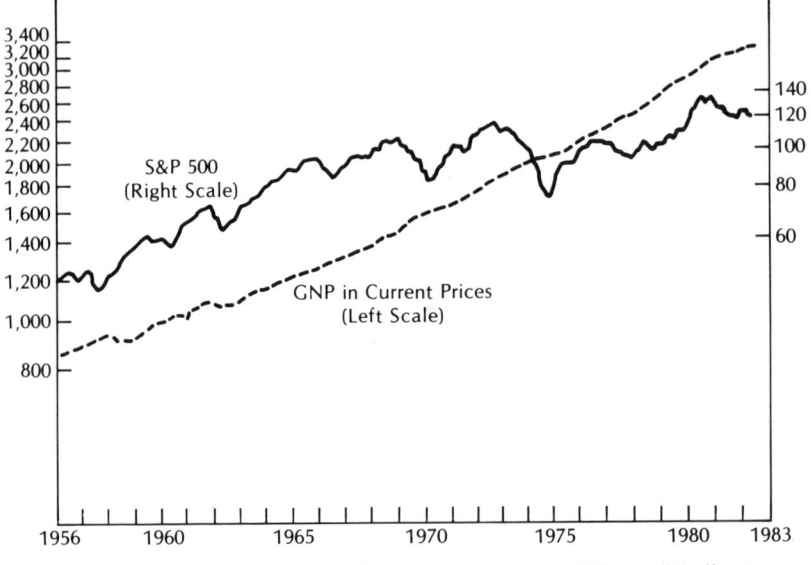

Figure 5.2 Gross National Product in Current Prices (Billions of Dollars) Versus S&P 500, 1956–83

general. The 1953–54 experience provides a good illustration. The S&P 500 reached its highest monthly average of 26.00—remarkably low in relation to today's index levels—in January 1953. By the time the business cycle had reached its peak the following July, the stock index stood at 23.00, having fallen for six months. When the business cycle reached its low in August 1974, the S&P index was at 31.00, nearly 30 percent above its level when the economy turned down thirteen months earlier. There was, as in every other case, a close connection between the decline and subsequent advance of the stock market and that of the economy, with the qualification that the market turns occurred earlier than at other times.

In all, the stock market has led the business cycle in twenty-five of the thirty peaks and nineteen of the same number of troughs recorded since 1854. The batting average since 1948 has been eight for eight. The average lead time has been between five and six months, although variations from the average have been sufficiently wide to make that an unreliable yardstick against which to forecast future turns.

Clue 2: Leading Indicators

We dared in an earlier chapter to make light of Hamlet's soliloquy—from Shakespeare to the Old Testament, the stock market is a universal study—in claiming that the key question is whether to buy or to sell. That remains unassailable. But in the present context, another key question is whether the stock market is the only business indicator that leads the economy. If it is, we are at an impasse because there are as yet no GNP or FRB index futures contracts, although anything is possible.

But if there are other elements of the economy that usually change their direction well in advance of the business cycle, we still have a fighting chance to get a fix on the stock market reasonably close to its highs and lows. Fortunately, there are such elements that have a demonstrable record of leading GNP and industrial production. Amazingly enough, they are called "leading indicators."

There are many ways to measure the level and trend of economic activity. Gross national product, industrial production, and common stock averages are only three of them. The number of people employed and the level of wages and new orders booked are three more. The list goes on and on. The Department of Commerce compiles on a continuing basis literally hundreds of such measures. The economist's problem is not one of obtaining data—the government does a heroic job of providing that—but rather of winnowing out and interpreting the most significant information.

The National Bureau of Economic Research is a private, nonprofit organization based in Cambridge, Massachusetts, that has done pioneering work in organizing and evaluating business cycle data. The NBER works closely with the Commerce Department and the Federal Reserve Board in identifying and monitoring those indicators that best reflect the performance of the overall economy. In so doing, the bureau has singled out twenty-two such indicators it believes are the most consistent gauges of economic activity. It has divided the twenty-two into twelve leading indicators, which normally move up and down ahead of most other statistical series; four coincident indicators, which move more or less with the majority; and six lagging series, which bring up the rear[5] (see table 5.3).

The group that is obviously of primary interest for forecasting purposes is the twelve leading indicators, one of which, as we noted early on, just happens to be one of the stars of our story, the S&P 500 index.

That poses something of a problem. If the purpose of our analytical exercise is to get a lead on what is going to happen in the stock market, how can we use the S&P 500 index to get a lead on itself—or its related futures contracts, for that matter? That idea conjures up the spectacle of a dog chasing its own tail. It might conceivably catch up with the tail, but the odds are heavily against that happening.

Moreover, GNP, in both current and constant terms, and industrial production are among the coincident indicators, so hoping for those series to provide us with clues to future stock price movements appears equally futile. If

Table 5.3 Leading, Coincident, and Lagging Index Components

Twelve Leading Index Components

1. Average workweek, production workers, manufacturing.
2. Average weekly initial claims, state unemployment insurance.
3. New orders for consumer goods and materials, 1972 dollars.
4. Vendor performance, percentage of companies receiving slower deliveries.
5. Net business formation.
6. Contracts and orders for plant and equipment, 1972 dollars.
7. New building permits, private housing units.
8. Net change in inventories on hand and on order, 1972 dollars.
9. Change in sensitive crude materials prices.
10. Change in total liquid assets.
11. Money supply—M_2—in 1972 dollars.
12. Stock prices, 500 common stocks.

Four Coincident Index Components

1. Employees on nonagricultural payrolls.
2. Personal income less transfer payments, 1972 dollars.
3. Industrial production, total.
4. Manufacturing and trade sales, 1972 dollars.

Six Lagging Index Components

1. Average duration of unemployment.
2. Manufacturing and trade inventories, 1972 dollars.
3. Labor cost per unit of output, manufacturing.
4. Average prime rate charged by banks.
5. Commercial and industrial loans outstanding, weekly reporting large commercial banks.
6. Ratio, consumer installment credit to personal income.

SOURCE: U.S. Department of Commerce, Bureau of Economic Analysis, *Business Conditions Digest*. May 1982, 12–15.

we were relying on the S&P index to forecast GNP and production trends, that would be another matter. But our objective is precisely the opposite one—that of employing business cycle analysis to help us in trading the S&P and other index futures contracts.

Yet all is not lost. Apart from the five-hundred-stock index, there are eleven other leading indicators on the NBER's list. If one of the eleven proves to be a "leader of leaders," our problems are solved. Even one or more series that move in fairly close harmony with the S&P 500—that reflect what we referred to in the previous chapter as a high correlation between them—would be extremely helpful.

The following is a brief description of the twelve leading indicators:[6]

1. *Average workweek, production workers, manufacturing.* The average workweek measured in hours is more sensitive to changes in economic activity than total employment is, because companies find it easier to adjust worker hours to product demand than to increase or cut back their work force. Research performed at the NBER suggests that the lead time of this indicator is somewhat longer at cyclical peaks than at bottoms.

2. *Average weekly initial claims, state unemployment insurance.* Due to the constant turnover in the work force, new unemployment claims rise faster than total unemployment during periods of slackening business activity and fall off more quickly when the recovery gets under way.

3. *New orders for consumer goods and materials.* This series is a reflection of the level of optimism (or pessimism) of retailers and manufacturers. Its importance is enhanced by a multiplier effect that radiates throughout the economy as suppliers respond to changes in the rate of incoming orders by stepping up or cutting back on the rate at which they place new orders with their suppliers.

4. *Vendor performance, percentage of companies receiving slower deliveries.* When the level of business activity is increasing, the "pipeline" for the new orders becomes congested, and firms tend to fall behind in filling them. As business begins to slacken, orders fall off, the pipeline clears, and delivery time decreases.

5. *Net business formation.* An increase in this index suggests rising optimism by entrepreneurs regarding the business outlook and is a forerunner of heightened economic activity. A decrease reflects growing pessimism and signals less activity.

6. *Contracts and orders for plant and equipment.* This is another indicator of growing or diminishing optimism. Like new orders for consumer goods and materials, an increase or decrease in plant and equipment orders exerts a multiplier effect through other sectors of the economy. Since there is often a lead time of several years or more in erecting new plants and major pieces of capital equipment, current expenditures on those items reflect contracts and orders of long standing. Current expenditures on plant and equipment accordingly are a lagging indicator.

7. *New building permits, private housing units.* With a lag of several months between the issuance of building permits and new housing starts, an increase in the number of permits currently being granted signifies heightened building activity in the future. A distortion in the normal lead time may occur due to seasonal weather factors and shortages of labor and materials.

8. *Net change in inventories on hand and on order.* Industrial and retail inventories customarily rise during periods of increasing business activity. When they enjoy a bullish outlook, businesspeople are intent on raising their inventories to be prepared for higher sales. When their optimism wanes, they have the opposite tendency to reduce inventory they're fearful they cannot readily sell.

9. *Change in sensitive crude materials prices.* Like inventories of finished goods, raw materials are stockpiled by executives who expect demand to increase. During a protracted period of inflation, however, the reliability of this indicator is compromised by a rise in the general price level.

10. *Change in total liquid assets.* A standard reaction to rising concern about the economic future is to "get liquid." As executives cut back on inventory and raw material supplies, money that otherwise would be committed to those resources is kept in cash or cash equivalents. When optimism revives, these liquid reserves are drawn down and invested in inventories, increased work force, raw material stockpiles, plant and equipment, and so on.

11. *Money supply*—This indicator is a measure of cash in circulation and demand and time deposits in commercial banks. A rising money supply, combined with declining interest rates, is the principal fuel for business expansion. On the other hand, limitation of the money supply is one of the primary means by which the government tries to cool off an "overheated" economy.[7]

12. *Stock prices, five hundred common stocks (S&P Composite Index).* Hopefully, after some hundred-odd pages, this indicator does not require further clarification. It should be reiterated, however, that our purpose in considering these leading indexes is not to predict the future course of the economy per se, but to gain insight into possible future movements of the S&P index itself, as well as the NYSE Composite and Value Line indexes, which we have tended to neglect in this discussion. Since the S&P 500 is included on the NBER's list of leading economic indicators, however, it seems reasonable to concentrate on that index for the purpose of this analysis.[8]

Clue 3: Corporate Profits

An important indicator that was dropped from the list of twelve leaders is after-tax corporate profits. The conventional wisdom of Wall Street holds that the primary underlying cause of stock price movements is anticipated earnings. The inference so far as this discussion is concerned is that declines in profits or slowdowns in their rate of growth serve to depress stock prices before business in general starts to contract. Conversely, a revival in profits sparks a recovery in stock prices before the business cycle reaches its ebb. Therefore, even though profits are no longer carried on the NBER list of leaders, index futures traders would do well to follow that series very closely.

Even better than following corporate profits is forecasting them—successfully, of course. That, once again, is far more easily said than done. Unfortunately, profits are among the most difficult economic series to predict. Although business cycles, as measured by changes in GNP, have moderated since 1948, profit fluctuations have not. That means a 1 percent drop in GNP has resulted in greater percentage drops in corporate earnings with each successive recession.

We have established that stock prices have consistently led business cycle downturns and upturns on average by about four months. Corporate after-tax profits have on average led peaks by six months and bottoms by two months. There are, as we've already observed, eight of the eleven official leading indicators (excluding stock prices) that have led business cycle peaks and valleys by a greater amount.

Another means of comparing the performance of related indicators is a method known as index diffusion analysis. It involves selecting those indicators that are believed to bear a close relationship to a particular value—in this case, corporate after-tax profits—and combining those indicators in a single index. One such indicator might be the ratio of prices to unit labor costs. Higher prices should produce higher dollar sales and, consequently, greater net profits if labor and other costs remain unchanged. On the other hand, a decrease in labor costs will produce higher profits if sales remain constant. A price/unit labor cost series would therefore be an appropriate choice for inclusion in a diffusion index representing the factors underlying corporate profits.

Similar analyses may be applied to the two main components of corporate earnings: corporate sales in dollars and percentage profit margins. Diffusion index analysis is sometimes criticized on the grounds that it can at best give an indication of turning points without providing any insight into another important consideration—that is, the future level of profits, sales, or margins. We will have a good deal more to say about the relationship between corporate profits and stock prices in the next chapter. Insofar as any of the other indicators mentioned above—such as new orders, housing starts, and inventory buildup—have a bearing on corporate profits, they deserve careful study as well.

Plunger

Enter Phil Plunger. Or reenter, to be more precise. Plunger is an everyman of financial futures trading, a veteran of many harrowing market engagements. He was trading interest rate futures in the days when 9 percent was thought to be an incredibly high rate of interest. Now, it is considered unremarkable. He traded foreign exchange futures during the darkest of days for the U.S. dollar, when people speculated that one deutsche mark might become equal to one dollar, and that one Swiss franc might someday be worth twice as much as either of them. Today, both the mark and the Swiss franc are worth less than fifty cents apiece.

Tempered in his more fanciful flights of impetuosity by Dan Decimal, his account representative at the venerable if not widely known brokerage firm of Stable and Company, Plunger is, if not exactly a winner in the futures market, at least a survivor. That is in itself an accomplishment not to be belittled.

Plunger's immediate reaction upon first reading about stock index futures was a somewhat skeptical "What will they think up next?" In this rare instance, he did not live up to his name and plunge. But as time passed and activity continued to increase at the several exchanges on which different index contracts were traded, his venturesome spirit was aroused, and he grew eager to try his hand at the new game.

"What about these index contracts?" he demanded of Decimal one day while seated at the latter's desk. "Are they an out-and-out crapshoot, or what?"

"No more than Treasury bond or Canadian dollar contracts are crapshoots," Decimal replied. "You didn't seem to have much of a problem swallowing them, as I recall."

"Well, are they riskier than stocks?" Plunger continued with his interrogatory.

"In most cases, they probably are," Decimal said. "The contract's life is limited, like any other futures. So whether you have a gain or a loss, you've got to realize it before its expiration date. There's no such thing as putting the contract away until the market turns around.

"Moreover, as if you didn't know," Decimal continued, "futures prices are much more volatile than stock prices. You'll win or lose in a shorter period of time with futures than with stocks. If you buy a hundred shares of a $60 stock, it has to go up six points for you to make 10 percent on your investment. That doesn't happen overnight. Even if you buy stock on margin, you'll probably have to sit with it for a while to realize a 10 percent profit. But if you put up

$6,000 to go long or short one index contract, at $500 a point you only need a move of little more than a point to make or lose 10 percent. That can easily happen in the course of one day, as we've repeatedly discovered."

"You're right. That's no different than Ginnie Mae or T-bill futures. I'm used to that fast action," Plunger allowed. "Which of them is the cheapest contract to buy? I see that the S&P 500 and Value Line contracts are in the 150.00–180.00 range, but the NYSE Composite contract is around 80.00. Is that the best buy?"

"If it is, it's not because it's at 80.00," Decimal answered. "We're dealing with index numbers here, not prices. The NYSE Composite index is measured against a historical base of 50, whereas the other two indexes have bases of 100. If the NYSE Composite had a base of 100, that index would stand at about 160.00 right now."

"How do I decide which of them to buy or sell, then?" Plunger asked, knowing from experience that he had to be equally willing to go short as to go long.

"It's not so much which contract as when," Decimal replied. "If you can call a rally in the stock market, all three contracts will go up by a greater or lesser degree. When the market falls, all three will fall as well. Concentrate on timing, and base your decision on the direction you think the market will take," Decimal counseled.

Armed with this advice, Plunger returned to his study and burned the midnight oil. In spite of his family name, he was a firm believer that the caveat "Investigate before you invest" applied as much to futures trading as it did to stock and bond investment.[9]

But all that Plunger was able to glean from his investigation was a welter of contradictions. He regarded himself as an adherent of the "fundamentalist" school of investment analysis, which holds that the stock market responds to business conditions, particularly the outlook for corporate earnings. But now, all of the business indicators he was accustomed to following were flashing confusing signals. The composite index of leading indicators, for example, had risen in each of the three preceding months. But early estimates by the U.S. Department of Commerce suggested that there would be a decline in the current month. To Plunger's knowledge, this leading composite had never fallen off at the outset of a business recovery. Moreover, the stock market, as measured by the S&P 500, had also fallen sharply over the past three months. That index had dropped from a monthly average of 166.35 to 159.70, its lowest level in over two years. If the current recession was nearing its end, as many economists maintained, it would be the first time that the stock market failed to turn up ahead of the recovery.

Other reports puzzled Plunger as well. The Federal Reserve Board's Index of Industrial Production was one of the coincident indicators that usually start to level off or even rise near the bottom of a recession. But the FRB index had fallen by about 0.6 percent each of the two preceding months. The inflation rate tended as a rule to increase in the early stages of a recession and then to decelerate in the late stages. But this time, Plunger noted, inflation decreased initially but then had shot up in recent months, the reverse of the customary pattern. Interest rates usually fell along with the inflation rate as a recession unfolded. But in this instance, the drop in interest rates had by no means matched the easing of inflation. In the prior month housing starts fell even as new building permits had risen for the fourth consecutive month. Both starts and permits were considered leading indicators, but they were now moving in opposite directions.[10]

Plunger scratched his head. Was the recession ending, or wasn't it? If it was ending, why hadn't stock prices, a reliable leading indicator, turned up by now? Should he buy index futures or sell them? To compound his dilemma, the latest composite leading index figure, when it was released, neither rose nor fell but remained unchanged from the prior month. Was that bullish or bearish? Plunger didn't know.

Finally, upon publication of a report that after-tax corporate profits had declined 0.8 percent during the second quarter of the year because the economy had turned out to be more sluggish than was expected, Plunger decided to act. He called Dan Decimal and asked for the latest quotation on the December S&P 500 contract. Decimal told him that the December S&Ps had last traded at 152.50, having been as high as 155.00 earlier that day.

"Sell two contracts at the market!" instructed Plunger. "This economy is still headed south, and stocks are going with it."

Decimal relayed Plunger's order to Stable and Company's floor broker at the Index and Option Market in Chicago and was soon informed that two December S&P 500 contracts had been sold for Plunger's account at 152.50.

Plunger had committed $12,000 of his account equity to sell the two contracts, and Decimal strongly advised him to limit his potential loss by means of a stop buy order. They agreed that $1,500 per contract, or about 25 percent of Plunger's initial margin commitment, was as much as he should risk on this short position. Decimal accordingly entered a stop buy order good through the month's end on two December S&Ps at 155.50, or three points above the initial sale price. If the contract price rallied to 155.50, Plunger would be "stopped out." His loss would amount to about $3,000 on the two contracts, plus brokerage commissions—Decimal's piece of the action.

Plunger had—if you'll pardon the expression—jumped off the fence. He was now a fully committed bear, on both the economy and the stock market. His reading of the latest economic indicators told him that the recovery was still a long way from being just around the corner and that stock prices had more to fall. He had decided to sell America short—for the time being, at least.

As it turned out, his short position was—if you'll again excuse the expression—a short-lived one. On the day following their sale, the December contracts rallied to 155.40, a hair (0.10 points) short of Plunger's stop price. On the day after that, they fell back to 153.50, again moving in the right direction so far as Plunger was concerned.

On the afternoon of the third day, Plunger called Decimal and said he'd just heard over the radio that stocks were soaring. What was going on, he wanted to know. Decimal told him that an influential economist had reversed his widely heeded opinion that interest rates would continue to rise and that a "buying panic" was carrying stock prices to their greatest one-day gain in history.

Even as they were speaking, Decimal received notification from Chicago that Plunger had just been stopped out of his short position at 155.50.

Upon being told the bad news, Plunger snapped, "You mean I studied those damned indicators backward and forward and then some Wall Street guru opens his mouth and stops me out? Those index futures are nothing but a crapshoot after all."

"You didn't complain when the same guru helped you to make a big profit on Treasury-bill futures last year," Decimal reminded his disgruntled client. "Are you going to let one loss knock you out of the box?"

"Not on your ticker tape," Plunger replied heatedly. "Phil Plunger never gives up!"

CHAPTER 6

Security Analysis and Stock Index Values

Phil Plunger, the protagonist of the foregoing vignette, regarded himself as a "fundamentalist." In another context that could have been an allusion to Plunger's religious convictions. But here it refers to his approach to investing and futures trading.

The distinction was made between company-related and market-related risks earlier in this book.[1] Fundamentalists are primarily company-oriented. They believe that stock prices are determined by corporate performance. That attitude stands in contrast to the position of the technicians, who maintain that stock prices are in the first instance influenced by trader psychology and by the buying and selling that spring from that psychology.[2]

A slightly ironical but fair description of a fundamentalist is one who "never measures the attractiveness of a stock by the fickle standards of the marketplace, but rather determines the price at which he is willing to invest, and then turns to the marketplace to see if the stock is selling at the required price."[3]

Fundamentalists are preoccupied with the value of a stock. Such value is not necessarily—in fact, it seldom is —equal to the prevailing market price of the stock. If its value is greater than its current price, a stock is considered to be underpriced and may on that account be regarded as a purchase candidate. If fundamental analysis shows a stock to be worth less than its market price, it is deemed overpriced, and if it should not for that reason alone be sold, it certainly shouldn't be bought.

Fundamentalists are students. They pore over financial statements and make their own calculations to verify those statements. In the old days a slide rule was their primary tool for making investment decisions. Now, fundamentalists probably spend their spare time writing programs for their home computers.

Technicians are also students in their own way. They concentrate on trading volume—that is, the number of shares bought and sold on any day, advance-decline ratios, chart formations, and what are to nonpractitioners of the (witch) craft, other occult signs. They are also starting to use personal computers to keep track of these things, including real-time visual displays of price charts. But to strict fundamentalists, technicians remain misguided souls, always running with the pack (or coven) after ephemeral "bubbles and bursts" in the market instead of behaving as serious investors should.

Fundamentalists' Bible

If this brand of fundamentalism were indeed a religion, it would come equipped with its own "Bible," entitled, appropriately enough, *Security Analysis*.[4] It was first published in 1934, decidedly not a very good year for books about investing in stocks, by Benjamin Graham and David L. Dodd, who were at that time both professors of finance at the Columbia University Graduate School of Business. Their names alone are even now sufficient to identify to practicing investment analysts the definitive text in their field. *Security Analysis* is a very good book, as germane to its subject today as it was in 1934.

The central idea of Graham and Dodd's work is their concept of *intrinsic value*. Moving through some seven-hundred-odd pages, a reader gains the impression the authors almost deplore the fact that stocks are traded in an open marketplace. One doubts that they would have had anything good to say about stock index futures.[5]

Graham and Dodd compared the relationship between security analysis and general market analysis to what was generally regarded in 1934 as a dubious link between conventional medicine and psychiatry. They urged analysts to preserve their mental health by ignoring the short-term fluctuations of the stock market, which, to their way of thinking, were signs of aberrant human behavior.[6]

Figure 6.1 illustrates the distinction Graham and Dodd made between intrinsic value and market price. It is a price chart of an unidentified stock, call it XYZ, setting highs and lows during alternating periods of investor optimism and gloom. Graham and Dodd would disregard these extremes in market price and concentrate instead on XYZ's intrinsic value, represented by line A-A' in the chart. In contrast to the jagged peaks and valleys traced by the market price, intrinsic value changes gradually as XYZ Company's operating record

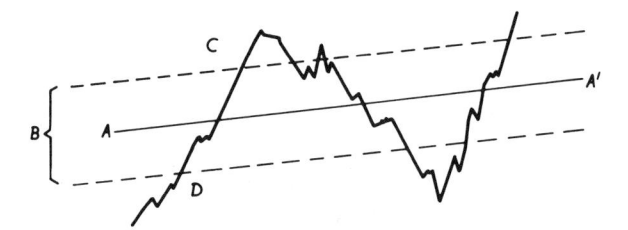

Figure 6.1 Intrinsic Value Chart. (Jerome B. Cohen, Edward D. Zinbarg, and Arthur Zeikel, *Investment Analysis and Portfolio Management* [Homewood, Ill.: Richard D. Irwin, 1977]. Reprinted by permission.)

and demonstrable prospects change. Conceding that they, too, are human and cannot establish a stock's intrinsic value to the dollar (even after seven hundred pages), the authors allow themselves a margin of error, range B, above and below A-A'.

Technicians and other misguided traders—they cannot in truth call themselves investors according to the fundamentalists—will continue to disregard value and push XYZ's price alternately above and below range B. When that happens, the fundamentalists shake their heads and hope—we won't go so far as to say pray—that their misguided brethren will someday see the light. Whether they do or not, XYZ's price will, by the nature of markets, eventually reenter the intrinsic value range and pass through it to the other extreme.

Three Important Elements

The fundamentalists believe there are three primary elements that impart value to a stock: a company's earnings, dividends, and assets. In most instances today, analysts and traders concentrate on earnings and dividends. If a company deteriorates to the point where its shareholders need to be concerned with its breakup value, its stock can't be much of an investment.[7]

Dividends are the immediate return a stockholder obtains on his or her investment. So it stands to reason that a stock on which three dollars in dividends are paid annually will be worth more to the stockholder, other things being equal, than one on which two dollars are paid. As a rule, companies that increase their dividend payout enjoy an immediate, if sometimes temporary, rise in the price of their stock, while companies that are forced to cut their dividends experience a drop in their stock price.

Higher earnings give a company the resources to raise its dividend payments. When its management does not choose to increase the payout, the added earnings can be reinvested in the business, enhancing the prospect of yet higher earnings and more liberal dividends in the future. Even those investors who are primarily "appreciation-minded"—that is to say, more interested in capital gains than they are in dividend income—are bound to pay attention to the dividend rate in estimating a stock's prospective value.

In the words of Graham and Dodd, a stock's intrinsic value is:

> That value which is justified by the facts—e.g., assets, earnings, dividends, definite prospects. In the usual case the most important single factor determining value is now held to be the *indicated average future earning power*. Intrinsic value would then be found by first estimating this earning power, and then multiplying that estimate by an appropriate "capitalization factor."[8]

Perhaps suspecting that they might have gone too far in intimating that analysts and investors who are attuned to market swings are slightly neurotic, Graham and Dodd continue:

> The investor does not actually have to make this choice between the world of value and the world of market prices. Experience affirms that the price and the independently ascertained value do tend to converge as time goes on. The valuation approach is thus not an unrealistic one, in the sense that it deals with concepts that play no part in the actual behavior of the market price. Its limitations and weaknesses stem rather from the lack of precision and of full dependability that are always associated with calculations of the economic future.[9]

Graham and Dodd don't claim that their valuation approach is a surefire system for beating the market. On the contrary, they seem to be saying that the way to investment success lies in disregarding the market most of the time or at least in avoiding the pitfalls of emotionalism and wishful thinking to which many investors succumb.

The "Intrinsic Value" Formula

Graham and Dodd wrote their masterly volume only several years following the speculative binge of the 1920s. They therefore witnessed at first hand a market driven to heights of euphoric frenzy and then to depths of unrelieved gloom the likes of which, fortunately, have not been experienced since. Their objective was to help their readers to avoid the ravaging consequences of such excesses by applying a quantitative measure of a company's long-term performance and financial condition rather than being swept along by the rosy or bleak views of the future that prevail at market peaks and bottoms.[10]

The formula Graham and Dodd devised to compute their concept of intrinsic value is:

$$\text{Intrinsic value} = M \left(\text{dividends} + \frac{\text{earnings}}{3}\right)$$
$$\pm \text{ possible adjustment for asset values}$$

The M in the formula is the capitalization factor, or price/earnings (and, in this case, dividend) multiple, they considered appropriate when a company paid out what they believed was a "normal" proportion of its earnings as dividends.

Graham and Dodd regarded a company's past earnings record as a reliable indicator of its future earnings potential as well as a primary determinant of the proper multiplier by which to capitalize those earnings. Its history of dividend payments was likewise held to be a valid guide to future payouts, and such asset factors as a company's working capital ratio and asset value per share were thought to influence the capitalization of earnings and dividends.[11]

In contrast to the practice of projecting corporate earnings for a limited period, usually over the coming year, that is customary on Wall Street today, Graham and Dodd tried to forecast earnings and dividends five and even ten years into the future. The price/earnings and dividend multiplier they selected for a particular stock incorporated their view of that company's dividend and earnings prospects beyond ten years.

An Analytical Look at GE

But before continuing to bandy ratios and formulas about with such abandon, it is a good idea to go back to basics for a brief spell and to refresh our memory about what these figures mean and how they are computed. To lend substance to our review, and by way of preparation for the weightier matters that follow, let us dispense with the ubiquitous XYZ Company and turn our attention to a true-to-life example of security analysis in action.

The General Electric Company is as good a choice as any and is probably better than most.[12] But readers are strongly urged to focus their attention on the analytical technique that is outlined rather than on the financial statistics regarding GE, which are in any case already dated. Of course, this exercise is for our purpose a building block toward gaining a better understanding of stock index futures rather than of individual companies per se. Nevertheless, readers should benefit by applying this type of fundamental analysis to one or more companies in which they may be interested.[13]

During its business year ended December 31, 1981, GE sold a staggering $27.2 billion worth of clock radios, television sets, electrical generators, jet engines, nuclear reactors, and other products in its diversified lines. After deducting from that figure its raw material costs, the year's depreciation of its plant and equipment, and assorted sales and administrative expenses, the company retained as operating income $2.5 billion, or about 9 percent of its total sales. The addition of other income earned from money market investments and other sources, and a further deduction of interest paid on its own bonds, gave GE before-tax earnings of $2.6 billion. The final deduction of about $1 billion for income-tax provision and an item labeled "minority interest in earnings of consolidated affiliates" brings us to the well-known bottom line: net earnings of over $1.6 billion (see table 6.1).

That is a lot of money no matter how you slice it. There are some underdeveloped countries that don't have a GNP of $1.6 billion. But so far as the individual stockholder is concerned, that figure is so massive as to be practically meaningless. Even when you confine the comparison to the corporate titans, how do you relate GE's bottom line to the $6.9 billion earned by AT&T in 1981? Or IBM's $3.3 billion and Exxon's $5.6 billion? There has to be among these meganumbers a common denominator, so to speak.

The denominator analysts find most useful is earnings per share (EPS). At the end of 1981, General Electric had 227.8 million shares outstanding. That is stock held outside the corporate treasury, whether by individual investors, institutions, or GE employees, executives, and directors. Dividing net earnings for 1981 by the number of shares outstanding produces an earnings per share figure for GE of $7.26—that is:

$$\frac{\$1,652,000,000}{227,760,000} = \$7.26$$

If, in subsequent years; net earnings rose and the number of outstanding shares remained unchanged, earnings per share would rise. If profits stayed constant and the outstanding shares increased by reason of an acquisition or a new stock offering, the EPS figure would decline.[14] For example, GE's net profit in 1980 was $1.514 billion while the number of shares the company had outstanding was virtually the same as it was in the year following, producing earnings per share in 1980 of $6.65. In addition to making the year-to-year record of profits earned by a single company more meaningful, the earnings per share figure makes it easier to compare the earnings performance of different companies, such as GE, AT&T, IBM, and Exxon.

Earnings per share also provide a convenient means by which the earnings of a company may be measured against the price of its stock. Once a company closes the books for its fiscal year, all of the reported figures are a matter of record. They don't change, except perhaps when earnings per share are restated in the event a merger or some other development causes a change in the company's capitalization. What does change continually is the relationship

Table 6.1 General Electric Company Consolidated Income Statement, Year Ended December 31, 1981 (Millions)

Net sales	$27,240
Cost of sales and operating expenses	
Cost of goods sold	18,945
Selling and administrative expense	4,966
Depreciation, depletion, and amortization	882
Total operating costs	24,793
Operating income	2,447
Other income	614
Less: interest and other financial charges	(401)
Earnings before income taxes and minority interest	2,660
Provision for income taxes	(962)
Minority interest in earnings of consolidated affiliates	(46)
Net earnings applicable to common stock	$ 1,652
Common shares outstanding	227,760,000
Net earnings per share	$7.26

SOURCE: Annual report, 1981.

of earnings to stock price. That is what Graham and Dodd referred to as the "capitalization factor"—*M* in their formula—and what is familiar to many investors as the price/earnings ratio.

The price/earnings (P/E) ratio changes as frequently as a stock's market price changes. The year's high for GE common in 1981 was, for example 69⅞, at which price the stock's P/E ratio on the basis of 1981 reported earnings was about 9½—that is:

$$\frac{69\ 7/8}{\$7.26} = \frac{69.875}{7.26} = 9.6$$

The 1981 low was 51⅛, where by the same manner of calculation, the P/E ratio was about 7. The problem was (and remains) that when those high and low prices were set, no one knew what GE's final earnings for 1981 would be. Analysts and investors had their choice of basing their calculations on 1980 reported earnings per share, which were then known to be $6.65, or else estimating the 1981 EPS figure and calculating an assumed P/E ratio on the basis of that estimate. Security analysts as a rule lean toward using an estimate of the current year's earnings and possibly those of the year following. Making such earnings forecasts is an integral part of their job.

Returning to our interpretation of the old masters, Graham and Dodd

Table 6.2   Selected Financial Data, General Electric Company, 1972–81

Income Data (Million $)

Year Ended Dec. 31	Revs.	Oper. Inc.	% Oper. Inc. of Revs.	Cap. Exp.	Depr.	Int. Exp.	Net Bef. Taxes	Eff. Tax Rate	Net Inc.	% Net Inc. of Revs.
1981	27,240	3,329	12.2%	2,025	882	424	²2,660	36.2%	1,652	6.1%
1980	24,959	2,950	11.8%	1,948	707	³335	²2,493	38.4%	1,514	6.1%
1979	22,461	2,754	12.3%	1,262	624	259	²2,391	39.9%	1,409	6.3%
1978	19,654	2,534	12.9%	1,055	576	224	²2,153	41.5%	1,230	6.3%
1977	17,519	2,220	12.7%	823	522	200	²1,889	40.9%	1,088	6.2%
¹1976	15,697	2,014	12.8%	740	486	175	²1,628	41.1%	³ 931	5.9%
1975	13,399	1,340	10.0%	448	419	169	² 950	37.7%	581	4.3%
1974	13,413	1,371	10.2%	672	376	180	²1,001	38.2%	608	4.5%
1973	11,575	1,289	11.1%	599	334	127	²1,012	41.4%	585	5.1%
1972	10,240	1,129	11.0%	436	314	107	² 897	40.6%	530	5.2%

Balance Sheet Data (Million $)

Dec. 31	Cash	Current Assets	Current Liab.	Ratio	Total Assets	Ret. on Assets	Long Term Debt	Common Equity	Total Cap.	% LT Debt of Cap.	Ret. on Equity
1981	2,471	10,804	8,734	1.2	20,942	8.4%	1,059	9,128	10,353	10.2%	19.1%
1980	2,201	9,883	7,592	1.3	18,511	8.6%	1,000	8,200	9,354	10.7%	19.5%
1979	2,577	9,385	6,872	1.4	16,645	8.9%	947	7,362	8,461	11.2%	20.2%
1978	2,463	8,755	6,175	1.4	15,036	8.6%	994	6,587	7,731	12.9%	19.6%
1977	2,278	7,865	5,417	1.5	13,697	8.4%	1,284	5,943	7,359	17.5%	19.4%
1976	1,613	6,685	4,605	1.5	12,050	7.7%	1,322	·5,253	6,694	19.8%	18.1%
1975	853	5,566	3,963	1.4	9,764	6.0%	1,038	4,069	5,191	20.0%	14.9%
1974	372	5,223	3,880	1.3	9,369	6.9%	1,195	3,704	4,971	24.0%	17.2%
1973	322	4,485	3,492	1.3	8,324	7.4%	917	3,372	4,340	21.1%	18.1%
1972	294	3,979	2,870	1.4	7,402	7.4%	947	3,085	4,075	23.2%	18.0%

Data as orig. reptd. 1. Reflects merger or acquisition. 2. Incl. equity in earns. of nonconsol. subs. 3. Reflects accounting change.

Per Share Data ($)

Yr. End Dec. 31	1981	1980	1979	1978	1977	¹1976	1975	1974	1973	1972
Book Value	38.63	35.67	32.08	28.71	25.90	23.05	21.92	20.11	18.35	16.75
Earnings	7.26	6.65	²6.20	²5.39	²4.79	²4.12	²3.17	²3.34	²3.21	²2.91
Dividends	3.15	2.95	2.75	2.50	2.10	1.70	1.60	1.60	1.50	1.40
Payout Ratio	43%	44%	44%	46%	44%	41%	51%	48%	47%	48%
Prices—High	69⁷/₈	63	55¹/₈	57⁵/₈	57¹/₄	59¹/₄	52⁷/₈	65	75⁷/₈	73
Low	51¹/₈	44	45	43⁵/₈	47³/₈	46	32³/₈	30	55	58¹/₄
P/E Ratio—	10–7	9–7	9–7	11–8	12–10	14–11	17–10	19–9	24–17	25–20

Data as orig. reptd. 1. Reflects merger or acquisition. 2. Ful. dil.: 6.15 in 1979, 5.35 in 1978, 4.75 in 1977, 4.09 in 1976, 3.12 in 1975, 3.31 in 1974, 3.18 in 1973, 2.87 in 1972.

SOURCE: Standard & Poor's Corporate Stock Reports. Stock prices and earnings per share figures contained in Table 6.2 and accompanying text are not adjusted for a 100% stock dividend (equivalent to a 2-for-1 split) effective June 1983. Reprinted with permission.

describe three methods by which future earnings may be estimated. The first method is to strike an average of past earnings over what is regarded as a normal sequence of years and to adopt that average as the earnings forecast. Table 6.2 contains a detailed summary of General Electric's operating and financial results since 1966. We note from the table that earnings per share between 1977 and 1981 ranged from $4.79 to $7.26. An arithmetic mean— our old friend from chapter 1—of those five years' earnings works out to $6.06 a share.

But there is a shortcoming to this method of straight averaging. GE's earnings were continually rising during the 1977–81 period, as they had been in nearly every year reported in table 6.2. A simple arithmetic mean would therefore appear to be a questionable estimate of the 1982 results. Graham and Dodd proposed to overcome the limitations of a straight average and take an evident earnings trend into account in their calculations by including what they called an "arbitrary percentage adjustment." GE's earnings grew at an average rate of about 10 percent a year from 1977 to 1981. Projecting an increase of that magnitude over 1981's results produced an earnings forecast for 1982 of $8.00 a share. That was probably a more realistic estimate than the straight average of $6.06 derived by the first method, but it was still only an extrapolation of the earnings trend over the previous five years.

Factors in an Analysis

The old masters conceded that the percentage-adjustment method could be too mechanical when business conditions are changing rapidly. They accordingly proposed what they called a "scientific" method of projecting future earnings by estimating potential sales, operating and nonoperating expenses, labor and material costs, and the numerous other factors that determine a company's bottom-line figure.

Present-day analysts refer to this third method as the "eclectic" approach. Whatever name it bears, it's the method that requires the greatest exercise of judgment on the part of analysts. Bluntly put, it's what separates the men from the boys in that profession—presumably the women from the girls as well—and determines who earns $250,000 a year and who just gets by. As an analyst who is at the high side of that range once observed, "We're not playing this game for Cracker Jack prizes."

The principal factors an analyst—whether at $250,000 a year or less—should consider in preparing a "scientific," or "eclectic," forecast of corporate earnings include:[15]

1. *Growth in revenues, expenses, net income, earnings per share, and assets.* General Electric's revenues, operating income, and net earnings grew at average annual rates of 11 percent, 9 percent, and 10 percent, respectively, between 1977 and 1981, well above the growth rate of the economy as a whole. The company's cost of goods rose an average 13 percent a year during those years. Selling and administrative expenses meanwhile increased 11 percent annually on average. Although the economy moved into a recession in the second half of 1981, GE continued to achieve gains in sales, net profits, and earnings per share.

2. *Management's record, long-range objectives, history of innovation, and business philosophy.* GE's management is among the most highly regarded in American business. The company's successful reorientation toward sophisticated and profitable high technologies and services while maintaining industry leadership in its traditional electrical appliance and equipment businesses attests to the strategic planning and execution capabilities of its senior management. During the nine-year tenure of its retired chairman and chief executive officer, Reginald H. Jones, the company's sales more than doubled from the $10-billion level of 1972, and net earnings increased from $573 million to over $1.5 billion by 1980.

3. *Earnings as a percentage of total capital and equity (common stock and retained earnings).* Between 1977 and 1981 General Electric earned annually an average of 17 percent of total capital and 19.6 percent of share owners' equity. Profits were consistently over 6 percent of total sales.

4. *Capital structure, credit rating, debt ratio objectives, and fixed charge (bond interest) coverage.* GE's long-term debt is a conservative 10 percent of the company's total capitalization, markedly lower than the 1977 level, when it swapped its common stock for $300 million worth of its bonds. The equity-for-debt swap secured for the company a substantial saving in annual interest charges. The annual interest expense is earned about seven times over. The company's bonds are rated AAA by both Moody's and Standard and Poor's. Value Line ranks GE's financial strength as A + +.

5. *Dividend policy, growth, and percentage payout.* Dividends were increased each year between 1977 and 1981 from an annual payment of $2.10 a share to $3.15. The company's recent policy has been to pay in dividends about 45 percent of annual net profits.

6. *Accounting policies.* GE's financial statements consolidate the accounts of the parent General Electric Company and those of all majority-owned subsidiaries except finance companies, principally the General Electric Credit Corporation, whose operations are not similar to those of the consolidated group. The nonconsolidated finance companies are included in the financial statements under the heading of investments and are valued at equity plus advances. The planned implementation of the Statement of Financial Accounting Standards No. 52 for foreign currency translation was not expected at the end of 1981 to have a material effect on GE's financial statements. The company employs the traditional methods of reporting in the preparation of its financial statements but appends certain supplementary information to indicate the effect of inflation on sales and earnings. The company believes the "current cost" method of price

adjustment is more representative of GE's results but emphasizes that considerable subjectivity is involved in the calculations.

7. *Key financial ratios.* The company's current ratio—that is, current assets divided by current liabilities—declined somewhat between 1977 and 1981, from 1.45 to about 1.30. Its ratio of net current assets to net worth also fell during those years, from 41 percent to 28 percent.

8. *Market position and market share.* General Electric revised its corporate structure in 1981 to emphasize its growing high-technology and service businesses. The company remains the largest U.S. manufacturer of electrical equipment. Sales to the U.S. government, primarily in fulfillment of defense contracts, comprised about 12 percent of total sales in 1981. Foreign business accounted for about 35 percent of net earnings.

9. *Employee relations, policies, and cost trends.* The company has 404,000 employees worldwide and has consistently pursued an active policy of employee support and advancement. As of the end of 1981, women accounted for 28 percent of total employment and minorities 12 percent. Efforts continued to advance women and minority employees to professional and managerial positions. The continuing emphasis on high technology and services makes the company's overall operations less labor-intensive and serves to improve profit margins.

10. *Economic environment, sensitivity to business cycles, long-term industry trends, and raw materials situation.* GE's expanded operations in defense contracting, medical equipment, nuclear fuel and services, and data processing reduce the company's vulnerability to cutbacks in consumer and industry spending.

11. *Technological leadership, research and development programs, plant obsolescence.* GE is an acknowledged leader in high-technology product development. The company's dominant positions in the design and manufacture of jet aircraft engines and nuclear reactors are but two of the most prominent examples of its technological leadership. Heavy investment has been made in its "factory of the future" automation equipment lines and in computer-aided engineering.

12. *Earnings per share stability and growth.* GE's record in this respect is excellent. Earnings declined in only one of the ten years from 1972 to 1981. Annual earnings gains during those years averaged 18 percent, aided by the merger with Utah International in 1976. As was noted above, earnings growth during the years 1977 to 1981 averaged about 10 percent annually.

13. *Stock price growth, volatility, price/earnings ratio.* GE stock has displayed moderate but consistent growth from its low of 30 at the bottom of the 1973–74 bear market. In five of the subsequent seven years, each year's low price was above the low of the year immediately preceding it. Average annual price/earnings ratios between 1977 and 1981 ranged from eleven times reported earnings in 1977 to an average of eight times earnings in 1979. The stock has a beta of .95, making its volatility nearly identical to that of the stock market as a whole. On the basis of a 1982 earnings estimate of $8.00 a share and a median price/earnings ratio of 10, GE stock could rise from its 1981 low of 51 1/8 to a target price of 80. Applying its 1977 high P/E ratio of 12 against the same $8.00-a-share earnings estimate, the stock could conceivably reach a price of 96.[16]

So What Is GE Stock Worth?

Having undertaken this typical analysis, what, according to the gospel of Graham and Dodd, was GE stock worth at the end of 1981? In applying their intrinsic-value formula now that we (hopefully) have a better idea of what it's all about, we still cannot say how the old masters would have evaluated the thirteen points concerning General Electric cited above. But for the sake of completing the exercise, let us assign to the Graham and Dodd formula a price-earnings multiple for GE of nine, as a fairly representative P/E ratio for that stock from 1977 to 1981. With that assumption, we can make the following calculation:

$$\text{Intrinsic value} = 9\ (\$3.15\ +\ \frac{\$7.26}{3})$$
$$= 9\ \times\ \$5.57$$
$$= \$50\ 1/8$$

According to this application of Graham and Dodd's intrinsic-value formula, GE common was "worth" 50⅛ at the end of 1981, when the stock was in fact selling at about 58. It is interesting to note that its low for 1981 was 51⅛.

But there is an inconsistency in these results that the astute reader—of Loosigian, not of Graham and Dodd—has assuredly spotted. The old masters said that value was based on the average *future* earning power of a corporation. An earnings figure of $7.26 a share and a $3.15 dividend were about ready to be entered in the record books—or in this case, GE's annual report—at the end of 1981. The stock market, including the $250,000-a-year analysts, wanted to know what lay ahead for the company, not behind it.

Starting with the Big Picture

Chapter 5 closed with our protagonist Phil Plunger puzzling over the "big picture." What were the leading economic indicators doing? Was the gross national product rising or falling? The Plunger interlude was not purely comic relief. For GNP is precisely where your high-powered, high-priced security analysts begin to develop their earnings forecasts. They start, as Plunger did, with the big picture and eventually work their way down to predicting how the earnings of a particular company will be affected by an estimated increase or drop in GNP.

The process begins by separating GNP itself into its four primary components: the currently employed work force, the average workweek expressed in hours, output per labor hour worked, and the general price level. When taken together, changes in the first three of these components produce a consequent change in real, or constant-dollar, GNP. By considering changes in the fourth component, the price level, as well, analysts can derive a projection of the change in current-dollar GNP.

Recent experience indicates that these component variables do not move in wide ranges. Yearly growth in the employed work force has usually been between 1.5 percent and 2.0 percent. The average hourly workweek has declined about 0.5 percent annually, and output per labor hour worked has gained between 2 percent and 3 percent annually. If they continue at the same rate, the combined effect of these changes is a possible growth in real GNP of 3 percent to 5 percent with most forecasts falling within the middle range of 3.5 percent to 4.0 percent. During the years from 1977 to 1981, real GNP grew in the United States at an average annual rate of about 2 percent.

The matrix of assumed growth rates, productivity gains, and price increases contained in table 6.3 offers an example of the way in which the analysis might proceed when estimated price changes are incorporated with the other variables. If an analyst predicts that GNP will rise 3.5 percent in the coming year, he or she will scan the two columns that are so labeled on the left-hand side of the table. If the analyst further projects a general price increase of 3 percent, he or she narrows the area of concentration further to the top tier of assumed price changes. Finally, if he or she projects that output per labor hour worked will rise by 2.5 percent rather than 3 percent during the coming year, and that total employment costs per labor hour will increase by 6 percent, the analyst has zeroed in on an estimated increase in corporate profits of 5 percent.

A period of extremely high inflation provokes greater price increases than those indicated in table 6.3. Expanded assumptions would in that case be incorporated into the matrix to provide for the possibility of virulent inflation. Generally, corporate profits are likely to increase at a slower rate than GNP in a high-inflation economy, and dividends are likely to grow more slowly than

Table 6.3 Matrix of Estimated Changes in Corporate Profits, Real GNP, Output per Labor Hour Worked, and General Price Levels

Total Employment Costs per Labor Hour	Assume 3.5% Real Growth: Output per Labor Hour		Assume 4% Real Growth: Output per Labor Hour		Assume 4.5% Real Growth: Output per Labor Hour	
	2.5%	3%	2.5%	3%	2.5%	3%
			Price Change of +3%			
5%	+ 8.5%	+10.2%	+ 9.0%	+10.7%	+ 9.5%	+11.3%
6%	+ 5.0	+ 6.8	+ 5.5	+ 7.2	+ 6.0	+ 7.8
			Price Change of +3.5%			
5%	+11.0%	+12.8%	+11.5%	+13.2%	+12.1%	+13.9%
6%	+ 7.5	+ 9.3	+ 8.0	+ 9.8	+ 8.6	+10.4
			Price Change of +4%			
5%	+13.6%	+15.3%	+14.1%	+15.9%	+14.6%	+16.4%
6%	+10.1	+11.8	+10.7	+12.4	+11.1	+12.9

SOURCE: The matrix is adapted from one presented by Henry A. Latane and Donald L. Tuttle in *Security Analysis and Portfolio Management,* (New York: Ronald Press, 1970), 305.

earnings. The chart in figure 6.2 depicts the relationship between after-tax corporate earnings reported by the Standard & Poor's 400 industrial stocks and current-dollar GNP from 1947 to 1975.[17] The comparison indicates that corporate earnings have failed to keep pace with GNP growth, indicating a steady erosion of corporate profit margins during those years.

Forecasting Sales and Earnings

Narrowing his or her study from aggregate corporate earnings to those of a specific company, the analyst prepares to make an earnings forecast by estimating future sales. Rising output and sales do not necessarily mean that increased profits will follow. Costs may rise faster. But the likelihood of an earnings increase is in most instances greater if sales are rising than if they remain steady or decline.

The sales forecast is derived from the analyst's projection of GNP. He or she estimates from historical data the effect that a 1 percent increase or decrease in GNP will have on the annual sales of the company being researched, taking

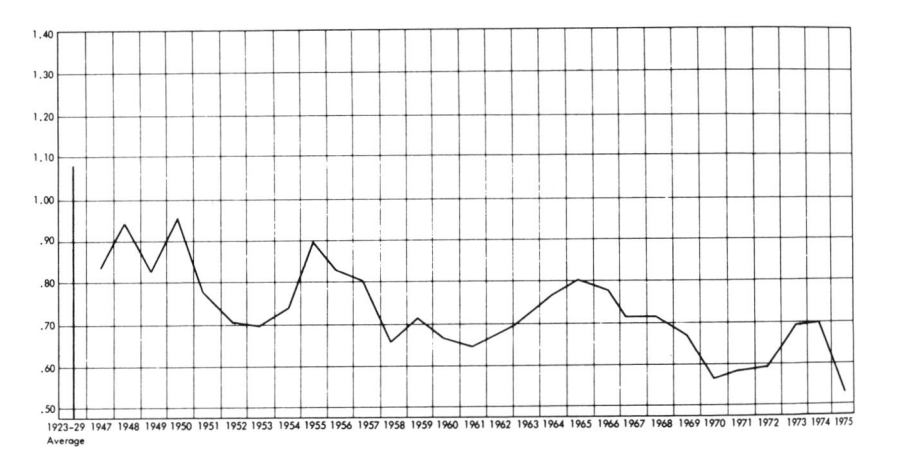

Figure 6.2 Ratio of After-Tax Earnings (S&P 400 Stocks) to Current-Dollar GNP Growth, 1947–75. (Jerome B. Cohen, Edward D. Zinbarg, and Arthur Zeikel, *Investment Analysis and Portfolio Management* [Homewood, Ill.: Richard D. Irwin, 1977]. Reprinted by permission.)

into account possible changes in consumer tastes, technology, inventory levels, and relative prices.

The analyst is now ready to develop an earnings forecast. There are a number of ways in which the task can be approached. He or she might undertake the direct method suggested by the matrix in table 6.3, moving from a GNP projection to an estimate of total corporate profits. The analyst would then derive from that aggregate profit figure an earnings trend for the particular industry in which he or she is interested. Finally, the analyst is in a position to formulate the desired corporate estimate, taking care to consider the particular characteristics that set the subject company apart from the industry standard.

Another approach is to produce from the sales forecast a complete projected income statement that proceeds via assumed profit margin, operating income, and before- and after-tax earnings figures to estimated earnings per share.

There are other alternatives. An analyst may prefer to make a probabilistic forecast in which he or she projects a range of values and assigns a percentage probability rating to those values considered most likely to be realized. The analyst may contribute to a conditional forecast that combines the specialized talents and experience of two or more analysts. For example, an economist might assume the responsibility for making a forecast of GNP, which he or she will then pass on to a security analyst as the basis for the latter's corporate earnings projection.

The final step is to select an appropriate price/earnings ratio to accompany the earnings forecast. Of the thirteen consequential factors listed above, those that are generally assigned the greatest weight in determining a P/E ratio include: the expected rate and consistency of the company's earnings growth, the anticipated level of dividend payments, the relative volatility of the stock (its beta), and the perceived image of the company and quality of its management.

Earnings Are Important, But . . .

Of all these factors, projected earnings growth is far and away the most decisive. Analysts generally agree—and the action of the market bears out their assessment—that the higher a company's rate of earnings growth is, the higher the price/earnings ratio of its stock should be.

Graham and Dodd pointed out early in their book that it is important to consider what they called "normalized" earnings in selecting and comparing P/E ratios. Even an average of earnings drawn over a period of years may not be what they would have regarded as normal if the period selected happened to include unusually high or low earnings years. Taken at their face value, abnormal earnings produce excessively high or low P/E ratios that may not reflect the present value of stocks measured by them except insofar as they are a sign of earnings instability.

Figure 6.3 presents in schematic form the linkages between the various factors determining share prices that have been discussed above. The conclusion to be drawn from the discussion is that a successful effort to predict future corporate performance, especially net profits, and the application to that estimate of an appropriate price/earnings ratio can be highly useful in predicting future stock prices and, by extension, future stock index levels. Like earnings themselves, however, the past behavior of a particular stock's P/E ratio is not a sure indicator of its future performance. Price/earnings ratios are, like profits, subject to near-term fluctuations around their longer-range trends. Such near-term movements can be misleading when it comes to using the current P/E ratio as a guide to a stock's future value.

Two prominent students of stock price behavior underscored the problems arising from attempting to forecast prices on the basis of corporate earnings in the following terms:

> The conclusions about prediction are discouraging in that they indicate the great difficulty of the task. The simple extrapolation of historical trends [is] not likely to be very useful in predicting future changes in earnings.
> Randomness in corporate earnings merely means that one's ability to forecast changes in earnings will not be significantly enhanced by studying changes in historical rates of growth in earnings.[18]

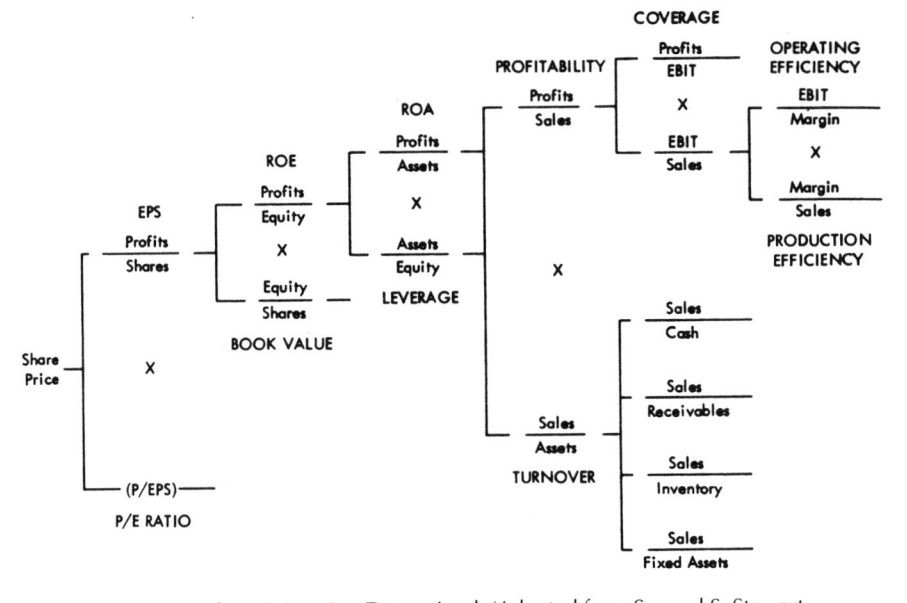

Figure 6.3 How Share Prices Are Determined. (Adapted from Samuel S. Stewart, "Corporate Forecasting," *Financial Analyst's Handbook*, vol. 1, *Portfolio Management,* Sumner N. Levine, ed. in chief [Homewood, Ill.: Dow Jones–Irwin, 1975], 912. Reprinted by permission.)

So much for the historical method. The crystal ball approach hasn't won universal acclaim either. Repeated studies have consistently arrived at the same verdict: Although there is a demonstrated relationship between corporate performance and stock prices, forecasting the former as a means of predicting the latter can be a futile as well as a tricky business. The reason for the futility is that the stock market reacts to changes in corporate performance and prospects so quickly that there usually isn't sufficient time for most investors—nor many analysts, for that matter—to take action on the basis of new information before that information is reflected in the current price.[19]

The studies also confirm the bad news noted above that the correlation between past earnings growth and future performance is quite low. There is, moreover, the possibility that a company's earnings have been, through the use of one "creative" accounting device or another, manipulated to such an extent that they cannot be regarded as "normalized" according to Graham and Dodd's standards.

The "bottom line"—if you'll excuse the expression—to all this is one that security analysts, especially the $250,000-a-year superstars, are not pleased to accept. And with good reason. The studies conclude that: (1) analysts' forecasts are no more accurate than simple extrapolation methods of projecting earnings, and (2) their forecasts do not help to secure higher-than-normal rates of return in the stock market.[20] By the law of averages, certain analysts are likely to have outstanding records in some years, and other analysts will do well in other years. But year in and year out, the superstars rarely if ever sustain their stellar performance.

But Wall Street analysts are not the only clay figures in this story. According to the studies cited above, corporate executives fare no better than outside forecasters in predicting their companies' future earnings. In many cases, their predictions prove to be less accurate because they are prone to emphasize their own firms' performance and prospects and to disregard the broader record of their competitors and of their industries in general.

Applying the Analytical Approach

What are we to make of all this so far as trading stock index futures is concerned? The question is whether an analysis of individual companies and their shares provides an insight into the probable behavior of the indexes and their related futures contracts. The answer is that if earnings and P/E ratios can be projected (even imperfectly) for individual stocks, it should be, and is, possible to derive and evaluate this information for the group of stocks that comprise a particular index. Even if the studies questioning the accuracy of corporate earnings are correct in their conclusions, there is still as much to be gained from an analytical standpoint by knowing where we are and where we've come from so far as aggregate index values are concerned as there is in the case of individual security prices.

As with the topics covered in previous chapters, the leap from individual stock to index analysis is most readily accomplished with respect to the thirty Dow Jones industrial stocks than with respect to the broader indexes. The procedure that was followed to evaluate the price and prospects of GE stock can be repeated twenty-nine times to appraise the other stocks contained in the DJIA.

Table 6.4 summarizes the results of such an exercise as of the end of 1981. The second and third columns of the table list the reported 1981 earnings and the P/E ratios derived therefrom for each of the thirty industrial issues. The last two columns are a similar listing on the basis of 1982 earnings estimated by the Value Line *Survey* at the close of 1981. In both cases the earnings per share for each stock are added and their total is divided into the industrial average itself to obtain current and projected P/E ratios for the thirty stocks as a unit as of June 30, 1982. On that date, according to table 6.4, the DJIA stocks had a combined price/earnings ratio on the basis of about-to-be reported 1981

Table 6.4   1981 and Estimated 1982 DJIA Earnings per Share and P/E Ratios

	6/30/82 Closing Price	1981 Earnings per Share	P/E on 1981 Earnings	1982 Estimated Earnings per Share	P/E on Estimated 1982 Earnings
Alcoa	22¾	$ 3.97	5.7	$ 2.00	11.4
Allied Corp.	30¼	9.17	3.3	6.50	4.6
American Brands	41¾	6.68	6.3	7.15	5.8
American Can	29	3.77	7.7	3.00	9.7
American Express	40¼	5.58	7.2	6.00	6.7
AT&T	51	8.55	5.9	9.10	5.6
Bethlehem Steel	15¾	4.83	3.3	d5.50	—
Du Pont	33	5.81	5.7	4.25	7.8
Eastman Kodak	73¾	7.66	9.6	7.75	9.5
Exxon	27¾	6.44	4.3	4.00	6.9
General Electric	63⅝	7.26	8.8	8.00	7.9
General Foods	37¾	4.47	8.4	6.00	6.3
General Motors	44⅝	1.07	41.7	3.75	11.9
Goodyear	24½	3.36	7.3	3.50	7.0
IBM	60⅝	5.63	10.8	7.00	8.7
Inco	8½	d0.10	—	d2.40	—
International Harvester	4¼	d20.44	—	d30.00	—
International Paper	36⅞	10.08	3.7	3.50	10.5
Merck	67½	5.36	12.6	5.90	11.4
Minnesota Mining and Manufacturing	53¼	5.74	9.3	6.00	8.9
Owens Illinois	23¼	5.15	4.5	3.50	6.6
Procter & Gamble	83	9.39	8.8	10.50	7.9
Sears, Roebuck	19⅜	2.00	9.4	2.25	8.6
Standard Oil (Calif.)	28¾	6.96	4.1	2.75	10.5
Texaco	29¼	8.75	3.3	4.50	6.5
Union Carbide	42⅜	9.56	4.4	6.75	6.3
United Technologies	39¼	7.05	5.6	6.75	5.8
U.S. Steel	18½	12.07	1.5	—	—
Westinghouse	25⅞	5.10	5.1	5.00	5.2
Woolworth	19	2.64	7.2	1.50	12.7
TOTAL	1095.34	153.62	5.2	99.00	8.1

DJIA Divisor 1.359   =   805.98
d = Deficit

earnings of 5.2 and a ratio of 8.1 on the basis of estimated 1982 earnings. Similar calculations can be performed to obtain five- and ten-year average price/earnings ratios to normalize earnings, as Graham and Dodd would put it, on the Dow stocks over an extended period.

Even with only thirty stocks to contend with, this calculation becomes cumbersome if it is repeated often enough. Fortunately, Dow Jones & Company has undertaken that task. Dow Jones performs the necessary computations quarterly and adds the results of the four most recent quarters to obtain the latest twelve-month DJIA unit earnings figure. The current P/E ratio for the unit is then calculated by dividing the industrial average by the most recent twelve-month earnings figure.

Table 6.5 lists the earnings per share, price/earnings ratios, and dividends by quarter for the thirty Dow Jones industrials taken as a unit from 1977 through 1981. The DJIA unit's latest twelve-month earnings per share over that five-year period ranged from a low of $89.23 on March 31, 1978, to a high of $128.99 as of June 29, 1979. Strangely enough, the unit's combined P/E ratio was 8.5 on the former date (DJIA: 757.36) and 6.5 as of the latter one (DJIA: 841.98), suggesting that—on those two dates, at least—the stock market did not respond more favorably to higher earnings as far as comparative P/E ratios were concerned.

Looking further into the past than the five-year period covered by table 6.5, the combined P/E ratio on the DJIA unit since 1968 ranged between 6.1 on the low side (September 30, 1974, DJIA: 607.87) and 17.3 at the upper extremity (March 31, 1971, DJIA: 904.37). When the industrial average reached its previous historical high of 1,020.02 on November 15, 1972, the combined P/E ratio stood at 15.2.

While such measurements are too broad to be of much direct help in trading stock index futures contracts on a day-to-day basis, it is nevertheless a useful point of departure to know when the stock market is relatively high or low in terms of corporate earnings and price/earnings multiples. A scalper or day trader in Kansas City (or anywhere else, for that matter) isn't immediately concerned with whether the Value Line Composite Average stands at ten or fifteen times its constituent stocks' current or estimated earnings. A trader who takes a longer-range view would, however, consider such information to be important, especially when it is considered in conjunction with other data that have a bearing on the current and prospective trend in stock prices.

Professors Graham and Dodd, were they on hand to speak for themselves, would probably be the first to maintain that their tenets of value do not guide the short-term behavior of stock and index futures prices. But as battlefield commanders do not make tactical decisions in a vacuum, the nearer-term technical and other trading decisions must be made against the backdrop of the overall investment environment. And within that context, the concept of

Table 6.5 DJIA Earnings, Dividends, and P/E Ratios, 1977–81

Dec. 31	Year-End DJIA	Latest 12-Month Earnings	P/E Ratio (Col. 1 ÷ Col. 2)	Dividends
1977	831.17	$ 89.10	9.3	$52.96
1978	805.01	112.79	7.1	57.36
1979	838.74	124.46	6.7	55.48
1980	963.99	121.86	7.9	57.60
1981	875.00	153.62	5.7	54.92

SOURCE: *Dow Jones Investor's Handbook,* (Homewood, Ill.: Dow Jones–Irwin, 1982). Reprinted with permission.

intrinsic value does indeed have a bearing. When the stock market and, in conjunction with it, index futures are priced at a historically high level in relation to corporate earnings, the risk of establishing a long futures position may be acute. When stocks are statistically cheap in relation to earnings, index futures traders should have very compelling reasons to undertake short positions in the face of the fact that prices will at some point appreciate from their depressed level.

Table 6.6 suggests a format for combining the individual company and unit analyses we have presented thus far. It compares the high and low prices and associated P/E ratios for General Electric and the Dow Jones Industrials at market peaks and valleys during the years from 1967 to 1982. As our abbreviated analysis verified, GE is a well-managed company, and its stock constitutes an excellent investment. But buying GE stock at any of its cyclical high price/earnings ratios, such as June 1976, July 1978, or April 1981, would not have proved especially rewarding in terms of capital appreciation during that five-year period. Investors who bought GE at one of those high points would subsequently have spent most of their time telling themselves what a fine company it is while awaiting a recovery back to the original purchase price. How much more satisfying—psychologically as well as financially—it would have been to be able to praise the company while at the same time enjoying the capital appreciation from one of the stock's recurring lows. That, in a nutshell, is what Graham and Dodd are all about.

But an investor can at least afford to sit and wait. A futures trader cannot. In the first place, a futures contract may expire before the hoped-for recovery takes place. And in the second place, even if it does not, the trader may be "eaten alive" by maintenance margin calls. If fundamental analysis—a consideration of present and projected earnings and price/earnings ratios—can

Table 6.6 Comparison of DJIA and General Electric Average Price/Earnings Multiples

Year	General Electric			DJIA		
	Price[a]	Average Earnings per Share for Preceding[a] Five Years	Ratio of Price to Average Earnings (Multiplier)	Price	Average Earnings per Unit for Preceding Five Years	Ratio of Price to Average Earnings (Multiplier)
1967	High 58	$3.75	15.5	High 943.08	$ 50.57	18.6
1970	Low 30			Low 631.16		
1973	High 75	3.30	22.7	High 1,051.70	63.28	16.6
1974	Low 30			Low 577.60		
1976	High 61½	3.18	19.3	High 1,014.79	84.94	11.9
1978	Low 43½			Low 742.12		
1982	High 100	6.70	14.9	High 1,070.55	122.33	8.7

SOURCES: General Electric Company, annual report, 1981, 52–53. *Dow Jones Investor's Handbook.* (Homewood, Ill.: Dow Jones—Irwin, 1982), 18–20.

aBefore two-for-one split, 1982, 100% Stock Dividend, 1983.

assist the trader in initiating and removing short and long positions in a timely manner (and it probably can) he or she would be advised to adhere to the Graham and Dodd teachings, at least in part.

Instructive though a study of the combined earnings and P/E ratios of the Dow Jones industrials unit might be at particular stages of a stock market cycle, the study must ultimately turn to a consideration of at least one of the broader indexes for which futures contracts are available.

Importance of Dividends

Dividends have in the foregoing discussion been relegated to a role secondary to corporate earnings. The de-emphasis of dividend income is especially noticeable during the latter stages of a bull market, when growth is the byword for nearly all investors. During such appreciation-minded periods, stockholders seem almost to begrudge companies' paying them liberal dividends for fear they will detract from their stocks' growth potential. Their preference appears to be to forego some dividends and have management apply the money instead to research and development of exciting new products or toward the acquisition of other companies.

But when the mood turns bearish, and the bright growth prospects appear to evaporate, dividends come back into vogue. A record of uninterrupted and—even better—steadily rising dividend payments again becomes a prime appeal of the stocks the brokerage firms are recommending to their disenchanted customers. Now, Graham and Dodd's emphasis on dividends no longer appears so archaic to the hotshot analysts and their followers. It no longer strikes them as hopelessly stodgy to accord to dividends a weight equal to and possibly greater than profits in the determination of intrinsic value. Suddenly, those glittering earnings forecasts appear to have lost their sparkle.

A projection of future dividend payments may be derived from an earnings forecast. As in the case of earnings, the record of past payouts is by no means an infallible indicator of future payments. But it is nevertheless a measure of the capacity to pay dividends. The compound total rate of return, including dividend income and capital gains, of the 400 stocks in the S&P Industrial (not the 500 Composite) Index has averaged about 9 percent over the past fifty or so years. During the same half-century, the average yield on U.S. government and highest-quality corporate bonds has been about 5 percent to 6 percent during low-inflation periods and about 8 percent to 9 percent during periods of relatively high inflation. Until the advent of double-digit long-term interest rates in the early 1980s, the generally held expectation was that common stock should provide a higher total return than bonds do because the ownership of stock entails a greater degree of risk. The level of risk associated with the volatile bond yields of 1980–82 cast doubt upon that piece of conventional wisdom, at least so far as the experience of those few years was concerned.

Analysts assume that the future dividends of a particular company will continue to grow at some predetermined rate and derive from that assumed rate of growth the "present value" of future dividend payments. They then proceed to calculate the current value of a stock by discounting its estimated future dividends by the prevailing interest rate. The formula for deriving the present value is:

$$\text{Present value} = \frac{\text{current dividend rate}}{\text{discount rate} - \text{growth rate}}$$

If the discount rate during low-inflation periods is 8 percent, and the dividend growth rate is assumed to be 5 percent, the so-called present value of current yield would be 3 percent. If, during high-inflation periods, the discount and growth rates were 11 percent and 7 percent, respectively, present value would be the difference between them, or 4 percent. Therefore, by dividing the current dividend rate on the four-hundred-stock S&P Industrial Index by 3 percent, analysts can estimate the present value of that index over low-inflation periods. A division by 4 percent provides the comparable high-inflation value.

Much like the practice of averaging several years' earnings to smooth out cyclical extremes, a number of consecutive annual dividend payments are employed to compute the estimated value of the stock index. The emphasis is in this regard the trend of dividend growth rather than the precise dollar amounts that are paid out in a given year or years.

"Intrinsic Values" of Indexes

Figure 6.4 traces an estimated value for the S&P industrial stock index against the actual movement of that index from 1959 to 1976. A so-called band of value is described by tracing an estimated upper value limit as determined by the 3 percent low-inflation figure and a lower limit set by the 4 percent high-inflation scenario. At current market prices within this estimated value band, stocks are adjudged to be fairly priced in relation to their current and anticipated dividends. When, according to figure 6.4, the index stands above the upper limit of the value band, as it did in 1972 and early 1973, it is a warning signal that investors as well as futures traders would do well to heed. The index's standing well below the estimated value band, as it did in late 1974, was by the same token an indication that stock prices were inordinately low in relation to their dividend-derived values.[21]

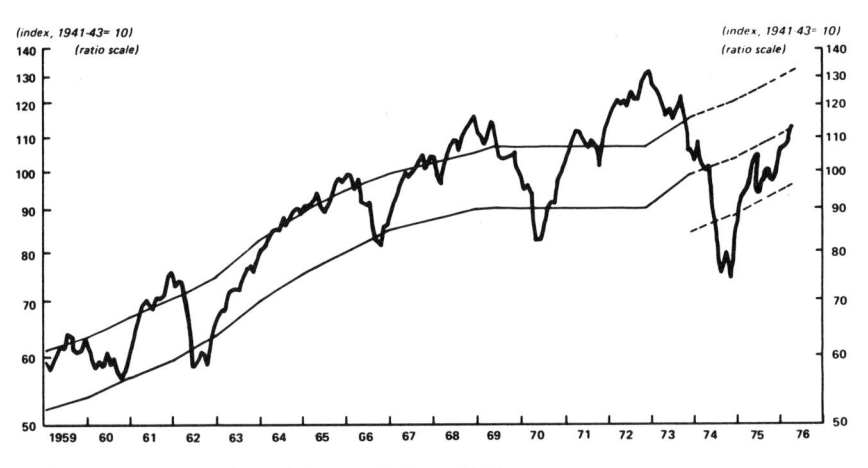

Figure 6.4   S&P Industrials Versus Estimated Value

Returning to the analysis of corporate earnings, price/earnings ratios for each of the constituent stocks in the S&P 500 index can, with the aid of a computer, be calculated as readily as we earlier calculated by hand the individual and composite P/E ratios for the thirty Dow Jones industrial stocks. From the early 1950s to about 1961, the composite P/E ratio on the S&P 500 stocks rose with few interruptions from about 10 to 20. During the 1960s and 1970s, the composite P/E ratio mainly fluctuated between 15 and 20, establishing a central value of about 17.5. The latter figure, incidentally, was not far removed from the average composite P/E of the DJIA during those years. During the 1973–74 bear market, the combined P/E ratios on both indexes fell back to their levels of the early 1950s.

Table 6.7 traces the annual range of composite P/E ratios for the S&P 500 index from 1964 to 1981, clearly showing the general decline in earnings multiples since 1973. Figure 6.5 displays the same information graphically for the years 1950–75. During the period from 1964 to 1973, a strategy of selling stocks—and index futures contracts, had they then existed—when the composite S&P 500 P/E ratio exceeded 18 and of establishing long positions when the ratio approached 12 would have been largely profitable. But in the aftermath of the 1973–74 bear market, the stock market's evaluation of corporate earnings, as reflected in the composite P/E ratios during those later years, changed drastically. Then, a ratio of 12 became the ceiling, a time to consider selling, and a ratio of 6 became the evident floor.[22]

Table 6.7 High and Low Price/Earnings Ratios, Standard & Poor's 500, 1964–81

	Price/Earnings Ratio	
Year	High	Low
1964	18.9	16.6
1965	17.9	15.7
1966	16.9	13.2
1967	18.3	15.1
1968	18.8	15.2
1969	18.4	15.4
1970	18.2	13.5
1971	18.4	15.8
1972	18.6	15.8
1973	14.7	11.3
1974	11.2	7.0
1975	12.0	8.8
1976	10.9	9.2
1977	9.8	8.3
1978	8.7	7.1
1979	7.5	6.5
1980	9.5	6.6
1981	8.9	7.3

SOURCE: Standard & Poor's *Stock Market Encyclopedia* (New York, 1982), 97.

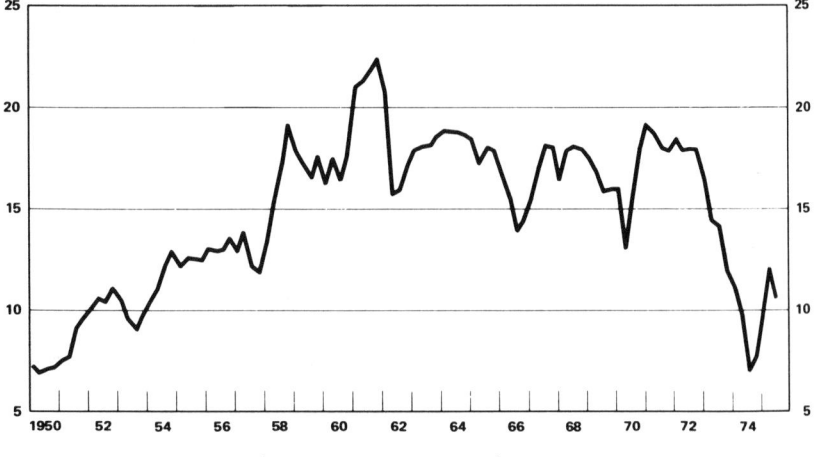

Figure 6.5 P/E Ratios of S&P 500 Composite Index, 1950–75

Analysis With Skepticism

As Graham and Dodd observed a half-century ago, alleged "new eras" in the stock market come and go with regularity, each new era bearing a striking resemblance to those that preceded it. The notion that "value will out" seems as valid now as it was then, whatever the precise method of establishing that value might be.

The evidence of the post-1973–74 years appears to confirm the continued soundness of Graham and Dodd's contention that dividends are as important as corporate earnings in determining a stock's value, if not more so. The price-earnings-dividend relationships we have summarized in the preceding pages suggest that an increase in dividend yield brings about a more than commensurate decline in a stock's price/earnings ratio if the dividend-to-earnings payout ratio is diminishing at the same time.

Taken in its entirety, the 1947–81 experience repeatedly reaffirms that a trader or analyst would be unwise to adopt without qualification and a healthy dose of skepticism past performance as his or her blueprint for the future. In the words of Graham and Dodd, if current circumstances so warrant, the analyst "must not hesitate to reject the past as his guide, and to construct some more reliable basis for his estimate of value."[23]

Even so, it is also true that the future begins where the past and present leave off. While they are struggling to find that new basis for value, investors and stock index traders should, as was noted earlier, have compelling grounds—other than the greater fool theory—for buying stocks or index contracts when their price/earnings ratios are at or close to the high side of their recent range or selling when they're near the low side. In addressing the question of what is cheap and what is dear with a measure of logic and objectivity, the application of fundamental analysis to the consideration of stock index futures values can be of significant help in correctly resolving the riddle of whether to buy or to sell.

CHAPTER 7

The Role and Influence of Government

More than 150 years before Graham and Dodd's *Security Analysis* saw the light of day—in fact, about the time the New York Stock Exchange found its origins in the Buttonwood Agreement among brokers—Adam Smith wrote *The Wealth of Nations*.[1] This early treatise on political economy argued for a government policy of *laissez-faire*, literally translated "let it be," that would keep the state out of a country's economic life.

During the first one and one-half centuries of the American nation, the political philosophy of a noninterventionist government went hand in hand with its pioneer ethic, underscoring the emphasis on personal initiative and self-sufficiency. This was especially true on Wall Street, even after the pioneers had long since headed west, and at the fledgling futures exchanges in Chicago and elsewhere after the members had moved their street-corner markets indoors. The members ran their exchanges like private clubs, and government meddling was not welcomed, either in their own affairs or in the economy at large.

But when these rugged nineteenth-century individualists wanted something from the government—lucrative land concessions and railroad rights-of-way, for example—laissez-faire took on a different interpretation. Then it meant, help us when we want it, but keep your nose out of our business the rest of the time.

Some presidential administrations—mostly Republican ones, as it turned out—were glad to oblige. The laconic Calvin Coolidge said it all when he declared, "The business of America is business." But the notion of keep your hands off and your nose out unless we want you ended abruptly with the stock market crash of October 1929 and the ten years of worldwide depression and six years of worldwide war that followed. Businesspeople—stockbrokers, in particular, it should be noted—were transformed from heroes to villains almost overnight. And Washington after the 1932 presidential election was no longer content to take a back seat to private business in managing the country's economic life. The newly elected President Franklin D. Roosevelt promised the American people a New Deal, and the relationship between government and business in the United States would never again be what it was before the 1929 crash.

Following the conclusion of World War II and the conversion to a peacetime economy that was in part interrupted and delayed by the Korean War, Dwight D. Eisenhower was elected president in 1952 on the strength of his wartime popularity and his pledge to "roll back the New Deal." That turned out to be a better campaign cry than it was a program for political action, and President Eisenhower talked less about rolling back as his administration progressed and more about sticking to "the middle of the road"—that is, preserving the substance if not the rhetoric of the New Deal's social and economic programs.

The same clarion call to restore to Americans the virtues of enterprise, self-reliance, and hard work by cutting back Big Government was sounded by Ronald Reagan during his 1976 and 1980 presidential campaigns. He succeeded in the latter effort and promptly set out to revive his image of an America that once was, through the enactment of a laissez-faire-minded program of "Reaganomics": reduce taxes, cut federal expenditures, eliminate cumbersome restrictions and regulations, and promote stable economic growth. Allow him to do those things, President Reagan assured the American people, and the United States would once again become the envy and the glory of the world.[2]

The planks in the platform of Reaganomics sounded like music to most businesspeople's ears. It was a tune that they themselves had been singing since the New Deal dislodged them from their perch in the 1930s. But the one area that they recognized as being an exception was the management of the nation's money. Bankers are businesspeople also, and money is their product. Other businesspeople, who rely on the bankers for funds with which to run their own enterprises, do not want that group to be the sole arbiters of how much money is available, to whom, and when. In spite of their distaste for government intervention, they saw the wisdom of some official body's serving as a disinterested regulator of the country's money and credit. Just as Clemenceau once observed that war is too important to be left to the generals, it was thought that money is too important to be left entirely in the hands of the bankers.[3]

The Supply of Money

Power to "regulate the coinage and the value thereof" is vested in Congress by the Constitution.[4] During much of the nineteenth century, monetary questions, government policy, and partisan politics were inextricably intertwined in debates over such issues as Andrew Jackson's suspending the federal charter of the Bank of the United States, the unregulated issuance of paper money by private banks, and the immense supply of "greenbacks" printed by the U.S. Treasury during and following the Civil War. Economic crises were usually in the first instance banking crises, and they often had something to do with the existence of either an excess or a shortage of whatever was at the time regarded as money.

Bimetallism, the acceptance of silver as well as gold as the backing for paper money, was a prominent and heated political issue during the closing years of the century, with the agrarian interests in the West pressing for the unlimited coinage of silver as a source of "easy" money. Their spokesman, many-times presidential aspirant William Jennings Bryan, declaimed that if elected, he would never allow the American people to be "crucified on a cross of gold."[5] Apparently unperturbed by this threatened fate, the people elected William McKinley instead, and the country remained on the gold standard.

Today, the mention of greenbacks—the term is still in use even though that type of paper currency is not—bimetallism and Bryan's cross-of-gold speech are but faint echoes of long-forgotten controversies. Yet the identical issues of the government's handling of money matters and the general availability of money in its various forms are still very much with us. It is also evident that today, as a century ago, these matters have an important bearing on overall economic conditions and, hence, on the behavior of stock prices.

Keynes and Keynesians

The growing involvement of government in business, monetary, and economic affairs has inevitably given rise to a debate not only over what the proper extent of this involvement should be but also over the precise forms it should take. At the depths of the 1930s depression, John Maynard Keynes—an English economist, Cambridge University don, and sometime civil servant and government adviser—wrote his epochal *General Theory of Employment, Interest, and Money*.[6] Although this work did not attract the popular attention of his earlier book, *The Economic Consequences of the Peace*, probably it's harder to read, it nonetheless had profound effects on economic and political thought and on the making of government policy that have lasted to the present day.

In *General Theory*, Keynes argued that the way out of the depression that was then gripping England and Europe as well as the United States was for the governments of the various countries to stimulate business activity by engaging in deficit spending—that is, by paying out more for public works, relief, and other socially useful purposes than they took in by way of taxes. That has since become a way of life—or a disease, as critics of deficit spending charge. But it was a new concept when Keynes proposed the idea. His "pump-priming" theory was adopted in the United States and elsewhere, and whether it was deficit spending or the onset of World War II that ended the depression, it did end. Since then, "Keynesianism" has become a major tenet of policy-making, if not an article of faith, for an entire generation of economists and government officials.

Keynesians are concerned with fiscal policy, seeing in the methods and levels of taxation, government spending, and budget management the most effective means of keeping the overall economy on an even keel. During a recession, the fastest way to "get the economy moving again," as politicians on the campaign trail are fond of expressing it, is for a government to undertake the same sort of deficit spending Keynes first proposed in the 1930s. But when the economy becomes "overheated"—the demand for goods and services outruns the available supply, with a resulting high rate of inflation— the cure is to incur a budget surplus to suppress demand.

Critics of the theory—or, more precisely, critics of the modern application of it—charge that Keynesians are always ready to implement the stimulation part, or as they baldly state, "to spend, spend, spend." But, the critics continue, when the time comes to apply the fiscal brakes and incur a surplus by raising taxes or reducing expenditures, the big spenders only know how to keep right on spending. Thus, instead of their avowed purpose of keeping the economy on an even keel, the criticism concludes, Keynesians make the economy dependent on a continuing regimen of government stimulation merely to keep it operating at a normal level.

The Monetarist Viewpoint

Adherents of the monetarist school contend that the most effective means of preventing a recession or overheating, or of eliminating either phenomenon if it does occur, is to manage a country's money supply. They allege that the money supply and its rate of turnover, which they call money velocity, are the key variables that affect a country's gross national product, corporate profits, interest rate structure, and—working through those factors—the level and direction of stock prices. They therefore conclude that it is the quantity of money that determines a country's levels of spending and taxation instead of, as the Keynesians maintain, the other way around.

To follow the monetarists' line of reasoning, it is first necessary to reach agreement on precisely what constitutes the quantity of money that circulates in a country. That is by no means a cut-and-dried matter. We live today in a checkbook and, increasingly, a credit-card economy. Bankers predict that the time is close at hand when computerized banking will make checks and possibly plastic cards largely obsolete. Cash money, the currency we carry around in pockets or purses, has become precisely that—pocket money. In today's commercial world, then, the money supply consists of this pocket money, coins and currency in public circulation, and—far more important in terms of the amount—the demand or checking deposits in commercial banks against which checks are drawn and credit-card charges are paid. In the case of credit-card payments, a check must still be written to make the necessary transfer of funds to the credit-card company.

But having included demand or checking accounts in our definition of money, how are we to treat funds held in other types of bank accounts—in time deposits or certificates, say, or even in money market funds? Monetarists address the problem of definition by classifying the money supply in at least three categories. Hence, M_1, the money supply narrowly defined, consists of the above-mentioned currency and coins in circulation, plus total checking accounts maintained in commercial banks. The broader definition of M_2 adds to that total time deposits in commercial banks. And M_3 consists of all of these amounts plus deposits in mutual savings banks and savings shares in savings and loan associations. In most instances a mention of the money supply in financial publications without further elaboration is a reference to M_1.[7]

Some monetarists contend that M_1 is the key variable in the economic scheme of things. Others favor M_2 or M_3. Whatever the measure, these monetarists argue that changes in the money supply produce proportionate changes in GNP, corporate earnings, and stock prices. Their rationale, most simply put, is that if people have more money to spend, they will go ahead and spend most of it. That increased level of spending on a fixed supply of goods, services, and financial assets, including stocks and bonds, serves to bid up the prices of those assets.

Conversely, as the money supply contracts, people have less to spend and in many cases refrain from spending what they do have. Company profits fall, and stock prices decline accordingly, along with the general level of employment, commodity prices, and interest rates.

The Role of the Fed

The central bank in most countries has the power to control, or at least to influence with an assortment of policy tools, the money supply in that country. The Federal Reserve System is the central bank of the United States, comparable to the Bank of England or to the Deutsche Bundesbank in Germany. When the expression *monetary authorities* is used, it is normally a reference to senior officials of the central bank.

The Federal Reserve System was established in 1914 during the Democratic administration of Woodrow Wilson. Until that relatively late date, Congress had resisted the creation of a central bank due to its reluctance to grant any one institution so much economic power. As a compromise, it passed legislation for a system of twelve district reserve banks to be overseen by a Board of Governors situated in Washington. But over the years, despite the system's geographic dispersal, the board has drawn to itself the principal power to formulate monetary policy, delegating to the district banks various supervisory and administrative duties and responsibility for executing certain of the policies established by the board of governors. By virtue of its location at the heart of the New York money market, the Federal Reserve Bank of New York has come to assume a special position in the execution of monetary policy and is on that account regarded as the first among equals.[8]

The primary responsibility of the Federal Reserve System in its entirety is to regulate the supply and flow of money within the United States and to buttress the value of the dollar abroad. Its policy goals, as stated in the Full Employment Act of 1946, are: (1) to achieve and maintain a high level of employment in the United States, (2) to promote a sustainable rate of economic growth, (3) to preserve a stable price level, and (4) to encourage a sound international balance of payments.

How the Fed Is Organized

The organizational structure of the system takes the form of a pyramid (see figure 7.1). At the base are approximately five thousand nationally chartered commercial banks that are required by law to be members and a lesser number of state-chartered banks that have joined the system of their own volition. Although less than half of the commercial banks in the United States are currently members of the Federal Reserve System, member banks' combined assets and deposits comprise over 70 percent of the total for all of the commercial banks in the country.

Commercial banks occupy a special position within the country's financial system because they are the only private institutions that have the capacity to "create" money. As a consequence of this special capability, they play a key role in the implementation of monetary policy.

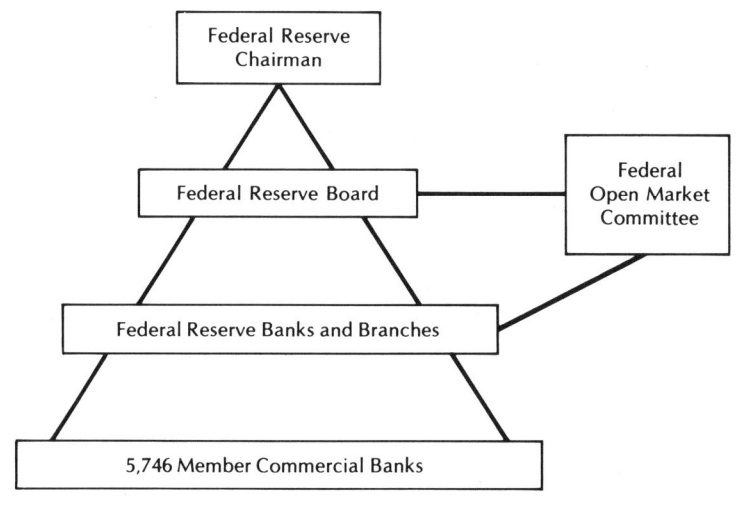

Figure 7.1   Diagram of Federal Reserve Pyramid

The second level of the organizational pyramid is that of the district Reserve Banks and their branches. Although each resembles a commercial bank in the sense that it has bank officers and a board of directors and earns substantial amounts on its loans and investments, the Reserve Banks are not intended to be profit-making institutions. Their primary responsibilities are to supervise and to regulate the member commercial banks in their districts. Any profits remaining after paying operating expenses, including staff salaries, and dividends on their stock owned by member commercial banks is remitted to the U.S. Treasury Department for disposition as "interest on Federal Reserve notes," the principal form of currency currently in circulation.

At the apex of the Federal Reserve System pyramid is the Board of Governors in Washington. This board is comprised of seven members appointed by the president of the United States with the advice and consent of the U.S. Senate. Board members are appointed to fourteen-year terms and are ineligible for reappointment after they have served one full term. The chairman and vice-chairman of the Board of Governors are named by the president from among the board members for four-year terms. They may be renamed by the president to serve repeated terms in those positions.

Like the district Federal Reserve Banks, the Board of Governors has certain administrative and supervisory duties, but its primary responsibility is the formulation, and in certain instances the implementation, of monetary policy. The board has at its command a variety of powers and policy tools by which it can regulate the availability of bank credit. Through that mechanism and by other means, it is able to bring about an expansion or contraction of the money supply.

An associated body that shares policy-making responsibility with the board, and that consists in part of the same members, is the Federal Open Market Committee, commonly referred to by its acronym, FOMC. In addition to the seven Federal Reserve Board governors, the FOMC is made up of the president of the Federal Reserve Bank of New York and the presidents of four other district Reserve Banks who serve on the committee in rotation. The FOMC meets in Washington at least monthly but is in telephone communication more frequently. Its function is to determine the extent and timing of security purchases and sales that reinforce the board's monetary policy and to issue the appropriate directives to the trading desk of the New York Federal Reserve Bank. The New York bank's role as executor of the committee's open market directives is the reason the president of that district bank is a permanent member of the FOMC.

Creating Money, and Vice Versa

Commercial banks have the ability to create money at the stroke of a pen or, to use a more modern metaphor, at the tap of a computer key. A bank simply enters a credit to a depositor's or borrower's checking account and, presto, the aggregate money supply is immediately increased by that amount. The only limitation on this money-creation process, and consequently on the potential volume of business and consumer spending, is the level of reserves that banks are required to maintain against existing and new demand deposits.

During the early years of the Federal Reserve System, member banks' reserves were simply regarded as a safeguard to prevent banks from overextending themselves. It gradually became apparent, however, that the power to set required reserve levels could become an important policy tool to regulate not only a bank's position but also the aggregate money supply. If a bank is required to keep a 10 percent reserve against its demand deposits or checking accounts, $1 million in reserves will support $10 million in demand deposits. But if the reserve requirement is increased to 20 percent, that same $1-million reserve will only support $5 million in deposits. If, in this simple example, the percentage reserve requirement were doubled to 20 percent, the bank would have to obtain an additional $1-million reserve to maintain its deposits at the $10-million level. Failing that, it would have to reduce its deposits in the amount of $5 million by calling in loans (or declining to make new ones) or by selling off some of its investments. If the bank took the latter course, the immediate result would be a reduction in the money supply of $5 million.

It's a fact of economic life that a rising level of business activity means increasing dollar expenditures. Consumers and businesses are, after all, buying more goods and services at higher prices. Increasing expenditures require in turn a larger money supply or else an accelerating rate at which a constant supply is passed from hand to hand or, as we determined at the outset of this discussion, from checking account to checking account. The latter instance is what economists refer to as an increase in the velocity of money.

If the quantity of money or its turnover velocity increases at a faster rate than the actual goods and services that are being bought and sold, the eventual result is inflation. If a shortage of money prevents demand from increasing at the same pace as real output, some sort of recession may be in store unless corrective steps are taken.

There are several policy tools at the disposal of the Board of Governors, the FOMC, and the district Federal Reserve Banks. As was noted above, the board has the authority to set *reserve requirements*. Changes in the percentage of permissible reserves, maintained in the form of either vault cash or deposits with its district Reserve Bank, compel a bank to adjust its level of reserves to maintain a given volume of deposits or else effect a change in deposit size to come into line with the new requirements. There is nothing to require a bank to utilize surplus reserves, but it must take prompt action to make up a shortfall.

Member banks that experience a deficiency in required reserves may borrow the necessary shortage from their district Federal Reserve Banks or from other commercial banks that have reserves to spare. The interest rate the district banks charge member banks that come to their "discount window" to borrow is called, appropriately enough, the *discount rate*. Changes in the discount rate are made by the individual district Reserve Banks, usually in line with the prevailing policy of the Board of Governors. Once the initial change is made by a particular district bank, the remaining eleven banks generally follow suit within a short period.

The third policy tool, and the one after which the Federal Open Market Committee is named, is the system's *open market purchases and sales* of government securities and other instruments in the New York money market. This market is comprised of a network of bank and nonbank dealers in U.S. Treasury bills and notes, commercial paper, bankers' acceptances, negotiable time certificates of deposit, and other short-term instruments. Other participants include nondealer banks, securities dealers, nonfinancial corporations, government bodies, and foreign entities that have a need to borrow or funds to lend for periods up to one year. For periods longer than one year, these institutions make use of the capital market.

The Federal Reserve System is the largest and most important participant in the New York money market, but for reasons that differ from those of the other participants. The FOMC directs the trading desk of the New York Federal

Reserve Bank to sell securities to dealers when the system's policy is to shrink the money supply by restraining or eliminating member banks' reserves. Conversely, the directive is to buy securities from dealers when the policy is to augment bank reserves and thereby exert a potentially expansive effect on the money supply. In addition to outright purchases and sales, the New York trading desk may execute repurchase agreements with dealers, obliging them to buy back within a matter of a few days the securities they sell to the Federal Reserve.

Besides the foregoing quantitative or general credit controls it has at its disposal, the Board of Governors has recourse to certain selective controls. The most important of these latter controls is the board's authority to set *margin requirements* on brokers' security loans to their customers and on such loans by banks to brokers and dealers. The board may also set *interest rate ceilings* on time and savings deposits held by member banks.

In pursuing a particular monetary policy, be it one of expansion or restraint, the Federal Reserve System endeavors to employ all of the foregoing tools in a concerted program of action. Any specific policy move, its extent, and its timing should therefore be assessed in light of what the Board of Governors, the FOMC, and the district Reserve Banks have done in the recent past and what they are likely to do in the near future.

The monetary authorities also try to coordinate their domestic policy measures with the steps they deem necessary in the international sphere and with the stated goals and actions put forward in the implementation of the government's fiscal policy.

Putting the Tools to Use

That covers the institutional setting and the available tools of monetary policy. The question is, how have the policies and tools worked in practice, and—more to our immediate purpose—what have been their effects on stock prices? A brief survey of the post–World War II record may offer some clues:[9]

- *1948–49.* The U.S. economy began to contract during the final months of 1948. The Federal Reserve moved to ease credit conditions in March 1949 by reducing member bank reserve requirements and by lowering margins on securities purchases from 75 percent to 50 percent. The economy began to recover in October 1949, seven months after the Federal Reserve moved to a policy of ease.

- *1953–54.* The Board of Governors again lowered margin requirements from 75 percent to 50 percent in February 1953, several months before the recession began. As late as April 1954, the discount rate was reduced from

2 percent to 1.5 percent, an incredibly low rate of interest by today's standards. It took until May 1954, over a year from the time the Federal Reserve took the first steps toward expansion, for the economy to reach bottom and turn upward.

- *1957–58.* Open market buying was undertaken in October 1957. Between November 1957 and April 1958, the discount rate was lowered in stages from 3.5 percent to 1.75 percent. Margin and reserve requirements also were reduced. The economy turned up in April 1958, six months after the initial easing moves.

- *1960–61.* The Federal Open Market Committee directed the purchase of securities in March 1960. The board lowered the discount rate from 4 percent to 3 percent the following June. Securities margins were reduced from 90 percent to 70 percent in July. Business conditions began to improve in February 1961, eleven months following the first moves toward easier conditions.

- *1969–70.* The recession began in December 1969, and the FOMC directed the New York trading desk to buy securities the following month. Stock margins and reserve requirements were reduced in stages, and in December 1970 the discount rate was cut from 6 percent to 5.5 percent. The recession ended in November 1970, ten months after the initial easing measures were undertaken.

- *1973–75.* This recession ran from November 1973 to September 1974 before the Board of Governors acted to reduce reserve requirements and the discount rate. Conditions began to improve in March 1975, six months following the first expansion moves.

- *1980.* The Federal Reserve stuck to a tight credit policy to contain inflation while the economy moved into a recession. By May 1980 the board acted to ease some of its consumer credit controls and reduced the discount rate to 10 percent from its high of 13 percent set earlier in the year. Because of the priority given to combating inflation, the first significant easing steps were taken a mere two months before the economy turned up in July.

- *1981–82.* The Board of Governors lowered the discount rate in line with other interest rates in November and December 1981, but the FOMC did not direct aggressive open market purchases of securities until May 1982. The economy appeared to have reached its bottom in July 1982, but the recovery that followed was somewhat insipid.

Figure 7.2 depicts the behavior of the S&P 500 Composite Index in relation to the first easing moves taken by the Federal Reserve in each of the foregoing

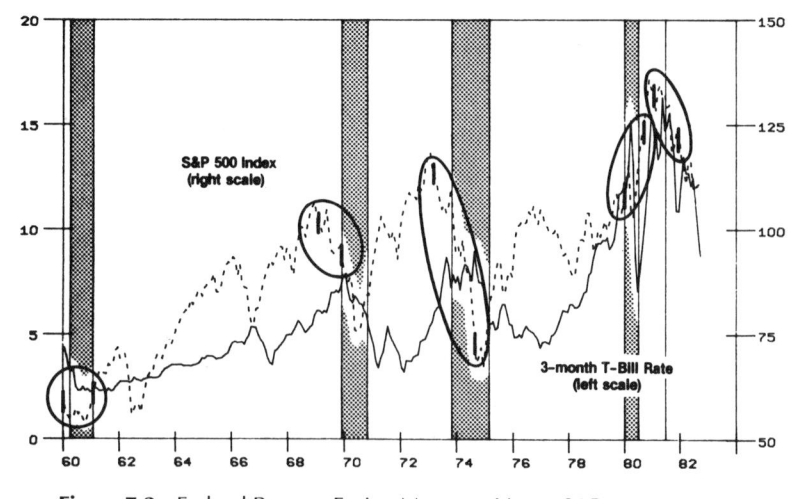

Figure 7.2 Federal Reserve Easing Measures Versus S&P 500, 1960–82

recessionary situations since 1960. The lead between the initial easing steps and a pronounced recovery in stock prices ranged between nine months in 1960 and in 1981–82 at the long extremity and four months in 1974–75 on the short side. The median lead time between monetary easing and stock price recovery was six months.

Money Supply and Stocks

We have already noted in chapter 5 that the S&P 500 index and M_1 are both among the leading economic indicators selected and monitored by the National Bureau of Economic Research.[10] Monetarists have given further study to the linkages between these two variables in an attempt to demonstrate that the money supply figures reported weekly by the Federal Reserve can provide an insight into the future movement of stock prices.[11] As evidence of a cause-and-effect relationship, they point to the fact that initial changes in monetary policy as outlined above precede turns in the business cycle by six to nine months, sufficiently longer than the average lead time in stock prices to provide a reliable signal of impending turning points in the S&P 500 and other major stock indexes.

One prominent researcher has observed in this regard that:

> All cyclically related stock price movements since at least 1918, as well as most intermediate movements have been closely associated with monetary change. . . . Similarly, changes in monetary growth are associated with the rate of change in corporate profits before taxes, with the money supply usually shortly in the lead.[12]

But another study was not as conclusive:

> Changes in the nominal money stock have little direct impact on the stock price, but a major indirect influence on stock prices through their effect on inflation and corporate earnings expectations.[13]

According to a typical monetarist scenario, stock prices climb during the early stages of an inflationary period because corporate profits are expected to rise at a faster pace than interest rates. But at a later stage in the business cycle, perhaps after the Federal Reserve has moved to a policy of restraint, interest rates outrun corporate earnings gains, and increasing inflationary expectations together with the likelihood of yet more diminished earnings growth serve to depress stock prices.

In summary, the so-called predictive version of monetary analysis argues that a tightening monetary policy—including an increased discount rate, higher securities margin and member bank reserve requirements, and open market selling—will bring about a decline in stock prices. Conversely, a policy of easing will stimulate higher stock prices.[14]

Not all monetarists accept this view wholeheartedly. Some of them are preoccupied with the efficient-market theory, which, as was noted in the previous chapter, holds that stock prices are continuously and immediately adjusting, not only to monetary data but to any and all information that affects them, from, say, a flare-up in the Middle East to the health of the president of the United States. Consequently, according to this view, the efficient market does not allow investors and traders sufficient time to study the most recent money-supply figures, form their conclusions, and take the appropriate market action before prices adjust to the latest developments.

Predicting—Or Guessing?

If the efficient-market view is a valid one, there is little to be gained from an investment or trading standpoint by deliberating over what steps the Federal Reserve took to regulate the money supply last month. That is old-hat information so far as the efficient market is concerned. The real trick is to divine what the Board of Governors and the FOMC are going to do next month or even tomorrow. Since the governors themselves often do not know what their policy will be one month in the future, that is a very neat trick indeed.[15]

Because this sort of anticipation is of necessity highly subjective—some traders and analysts are simply better guessers than others—there is according to the efficient-market theorists no systematic or predictable lag between the Federal Reserve's policy moves and money-supply data on the one hand and the behavior of stock prices on the other. Trading strategies that take their cues from such monetary considerations therefore, cannot produce above-average gains.

Table 7.1 Money Supply Growth Trading Signals and S&P 425 Index Performance, 1946–60

Buy Signal	S&P 425	Sell Signal	S&P 425
July 1946	17.42	Oct. 1947	15.19
Sept. 1948	15.53	April 1953	24.84
Feb. 1954	26.12	May 1956	49.64
Dec. 1956	49.79	April 1958	45.09
June 1958	47.62	Feb. 1960	59.60

SOURCE: Adapted from Michael S. Rozeff, "The Money Supply and the Stock Market—The Demise of a Leading Indicator," *Financial Analyst's Journal,* September–October 1975, 20.

Table 7.1 is a summary of such a monetary trading program conducted between 1946 and 1960. The results unfortunately confirm the efficient-market position that there is not a direct cause-and-effect relationship between monetary policy measures and subsequent stock price behavior. Accordingly, current money-supply data, are not a reliable indicator of future stock price movements.[16]

There may, however, be a middle ground between the predictive and efficient-market viewpoints. The alleged weaknesses of the predictive case are twofold: First, the average lag between changes in the rate of monetary growth and ensuing stock price trends is sufficiently varied from cycle to cycle as to make an average struck from past cycles inadequate information on which to base current trading decisions. Second, the predictive argument assumes a recognition of business cycle peaks and troughs at the time they occur. In fact, these turning points are only evident in retrospect, as much as several months after the event.[17]

But there is still insight to be derived from the discernible relationship between *current* changes in money growth and *current* trends in stock prices. If the stock market does in fact anticipate, among other things, future monetary growth, is there a point to studying current money-supply figures for hints of future changes in those numbers? And is that the same thing as trying to read the minds of the Federal Reserve Board governors?

And where do interest rates fit into this puzzle? What is their place in relation to monetary policy, money supply, and stock prices? The Federal Reserve Board raises the discount rate when it wants to tighten up on money. When that occurs, other types of interest rates are usually climbing as well. Therefore, we might postulate that rising interest rates portend falling stock prices and, conversely, that declining rates are usually a precursor to higher stock prices. The big question, as always, is: when?

Interest rates are generally thought of as the price of money. More precisely, they are the price of borrowed money—that is, credit. That price, like every other, is determined by supply and demand. Demand, as was noted earlier in this chapter, usually rises during periods of business expansion and declines during recessions. But supply and demand are not allowed free rein. In its role as monetary regulator, the Federal Reserve System is a significant, if not the paramount, force influencing the supply of—and, less so, the demand for—money and credit.

The supply of money and the level of commercial bank reserves determine the supply of available credit. Other factors remaining equal, the slower the rate of money-supply growth, the greater the upward pressure on interest rates. During only two of the twenty-one years between 1961 and 1982 did interest rates decline at the same time that M_1, adjusted for inflation, was contracting.[18]

Short- and long-term interest rates—the line dividing them is generally considered to be one year—are connected because borrowers and lenders can often choose the most advantageous rates and maturities to obtain or commit funds, at least temporarily. But the two sets of rates are affected by different factors.

Short-term interest rates are almost exclusively determined by prevailing supply/demand considerations. These would include the current level of credit demand by consumers and corporations and, as was just mentioned above, present Federal Reserve policy.

The current and anticipated future rates of inflation play very important roles in the determination of long-term interest rates, such as those that apply to bonds. The purchase of a long-term bond entails a commitment of capital for possibly up to twenty or thirty years. An investor therefore has good reason to be concerned about the purchasing power of the interest payments and the capital value of such bonds as they approach their maturity. If the outlook is for a high rate of inflation, prospective bond buyers will require a higher nominal interest rate to compensate them for the anticipated loss of purchasing power over the life of the bonds.[19]

The federal funds rate is an important short-term interest rate and money market indicator. As an alternative to borrowing at the prevailing discount rate from their district Federal Reserve Banks to make up deficiencies in their reserve positions, member banks may borrow from other banks that have surplus reserves.[20] As an open market rate determined by what banks are willing to pay to borrow reserves, the federal funds rate is far more volatile than the administered discount rate. But over time the federal funds rate rises in response to tightening policies that compel banks to borrow to make up deficient reserves. When the Federal Reserve Board adopts an expansive policy, most likely including a reduction in the discount rate, member banks are under less pressure to borrow, and the federal funds rate declines along with other money market rates.

Interplay of Money and the Economy

Stock prices, according to the monetarist view, are tied to the money supply and interest rates through the effect of the latter on corporate earnings. To reiterate what was covered in some detail in the preceding chapter, stock prices are pushed up by the anticipation of rising earnings, higher price/earnings ratios, or some combination of the two. A restrictive monetary policy and high interest rates choke corporate earnings, serve to suppress P/E ratios, and keep stock prices at a depressed level. An expansive policy helps to achieve the opposite effect.

The comparative performance of M_1 and the S&P 400 Industrial Index between 1969 and 1982 is charted in figure 7.3. The chart confirms the supposition that when the Federal Reserve pursues a policy of restraint, the resulting retardation of money growth helps to keep stock prices depressed.

The interaction of the money supply, interest rates, the rate of inflation, and economic growth, with the resultant effect on corporate earnings and stock prices, forces the Federal Reserve to walk a fine line in shaping and executing monetary policy and occasionally lands it in a pickle. Too much expansion means a larger money supply and higher prices—including higher interest rates once the initial easing effects have worn off. In fact, money expansion without a corresponding increase in real output is synonymous with inflation.

A policy that is too tight also keeps interest rates high but contracts the money supply so that corporate earnings stagnate and, if the restrictive pressure is applied long enough, people are put out of work.

Inflation or unemployment—that is not a very appealing choice. The Federal Reserve's dilemma becomes even more acute when monetary policy is working at cross-purposes with the taxation and spending policies pursued by other departments in the government. If the central bank is applying a restrictive policy with a tight fist to wring inflation out of the economy once and for all, and the Treasury and budget departments are running up large deficits, the populace and their elected representatives (especially those who belong to the party out of office) complain that they are getting the worst of both worlds and wonder in very vocal terms whether the administration can do anything right. The stock market mirrors the prevailing gloom and frustration by sinking to new lows.

That was the situation during the summer of 1982. The unemployment rate was 9.5 percent, the highest level it had reached in the United States since the 1930s. Housing starts and the utilization of plant capacity had fallen to alarmingly low levels, and corporate profit margins reached a postwar record

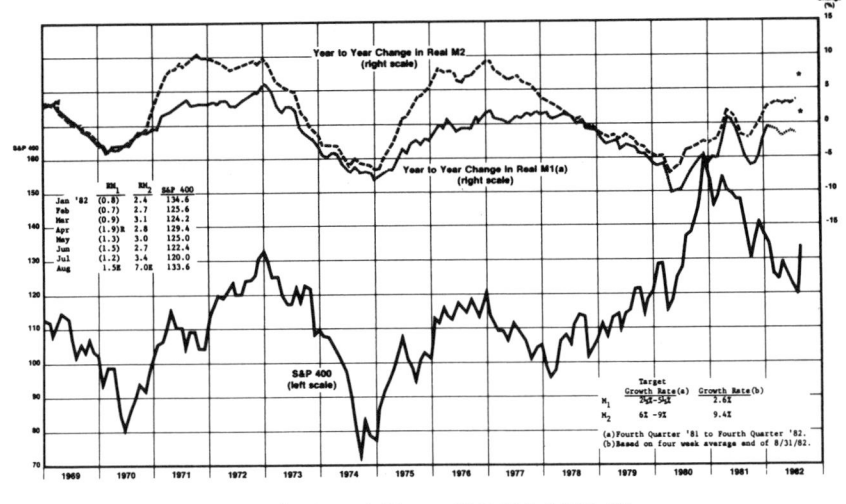

Figure 7.3 Money Supply Growth Versus S&P 400, 1969–82

low of 6 percent. The only good news, and the justification for the Federal Reserve's tightfisted policy, was that the rate of inflation had abated considerably, from an annual rate of 13 percent in 1980 to less than half that figure.

Combined earnings per share on the S&P 500 stocks were expected to drop an estimated 10 percent or more in 1982 to $13.75, from the 1981 earnings figure of $15.13. On an inflation-adjusted basis, the 1982 estimate indicated a 30 percent decline in corporate earnings from their 1979 level, while stock prices dropped 20 percent on an inflation-adjusted basis during the same period. The S&P 500 index had fallen from 132.50 to 102.00 during the preceding fifteen months. The other major stock indexes had sunk to comparably low levels.

During this unsettling period the administration was having a difficult time placating its critics. The program of Reaganomics that stressed the reduction of both federal taxes and expenditures was manifestly not delivering the promised gains in productivity and economic growth. What was worse, the program seemed in danger of being scuttled by the very people who had so confidently espoused it for so long.

After achieving what administration spokespersons had trumpeted as the largest tax cut in U.S. history, the architects of Reaganomics acceded to the Senate's demands to reinstate nearly $100 billion of the tax reduction a year later. When asked by reporters whether that did not constitute the biggest tax increase in history, the president chided them for misreporting, saying that the new plan was not a "tax increase" but a "tax reform."

Some relief arrived in the form of declining interest rates. Was Reaganomics working at last? The media sages, chastened but not subdued, still harbored doubts. Titillating gossip items such as the following about back-room dealings deep within the corridors of power appeared in national news magazines:

> Before the Federal Reserve Board reduced its discount rate, at least two top White House aides bluntly told Chairman Paul Volcker that President Reagan wanted to see faster expansion of the money supply to cut interest rates and boost economic recovery before Election Day.[21]

Some journalists were even more cynical, as one reported:

> Many suspicious Democrats in Congress openly predict that the drop in interest rates won't last. Their scenario: The Federal Reserve Board will permit borrowing costs to decline only until after the November 2 elections—to take Reagan and the Republicans off the hook.[22]

The congressional Democrats might well have been suspicious, inasmuch as that was precisely the scenario that unfolded in 1980 when a Democratic president was running for reelection. As one former Federal Reserve Board Chairman observed after his term was over, "You don't say no to the president."

Plunger Triumphant

Phil Plunger had a problem. During the palmy days of the last bull market, he decided it would be a good idea to diversify his investments. A friend recommended Florida condominiums, so after a cursory investigation—his cash flow was free and easy then—he bought one in Boca Raton for $120,000.

But now, the worm had turned. The stock market had been going down for over a year, some other side ventures had turned sour, and Plunger was strapped for cash. He called the condominium management agent to inquire about selling his place and received further bad news.

He related his troubles to Dan Decimal, his broker at Stable & Company.

"They told me I'd make 25 percent a year in appreciation, virtually guaranteed, over and above the rental income. That was more than three years ago. Now they tell me they doubt they can get $80,000 for my place. What's going on?"

"Conditions were different then," replied Decimal sympathetically. "You've seen what's happened in the stock market. The housing market has been just as badly affected, in Florida and elsewhere."

"What's causing this mess?" asked Plunger, bewilderment drawn all over his face.

"Interest rates."

"Interest rates?"

"What rate are you paying on your mortgage down in Boca Raton?" asked Decimal.

"Eight percent," replied Plunger.

"Would you be willing to pay 17 percent?" asked Decimal again.

"Certainly not!" said Plunger. "But isn't the government supposed to step in when interest rates get too high? Manufacture easy money or something like that?"

"Something like that," responded Decimal. "Normally it would. But its first priority, or at least the Federal Reserve's, is to stamp out inflation, and the only way it can do that is to limit the money supply and keep interest rates high. That's why you aren't getting any offers for your Boca Raton dream house."

"Money supply? What's that?" asked Plunger, starting to show his exasperation.

"Here, on page 28 of the *Journal*," Decimal pointed, "in the Federal Reserve Report under 'Monetary and Reserve Aggregates,' it says that M_1 grew from \$451.4 billion to \$453.4 billion. That's an increase of \$2 billion."

"I thought that M_1 was a type of Army carbine," Plunger riposted, adding hastily, "That's a joke, of course."

"I thought it might be," replied Decimal, showing no trace of amusement. "You don't survive for very long in the stock or futures markets these days without knowing all about M_1—and all the other M's for that matter."

"Sort of like M&Ms, the candy that melts in your mouth, not in your hand," Plunger chortled. "Speaking of futures, how are those stock index futures of yours doing these days? I've got to make up for the bath I'm taking on that oceanfront white elephant somehow."

"The December Value Line contract is at 111.50, close to its low for the year. The S&P 500 and NYSE contracts are also near their lows. The stock market has been severely depressed, as you know, and the index futures contracts are projecting more of the same."

"Well, what do your M_1s and M_2s have to say about what's going to happen to stocks? Maybe we can get a fast play out of one of those contracts."

"Actually, that might not be such a bad idea," replied Decimal spiritedly. "M_1 has been rising at an annual rate of 3.7 percent thus far this year. That's a far cry from its 8 percent growth rate when you bought your oceanfront white elephant. The inflation rate has dropped from over 13 percent to less than half that, and judging from the dip we've seen in interest rates lately, the stock market could very well stage a turnaround in the near future."

Decimal could not know how prophetic those words were. And Plunger was interested. In spite of his wisecracking about monetary jargon, he knew that declining interest rates were a bullish influence and that a further drop could present him with a profitable opportunity. The question was, was the fall in rates over the past several weeks merely a temporary phenomenon—he had, in fact, heard that the drop was politically motivated—or had the long-awaited return to the rate levels of happier days actually begun?

Plunger decided not to wait to find out. He instructed Decimal to enter an open order good through that week to buy three December Value Line contracts at the round figure of 110.00 or less.

As it turned out, December Value Lines sold down to 110.00 the following day, at which price the buy order was executed. Following Plunger's purchase, the contract price turned up to close the day at 112.40.

"Wow!" exclaimed Plunger. "A $3,600 profit in less than a day. That's what I call action. Let's take the money and run!"

"It's your money," replied Decimal. "But that contract dropped from 123.00 to 110.00 in less than three weeks. This rally should run for more than a couple of points. Why don't we put a sell stop order in at your buy point to protect your margin money and see what happens?"

"Well, if you feel so strongly about it," said Plunger dubiously. "But it's been a dog's age since I had a fast profit like this one. I'd hate to see it slip through my fingers."

It was touch and go for the next three days as the December Value Line contract moved back and forth between 110.50 and 112.50, coming close to, but not quite "triggering," the sell stop price.

But on the fourth day, the world turned rosy for Plunger and, by association, Decimal, who did well when his clients did well. The Federal Reserve had reported the night before that M_1 had not risen but had *declined* by $2 billion that week, and the Board of Governors announced a further one-half point reduction in the discount rate.

The Fed was easing with a vengeance at last, and the stock market was euphoric. The December Value Lines shot up five points that day alone and, scarcely pausing to digest that eruption, soared another eight points during the following week.

"Great Caesar's ghost!" exploded Plunger. "A $24,000 profit in two weeks. You can have your Florida condos. It's stock index futures for me from here on in!"

hnical Analysis,
chology, and
ectations

offers the technicians their promised turn at bat. Fortunately for
ave a very heavy hitter playing on their team—or at least the
e. Although he was probably never aware that he was in the
less an important personage in our story than Charles Dow himself
is accorded the distinction of being the father of modern technical analysis.

Perhaps "uncle" would be more genealogically correct. Having devised
and refined his stock market averages in the manner described in chapter 1,
Dow periodically referred to them in his *Wall Street Journal* editorials.[1]
William Peter Hamilton, who succeeded Dow as editor of the *Journal*,
continued to make mention of them. But where Dow regarded his averages in
the first instance as what he called a barometer of business conditions,
Hamilton stressed their value as indicators of general stock market behavior,
precisely what they are considered to be today.

It was Hamilton who developed a set of principles and precepts governing
common stock investment based on the behavior of the industrial and rail
averages that he spelled out in his 1921 book, *The Stock Market Barometer.*[2]
But it was Dow who got the credit when Robert Rhea subsequently refined
Hamilton's ideas and incorporated them in his own book, *The Dow Theory.*[3]

The Dow Theory

As set forth by Rhea and developed further by later interpreters, the Dow
theory presents a methodology for identifying major stock market trends.

159

Although Hamilton and Rhea never claimed that the application of their ideas could help an investor to predict the extent and duration of price swings, their concepts have frequently been employed to forecast future price movement.

The Dow theory can best be described by listing its six basic principles:

1. The rail and industrial averages discount all the external factors that affect stock prices.

2. There are three distinct types of stock market movements. The primary moves are those that are popularly labeled bull or bear markets. They last from one to several years but are regularly interrupted by secondary movements, which retrace from one-third to two-thirds of the immediately preceding movement. These secondary moves run from one to several weeks. The third type are the minor "bubbles and bursts," which last from a few hours to several weeks. They have no analytical significance so far as the Dow theory is concerned.

3. The underlying trend of stock prices is revealed by the movement of the averages. The stock market is held to be in a bullish trend when each price rally surpasses the previous high point and each reaction stops short of the prior low. Conversely, a bear market is characterized by a series of successively lower peaks and troughs. Figure 8.1 illustrates these series of highs and lows.

4. The industrial and rail averages must confirm each other to verify a new primary movement. A key consideration in the application of the Dow theory, but a cause of some uncertainty, is that the two averages must be regarded jointly. A signal from one of the averages is not held to be valid until it is confirmed by a comparable signal from the other average.

5. The relationship of daily trading volume to price movement is an important consideration. Volume normally expands during the upward "leg" of a bull movement and contracts during the ensuing secondary reaction. If volume begins to flag during the upswing and expand on the decline, it is an indication that the bull move is drawing to a close. Even so, the conclusive signal of a trend reversal must be given by the movement of the averages themselves.

6. Price movements occur between successive periods of accumulation and distribution. Accumulation of stock in "strong" hands is taken to be a bullish sign. The distribution of shares into "weak" hands has a bearish implication.

As was noted above, a cause of confusion and uncertainty in the application of the Dow theory is the stipulation that the rail and industrial

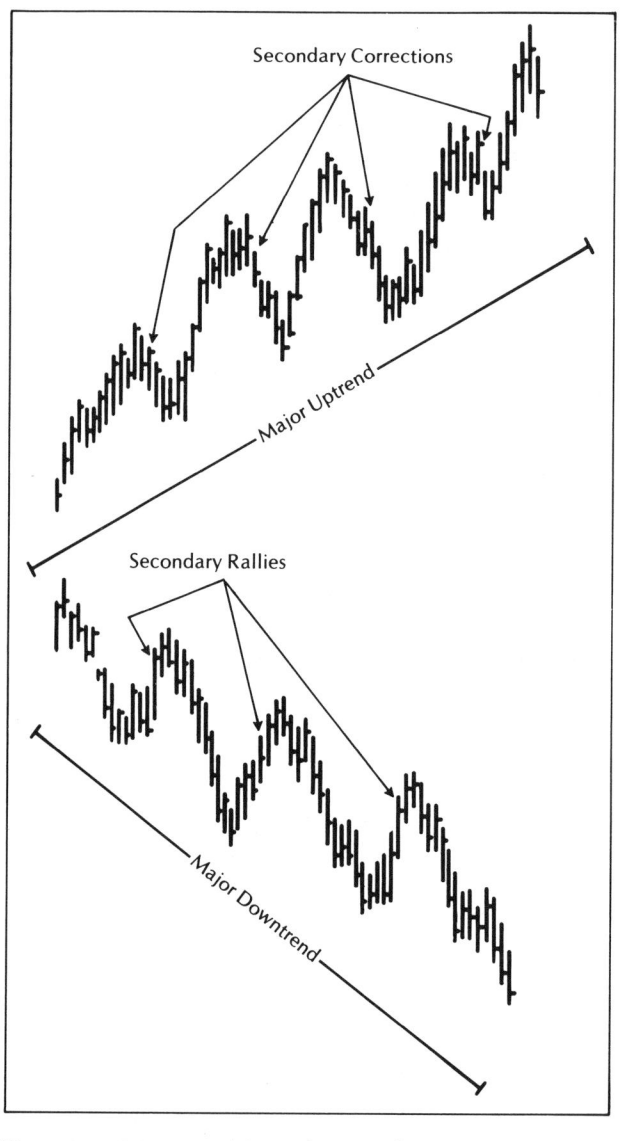

Figure 8.1 Primary and Secondary Trends

averages confirm each other in signaling a change in the primary trend. It is to be expected that in an expanding economy an increased volume of industrial output will result in greater freight traffic. There is decided logic, therefore, in requiring that the rail average confirm the industrials or vice versa. On the other hand, the modification of the rail average to a broader transportation index in 1970, with the inclusion of airline stocks (as well as truckers and freight forwarders) disrupted the initial connection between production and traffic.[4] Moreover, the regulation of common carrier rates and other aspects of their business insulates the railroads and other carriers to a certain extent from the supply/demand forces that affect the performance of the less-regulated industrial corporations.

In the face of criticism by the avant-gardists, who find it difficult to accept that in this day of computers and advanced calculus, such a simple 80-year-old system can produce results, the Dow theory has proved to be surprisingly effective in its application. Table 8.1 contains a scorecard of its performance since the theory was formulated. Of course, if it were as simple as it appears on the surface, everyone who tried it would make money, and its usefulness would come to an abrupt end. Judgment and interpretation are key ingredients in the profitable application of the Dow theory, just as they are in the many technical approaches that have followed it.

Modern-day technicians subscribe to the same basic belief that inspired William Peter Hamilton to formulate the Dow theory three-quarters of a century ago. It is that the prices of individual stocks and, consequently, the level of the various indexes are a continually changing distillation of the countless economic, monetary, political, and psychological forces that motivate investors to buy and sell stocks. Rather than analyzing each of these factors in detail, as we've endeavored to do in the last three chapters, technicians paraphrase Alexander Pope's observation that "the proper study of mankind is man." They believe that the proper study of the stock and futures markets is the markets themselves.

Three Technical Indicators

Technicians are essentially price historians, with a few other wrinkles thrown in. They believe that the same human impulses and expectations that caused stock prices to behave in a certain way in the past will produce the same results if and when these impulses and expectations recur. The way to detect their recurrence, the technicians maintain, is to study and interpret such attributes of market activity as price, volume, time, and breadth.

Technical analysis is concerned with three types of indicators: those that measure the sentiment of investors (including financial institutions)—that is,

Table 8.1 Application of the Dow Theory—An 80-Year Record

	Buy Signals			Sell Signals	
Date of Buy Signal	DJIA	% Gain from Sell Signal When Short	Date of Sell Signal	DJIA	% Gain from Buy Signal
July 1897	44		Dec. 1899	63	43
Oct. 1900	59	6	June 1903	59	0
July 1904	51	14	Apr. 1906	92	80
Apr. 1908	70	24	May 1910	85	21
Oct. 1910	82	4	Jan. 1913	85	3
Apr. 1915	65	24	Aug. 1917	86	32
May 1918	82	5	Feb. 1920	99	22
Feb. 1922	84	16	June 1923	91	8
Dec. 1923	94	Loss 3	Oct. 1929	306	226
May 1933	84	73	Sept. 1937	164	95
June 1938	127	23	Mar. 1939	136	7
July 1939	143	5	May 1940	138	Loss 7
Feb. 1943	126	8	Aug. 1946	191	52
Apr. 1948	184	4	Nov. 1948	173	Loss 6
Oct. 1950	229	Loss 32	Apr. 1953	280	22
Jan. 1954	288	Loss 3	Oct. 1956	468	63
Apr. 1958	450	4	Mar. 1960	612	36
Nov. 1960	602	2	Apr. 1962	683	13
Nov. 1962	625	8	May 1966	900	43
Jan. 1967	823	9	June 1969	900	9
Dec. 1970	823	9	Apr. 1973	921	12
Jan. 1975	680	26	Oct. 1977	801	18
Average of all cycles:		11%	Average of all cycles:		36%

Source: Martin J. Pring, *Technical Analysis Explained: An Illustrated Guide for the Investor*, (New York: McGraw-Hill Book Company, 1980), 21. Reprinted with permission.

are they bullish or bearish; the flow of funds into and out of the stock market; and the price and volume structure of the market itself.

A frequently cited example of a sentiment indicator is the level of odd-lot transactions conducted on the New York Stock Exchange and on other exchanges. Technicians subscribe to the notion that "the public is always wrong." They accordingly monitor the latest odd-lot statistics in an effort to learn what *not* to do.

The only problem with this discriminatory approach is that the great unwashed public hasn't done all that badly at recent major turning points in the stock market. Whatever the reason, average folks haven't been as dumb in handling their investments lately as the odd-lot elitists would have us believe they are.

The reciprocal of odd-lot elitism is the conviction that insiders, however they may be defined, are always "in the know." That is to say that if you are the vice president of finance of a major corporation, or even just the assistant comptroller of a small-to-middling company, you can get your information from the horse's mouth because *you* are the horse. In spite of the numerous restrictions the Securities and Exchange Commission imposes on insider trading, technicians believe these favored few will find a way to profit by their privileged knowledge. To gain a peek into this rarefied world, they snap up the most recent SEC report on insider trading as if it were the latest issue of *Penthouse* magazine. By aping what the report says the insiders did two or three months ago, technicians believe there is sufficient mileage left in the stocks for them to make a few dollars on this information.

A second technical approach is the study of the flow of funds into and out of the stock market. In contrast to the odd-lot buying and selling statistics, flow-of-funds indicators reveal the amounts big institutions such as mutual funds, insurance companies, and bank trust departments have at their disposal to buy stocks if they so choose. The problem with this approach is that while it may tell you what cash resources these heavy hitters have available, it doesn't tell when they plan to use them or how. The institutions themselves won't know that until the portfolio managers who work there decide that the time has come to act.

The third approach is concerned with an analysis of market structure. This is the primary grist for a technician's mill, and the one that stock index futures traders can most readily employ. It is a study of market price, volume, timing, momentum, and breadth. To technicians, "the market" consists of the leading stock indexes. In that respect, every index trader is at least in part a technician whether he or she wants to be or not.

Technicians talk a great deal about panic, fear, greed, pessimism, optimism, and euphoria—some of the worthier manifestations of human nature. But when it comes to doing their homework, they are just as intent on punching out the numbers as are the fundamental analysts, who are concerned with such matters as estimated corporate earnings and the Federal Reserve's open market policy.

Technicians are by no means flaky. There may have been a time—though you'd have to go back to the 1950s and early 1960s to find it—when the most profitable investment strategy was to buy a solid stock and put it away. But that has seldom been the case since those golden years. Looking at stock performance from the perspective of the Dow Jones Industrial Average, a buy-and-hold type of investor who bought in 1966 and held until 1978 had very little in the way of capital appreciation to show for his or her patience and fortitude.[5]

But the technician who was disposed to buy and sell as frequently as his or her indicators instructed had the potential of an aggregate movement in the DJIA, up and down, of over 1,600 points from which to glean profits. He or she had the opportunity to capture 227 points on the S&P 500 during the same thirteen-year period. That works out to $113,500 for each S&P 500 futures contract ($500 × 227). To be sure, no one can expect to hit the top and bottom of one stock market cycle, let alone three of them. But the profits to be amassed by capturing 50 percent of those moves are still considerable.

The Basic Tool: Charts

A technician's basic tool is a price chart, of which there are three principal types—line, bar, and point-and-figure charts. A *line chart* is a type that has appeared frequently in this book. It plots the change over time of a single price, index, or other quantity. Often two values are charted over the same time period to obtain a comparative analysis.[6]

In that they display a single value for each unit of time that is measured—be it a day, week, or month—line charts are not suitable for presenting an accurate picture of daily or weekly changes in stock or futures prices. Where it is desirable to show the daily or weekly range of prices over the course of numerous trading sessions, a *bar chart* is the preferred format. It, too, is a line chart in the sense that the indicated bar is a vertical line that spans the high and low prices during the designated unit of time. Another line—a short, horizontal one—marks the closing or settlement price within the daily, weekly, or monthly range.

Table 8.2 lists the daily high, low, and closing figures for the NYSE Composite Index for August 1982. That information is translated into a chart in figure 8.2, where the horizontal axis of the chart is divided according to trading sessions and the vertical axis spans the range between 55.00 and 70.00 on the index.

Table 8.3 and figure 8.3 contain the same type of information concerning the December 1982 NYSE Composite futures contract during August 1982. The benefits of the charts are obvious. Whereas the tables, though perfectly accurate, present a jumble of hard-to-compare numbers, the related charts give a clear picture of the low August 9 and high August 26 points for both series and make it much easier to compare them.

Bar charts may be drawn to either an arithmetic or semilogarithmic scale. The latter makes it easier to evaluate the percentage advance or decline of a

Table 8.2 NYSE Composite Index Performance, August 1982

August 1982	High	Low	Close	Daily Change
2	62.54	61.45	62.49	
3	62.98	61.91	61.91	−0.58
4	61.88	60.95	60.97	−0.94
5	60.91	60.24	60.44	−0.53
6	60.45	59.66	59.69	−0.75
9	59.60	58.85	59.25	−0.44
10	59.64	59.10	59.13	−0.12
11	59.16	58.88	58.95	−0.18
12	59.23	58.78	58.80	−0.15
13	59.54	58.80	59.54	+0.74
16	60.51	59.50	59.75	+0.21
17	62.41	59.74	62.41	+2.66
18	63.95	62.29	62.32	−0.09
19	62.93	62.18	62.57	+0.25
20	64.65	62.57	64.65	+2.08
23	66.36	64.48	66.36	+1.71
24	66.57	65.94	66.10	−0.26
25	67.64	65.94	67.39	+1.29
26	68.94	67.36	68.01	+0.62
27	68.02	67.02	67.23	−0.78
30	67.52	66.53	67.52	+0.29
31	68.56	67.50	68.54	+1.02

SOURCE: *Wall Street Journal,* August 2–31, 1982 inclusive.

particular price movement. While in percentage terms a move from, say, six to twelve is equal to a move from two to four—both are 100 percent gains—in arithmetic terms it is three times greater.

The third method of price charting, one that is something of a puzzle to most nontechnicians, is the *point-and-figure* system. Consisting solely of adjacent columns of Xs and Os, point-and-figure charts resemble some advanced form of ticktacktoe (see figure 8.4). In addition to these unusual notations, the method is unique in that it does not adhere to any time scale but is determined solely by changes in price trend.

So long as the value being charted is rising in price, a chartist using the point-and-figure technique keeps on extending an ascending column of Xs. When the price declines by a predetermined amount, possibly one point, the

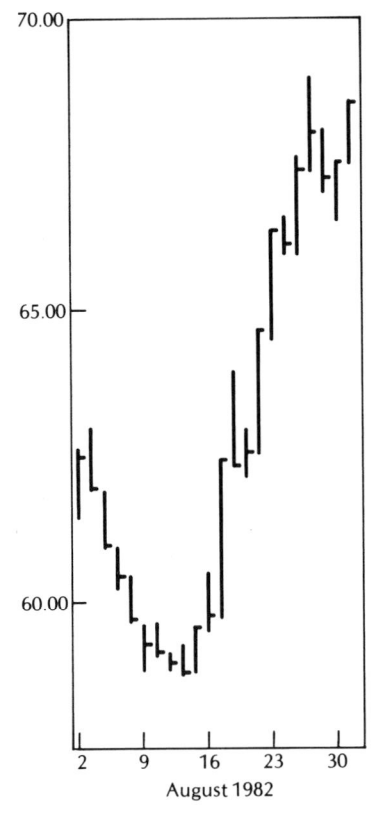

Figure 8.2   NYSE Composite
Index, August
1982

chartist moves one column to the right and begins marking continuously descending Os. A point-and-figure chart therefore moves laterally across the page as the price trend keeps reversing itself, while a bar chart proceeds according to the stated units of time, be they days, weeks, or months.

The question invariably arises of which method of charting is best. The choice really lies between bar and point-and-figure charts, since line charts are in any case inadequate for the purpose of technical analysis except in the use of moving averages, which will be discussed presently. The fact is that there is no consistent and overriding advantage to be gained from employing one or the other technique. Analysts often employ the two simultaneously as a sort of fail-safe measure.

Table 8.3 December 1982 NYSE Composite Index Futures Contract Performance, August 1982

August 1982	High	Low	Settle	Daily Change
2	63.70	62.30	63.65	+1.60
3	63.55	61.40	61.45	−2.20
4	61.80	60.20	60.45	−1.00
5	60.75	59.75	60.60	+0.15
6	60.75	58.80	58.90	−1.70
9	60.05	58.10	60.00	+1.10
10	60.40	58.80	58.95	−1.05
11	59.85	58.85	59.35	+0.40
12	60.10	58.90	59.05	−0.30
13	61.00	59.10	60.70	+1.65
16	61.75	59.50	59.65	−1.05
17	63.80	59.90	63.60	+3.95
18	64.85	62.05	62.40	−1.20
19	63.40	61.90	63.40	+1.00
20	66.60	63.25	66.20	+2.80
23	67.95	65.00	67.60	+1.40
24	68.00	66.40	66.55	−1.05
25	68.10	66.30	67.90	+1.35
26	69.00	67.20	68.20	+0.30
27	68.00	66.60	66.90	−1.30
30	68.15	66.20	68.20	+1.30
31	69.10	67.70	68.45	+0.25

SOURCE: *Wall Street Journal*, August 2–31, 1982 inclusive.

By way of comparison, figure 8.4 (mentioned above) reproduces in point-and-figure form the bar chart of the December 1982 NYSE contract that is presented in figure 8.3.[7]

Fathoming the Future in Charts

There can be no question that charts are a convenient way of recording and displaying past price behavior. The uncertainty arises over the ability of technical analysts to predict from chart patterns and related data what prices will do in the future. Just as the ability to forecast corporate earnings correctly separates the men from the boys—and, of course, the women from the girls— among the fundamental analysts, so the ability to look at a price chart and

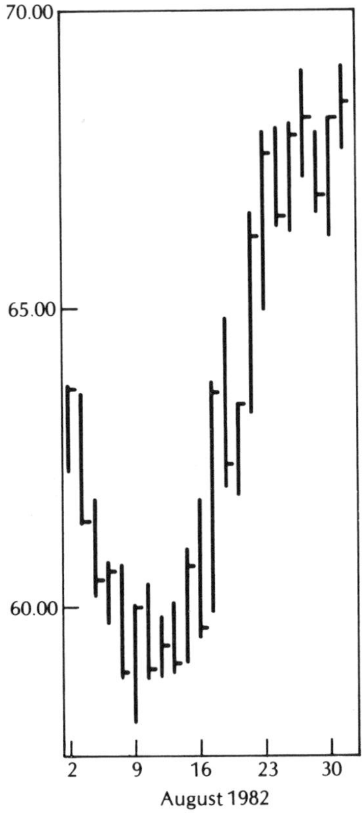

Figure 8.3 December 1982
Contract, NYSE
Composite,
August 1982

discern what is going to happen next is the acid test for technical analysts. If
they cannot pass that test, they might just as well be playing ticktacktoe.

The price of a stock, commodity, or index can only move in one of three
ways: up, down, or sideways (that is, it can remain unchanged).[8] These
movements are held to establish price trends, and success in any sort of trading
comes from the ability to identify trends in their incipient stages. It is here that
we return to the tenet of the Dow theory that holds that an uptrend is defined
by a series of ascending highs and lows, and a downtrend by a series of
descending intermediate tops and bottoms. This wavelike effect was well
described by Charles Dow in "Watching the Tide" and in other editorials. In

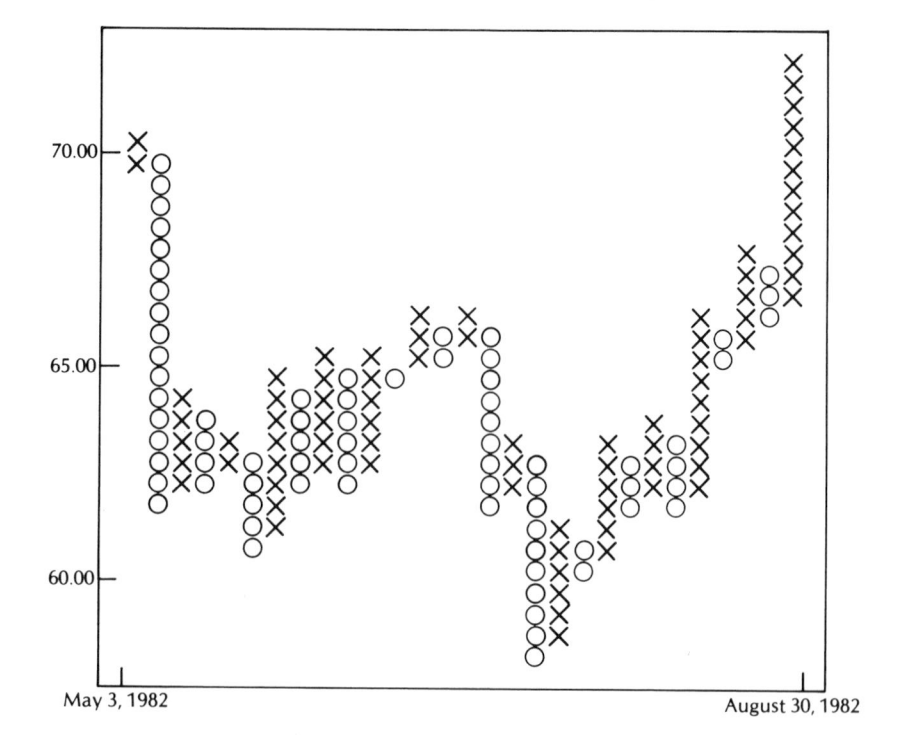

Figure 8.4   Point-and-Figure Chart for December 1982 NYSE Composite

terms of the Dow theory, the major feat in trend analysis is distinguishing between a secondary reaction to an existing primary trend and the first wave of a new and opposite primary trend. The latter means a shift from a bull to a bear market or vice versa.

A simple but effective means of identifying a primary or major trend and the several secondary or minor trends that occur within it is to draw a *trendline*. In the case of an uptrend, it is often possible to draw a single line, such as the lower of the parallel ascending lines in figure 8.5, that joins the ascending lows of the secondary reactions. This trendline gives the technical analyst a bench mark against which to gauge future price action. So long as the secondary-reaction lows stop at or above the trendline, the uptrend is held to remain intact, and the analyst's next consideration is to pick a point at which to go long. If a minor reaction carries the price through and below the trendline, the uptrend is considered to have been violated, a signal that a reversal of the primary trend is imminent. In that case, the analyst's indicated course of action is to get out of his or her long positions and establish short ones.

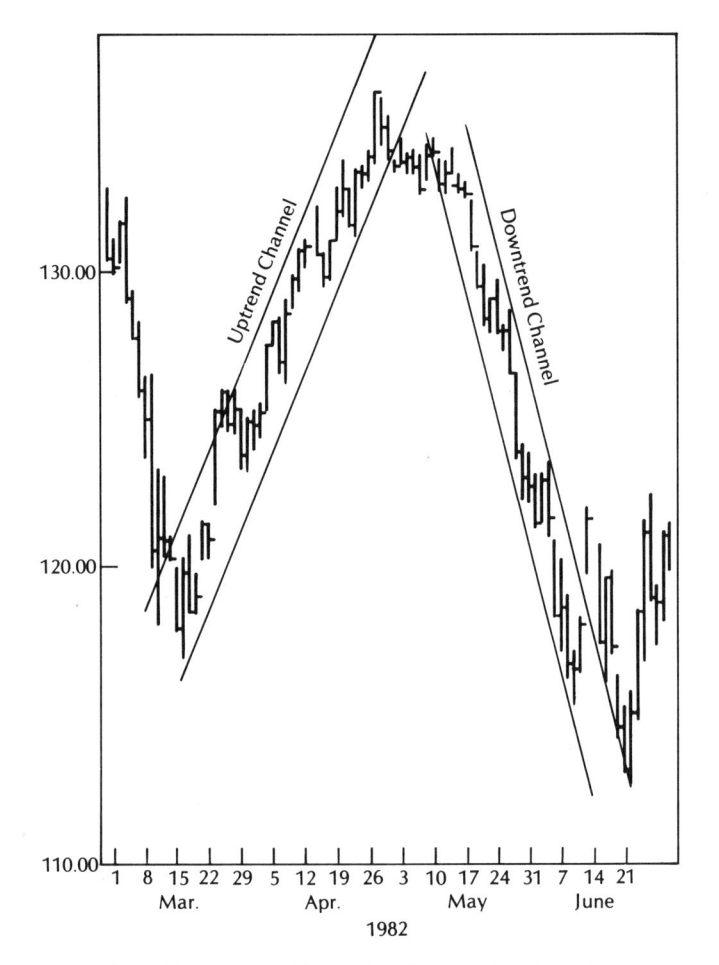

Figure 8.5 Up- and Downtrend Channels, December 1982
Value Line

Conversely, when the primary trend is down, as is also illustrated in figure
8.5, the trendline is drawn through the peaks of the secondary rallies that
intermittently interrupt the downtrend. As in the case of an uptrend, so long as
the secondary movements stop at the trendline, the primary trend remains
down, and the technical analyst is advised either to stay short or to get short if
he or she has not already done so. When one of the minor rallies penetrates
the trendline, the analyst should think in terms of reversing his or her position
from short to long, inasmuch as that penetration could signal the end of the
downtrend.

Readers have a right to become irritated by the repeated use of qualifying words like *could* or *might*. Technicians become equally exasperated with chart signals that turn out to be false alarms, but they learn to accept them as part of the game. A trendline could be penetrated, with the primary trend then continuing in the same direction as if nothing happened. What does the technician do? He or she simply erases the discredited line and draws a new one. Or the technician may "fudge" and bend the old one a little bit. After all, he or she may reason, nothing is perfect in this life, and a warped trendline is better than no trendline at all. Not so, protest the straight-arrow technicians, who brook no compromise. They don't fudge. Once a trendline is violated—such a quaint, Victorian expression!—the straight arrows unhesitatingly prepare to reverse their course. It's hard to say who's right, the fudgers or the straight arrows. In the final analysis, it's the ones who make the most money who are right.

Channels, Support, and Resistance

On occasion, it is possible to draw a parallel line above or below the trendline to define what is known as the *trend channel*. These lines do not appear as consistently as basic trendlines, but when they do, they provide a fair indication of the duration and turning points of secondary movements (see figure 8.5). In the most perfect of worlds, it should be possible to sell at the upper boundary of a trend channel and buy at the lower boundary, running in between to the bank to deposit the profits. But we have already reconciled ourselves to the fact that imperfection is the essence of the human condition, so it should come as no surprise that such an idealized strategy rarely succeeds in practice.

It may seem as if the Great Spirit has ordained these trendlines and channels. Market technicians prefer to think of the forces that shape them as support and resistance. It stands to reason that a great many analysts who separately examine the same chart will arrive at roughly the same conclusions. After all, how many ways are there to look at a road map? If these analysts and their followers act on the strength of their conclusions, they'll all be trying to buy and sell at around the same points. Hence, trends—reflecting the actions of the people who make them—have a tendency to prolong themselves, at least until there occurs a major change in analyst and trader sentiment that forces a trend reversal.

Other terms for support and resistance are *accumulation* and *distribution*. A host of traders buying stock or futures contracts at a particular price level support the price at that level for as long as their buying lasts. The same or another group of traders who sell at a different price level impose a temporary barrier at that point. The establishment of these accumulation and distribution levels can be visualized in the case of individual securities and futures contracts. It's harder to imagine the process when the various stock indexes are involved. Yet support and resistance are in effect in their case as well. In general terms, a stock, contract, or the market as a whole will undergo an accumulation phase before a sustained advance and a distribution phase prior to an extended decline. Technicians believe that the longer an accumulation or distribution phase lasts, the more sustained the ensuing price movement will be.

Questions and Answers

There are several key questions technical analysts should ask themselves regarding the current trend and the prospects for its imminent reversal. They include:

1. How long has the current trend been underway?

2. How does that compare with the duration of previous trends in the same or the opposite direction?

3. Has the stock or contract price violated its trend?

4. Are there any signs of current accumulation or distribution?

5. Are the chances greater for a continuation of the prevailing trend or for its reversal?

In preparing their answers to the above questions, analysts should consider the following guidelines:

1. Each time a secondary movement tests the trendline and it remains intact, the prevailing trend gains strength, and the prospects for its continuation are enhanced.

2. The trend of a specific index futures contract is reinforced if other expirations of the same contract behave in the same fashion, and even more so if the spot index exhibits the same trend.

3. Trends have greater momentum and staying power if the trend channel is narrow than if it is wide.

4. An acutely sloped trend has greater momentum and staying power than one that has a shallow slope.

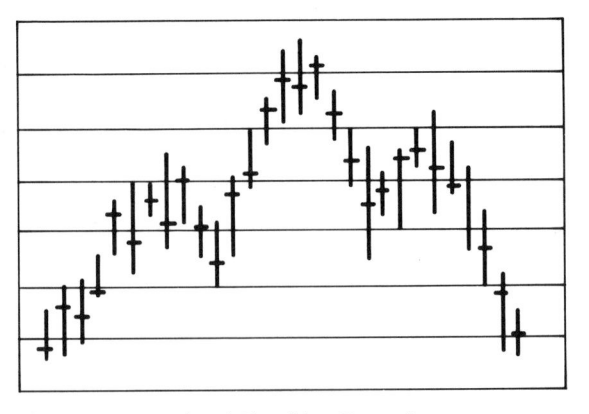

Figure 8.6 Head-and-Shoulders Formation

Bull and bear markets obviously do not last indefinitely. A trend must eventually run its course and reverse itself. The conservative strategy is to buy or sell into a trend—whichever is the appropriate move—after the trend has become established and the trendline has withstood one or two tests.

Recalling a baseball analogy, moving with an established trend is analogous to striving for a high batting average. Steady base hits aren't very exciting, but they win a lot of ball games. The alternative is to swing from the heels and try to belt the ball out of the park each time at bat. That involves spotting a trend reversal while it's happening and getting aboard a new trend at the very beginning. Deep in his or her heart, a technician knows that the risk of such a go-for-broke approach can involve just that. Babe Ruth also holds the strikeout record—as a batter, not as a pitcher. Although they are aware of this, many traders go ahead and swing for the fence anyway. Everyone likes to hit home runs.

Calling the Turns

There are a number of chart formations that purportedly give technical analysts advance warning of a trend reversal. Most people can follow a prevailing trend. That, after all, mainly involves the application of common sense. But trying to call a turn in a trend by reading meaning into a lot of fuzzy chart formations is a horse of a different color.

Entire books have been written on the subject of chart analysis.[9] It would not do the topic justice to try summarizing it within a few pages. But one or two commonly seen chart formations are worth mentioning by way of illustration.

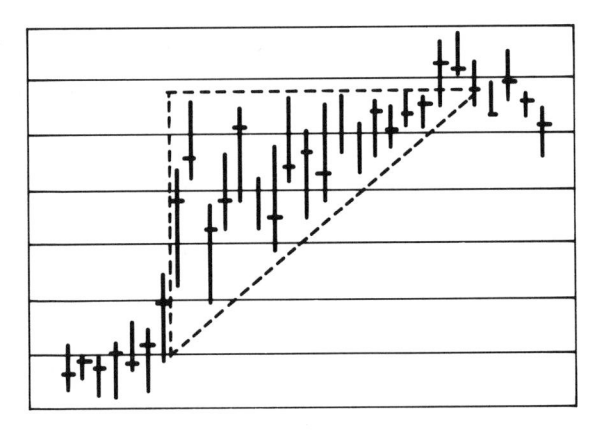

Figure 8.7 Ascending Triangle Formation

Technicians believe that a very reliable signal is the so-called head-and-shoulders or multiple-top-formation (see figure 8.6). This formation consists of three successive attempts by a stock or contract price to reach a new high level. The second thrust, the so-called head, manages to exceed the tops of the two rallies that adjoin it, but all three rallies lack the steam, moxie, new buyers, or whatever is needed to keep the advance going. When the third rally attempt fails and the price falls below the "neckline" of the head-and-shoulders formation, chart watchers take that to mean that the advance is over and that the smart money should go on the short side.

Conversely, the failure of a triple-bottom or inverted head-and-shoulders formation to continue to set new lows is held to signal the beginning of an uptrend. Analysts maintain, however, that multiple bottoms do not have the same reliability and predictive value that multiple tops do.

Triangles are another type of formation (see figure 8.7). There are three kinds—symmetrical, ascending, and descending—but all are taken as evidence of a continuing trend rather than as reversal patterns. Triangles typically occur within so-called congestion areas, where an uptrend or downtrend pauses to gather fresh momentum for a continued advance or decline.

A third type of technical phenomenon is not a chart formation per se but is rather the absence of one. Gaps are areas on a chart where no trading activity is noted. They are further divided into three types, according to the time and place within a trend that the gap occurs (see figure 8.8).

A "breakaway gap" usually occurs at or shortly following a trend reversal. It is taken as confirmation that a new trend is getting underway. A "runaway gap" may occur at or near the midpoint of a trend and is considered a sign that

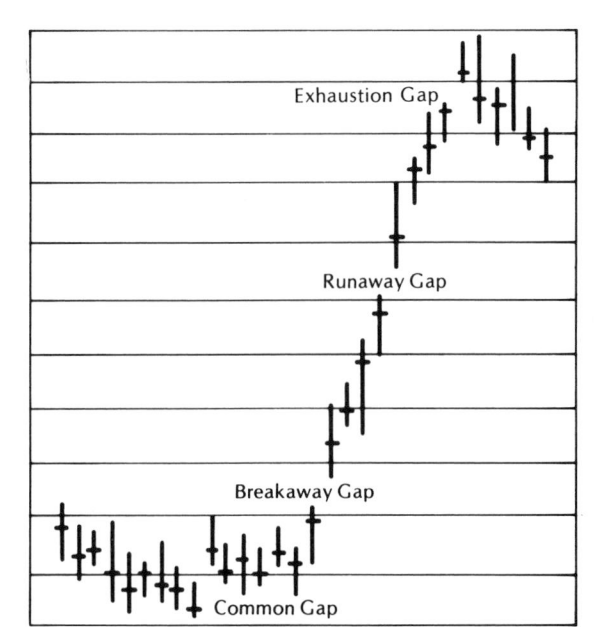

Figure 8.8 Gap Formations

there is sufficient momentum to propel a further push. Third is the "exhaustion," or "key reversal," gap, which signals the termination of a trend. In the case of an uptrend, an exhaustion gap is said to have occurred when a contract price opens a trading session appreciably higher than the previous day's high but fails to sustain the advance, closing the session at or near the low price for that day. The reverse sequence is likely to occur at the culmination of a prolonged bear market—namely, an opening price that is sharply lower and then an appreciably higher closing.

Volume and Open Interest

In conjunction with their study of price activity, technical analysts keep a close watch on trading volume and, in the case of stock index futures, on changes in open interest. Volume consists of the number of shares or contracts that are traded daily. Open interest is the number of futures contracts that are in existence at any time. When they are considered along with price movement, both are helpful indicators of whether the market's bullish or bearish tone is increasing, remaining constant, or waning.

As a general rule, an indication of a trend reversal, such as the completion of a head-and-shoulders formation or a breakaway gap, has greater validity when it is accompanied by a substantial increase in trading volume and open interest. High volume is essential to power a continued advance or decline.

After an extended price rise, an inability to sustain the advance coupled with extremely high volume suggests that traders are "reversing gears" and that a trend reversal is in the offing. Conversely, a great increase in volume following a prolonged bear market often culminates in a so-called selling climax, which exhausts the theretofore preponderant selling pressure and sets the stage for a rally and possibly an extended uptrend. This activity is manifested by the exhaustion gap described above.

According to two veteran analyst-traders, changes in open interest, when taken in conjunction with price activity, have the following significance so far as market participation is concerned:

If contract price and open interest change in the following manner:	The significant change in market activity is believed to be:
Both prices and open interest rise;	New buyers are entering.
Prices rise and open interest declines;	Short positions are being covered.
Prices decline but open interest rises;	New sellers are entering.
Both prices and open interest decline;	Long positions are being liquidated.[10]

The related guidelines linking volume and open interest are:

1. During an uptrend a combination of high volume and rising open interest indicates a technically strong market condition and suggests a continuation of the trend.

2. During a downtrend a combination of high volume and rising open interest indicates a technically weak market and suggests a continuation of the trend.

3. During an uptrend a combination of high volume and shrinking open interest suggests that the current price strength is due to short covering, signifying a technically weak market.

4. During a downtrend a combination of high volume and declining open interest suggests that the current price weakness is due to the liquidation of long positions, signifying a potentially stronger market because prospective selling pressure is being cleared away.[11]

In summary, the foregoing observations suggest that the joint movement of price and open interest up or down is a bullish indicator and that their divergence is a potentially bearish indicator.

Moving Averages and Momentum

Moving-average and momentum studies are additional techniques that are used to assess the tone and technical condition of both the stock and futures markets. A moving average is a computation that is used to smooth out minor price fluctuations for the purpose of clarifying the underlying trend.[12] When charted concurrently with a regular daily bar chart, the crossing of the moving average and the daily price is held to indicate a change in the underlying price trend. If the moving average crosses over the daily price, the stock or contract in question is adjusted to have moved into an upward trend. Conversely, a crossover from above to below the daily price is taken as a confirmation that a downtrend has gotten under way.

The purported benefit of the moving-average crossover technique is that, being mechanical and clear-cut, it does not demand the subjective type of interpretation required of the indicators discussed above. An important consideration in the successful use of this analytical tool is the selection of a suitable time period to be averaged. Some technicians calculate averages with two or more different time frames to measure the trend of a certain index or contract. Figure 8.9 shows such a multiple average, measuring the Dow Jones Industrial Average against ten-week and thirty-week moving averages during the four-year period from 1974 through 1977. The crossover of both moving averages signaled the declines in the DJIA of March–December 1974 and August 1976–October 1977 and the rallies of February–June 1975 and January–March 1976.

Momentum analysis is another technique used to identify trend reversals as they occur. The rationale behind these measurements is that the momentum of a particular price movement, what we have offhandedly referred to as steam or moxie, tends to decline markedly as the particular stock or contract reaches its peak or trough.

For example, if an analyst wants to measure the five-week price momentum of an S&P 500 futures contract, or of the spot index itself, he or she will divide the current contract price or index by the price five weeks earlier. If the prices in question are, say, 115.00 now and 120.00 five weeks ago, the momentum figure would be $\frac{115.00}{120.00}$, or .96. By repeating the calculation at frequent intervals, the rate of price change, or the momentum, can be ascertained.

The breadth of a market trend is measured by means of an advance-decline line that represents the total number of stocks that advance during the course of a particular day or week minus the number that decline. As a rule, the advance-decline line rises and falls along with the indexes, an indication that as the market as a whole rises, the number of stocks that participate in the move also rises. Conversely, as the averages fall, the number of stocks that decline exceeds those that advance by an increasing margin.

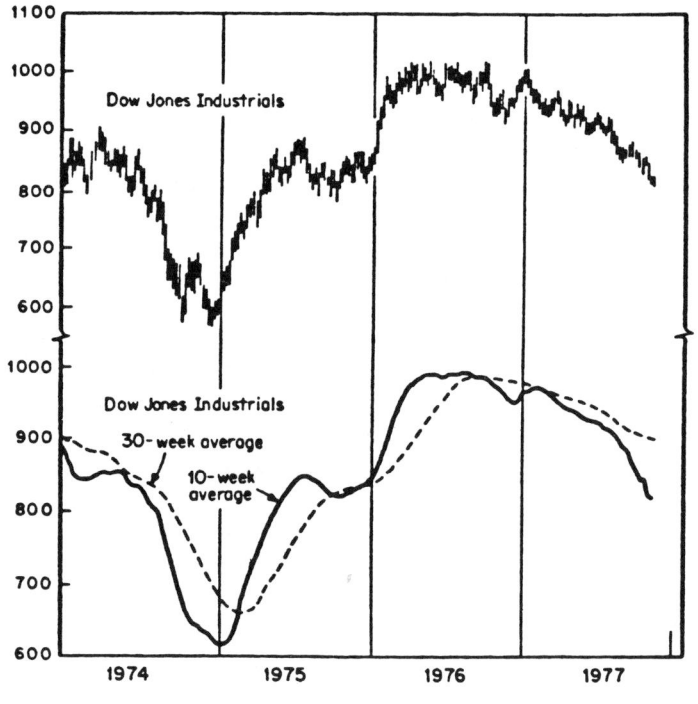

Figure 8.9 Dow Jones Industrial Averages Versus 30–Week/10–Week Moving Averages, 1974–1977

The momentum of market breadth is calculated by dividing the number of stocks that advance during a chosen period by the number that decline. It is procedurally similar to the computation of price momentum explained above. The movement of momentum and price together indicate a continuation of the prevailing trend. Their divergence signals a possible trend reversal.

Psychology and Attitudes

Some analysts supplement these measurements with nonquantitative methods of assessing the mood and expectations of investors and traders. Such psychologically oriented studies stand in contrast to the trend analyses and the volume, open interest, and momentum studies described thus far in this chapter.

In advancing the advantages of their approach, the opinion-samplers denigrate the poor results of more conventional methods of forecasting. They prefer to rely instead on direct polling techniques to ascertain the psychological attitudes that underlie collective spending, saving, and investment decisions of individuals and business entities.

Researchers at the University of Michigan have since 1955 published an index of consumer sentiment that incorporates attitudes concerning the stock market and interest rates as well as such conventional consumer items as durable goods, automobiles, and so on.[13] The premise underlying the attitude surveys is that once a set of expectations is established throughout the population, it will only be modified slowly and gradually. Since the public's expectations are not expected to change during the period for which a forecast is made, the attitudes revealed by statistical opinion sampling are held to comprise the basis for an accurate forecast.[14]

In 1969 the Michigan research unit surveyed a sampling of nearly five thousand stockholders regarding their attitudes toward stock ownership and their investment goals. The respondents were divided into three categories. Over 60 percent of those sampled perceived themselves to be conservative investors whose objective was to own "safe" stocks and thereby avoid risk. Investors who were disposed to speculate for the sake of amassing sizable capital gains comprised another 20 percent of the sample, and the remainder were individuals with mixed objectives. The majority of those sampled who owned shares in more than two corporations held both "safe" and "speculative" stocks.

Most of the investors who were surveyed admitted to having little information about the stock market except when big upward or downward movements resulted in large newspaper headlines or extensive television coverage. When they were asked what they thought the causes of these big movements were, a large proportion of those sampled attributed large price advances as well as declines to "speculation" or to "manipulation."[15]

Investors' attitudes regarding the stock market changed markedly during the 1960s—probably because the market was climbing during most of those years. The belief that successful investing was largely a matter of luck or of access to inside information became less widely held, and there was a greater appreciation of the importance of economic news and corporate developments. Despite this, only a small proportion of investors who responded to the Michigan survey, even among those with substantial holdings, said they devoted much time to the study of economic and financial news.

Three-quarters of all the stockholders who were surveyed, and half of those with holdings in excess of $100,000, claimed not to know enough about stocks to invest successfully. Many felt that reliable information and advice were not available to them. In fact, a substantial proportion devoted more time and effort to researching automobiles before buying than they did to stocks worth many times the price of a car. A lot of them ultimately took the recommendations of their friends and neighbors in making their investments.

The Michigan survey concluded that for stock ownership to become more widespread among Americans, it would require "a substantial change in the opinions and even the convictions of a great many people. Information on stocks would have to be more readily available and confidence in the reliability of that information would have to be strengthened.[16]

The Role of News

One hoary adage that still has currency on Wall Street is, "Buy on the rumor, sell on the news." The influence of expectations is so pervasive in the stock market that even when the news concerning a certain company is deemed to be good, its stock could very well be dumped if the opinion-molders in the Street decree that the news didn't measure up to their expectations. On the other hand, if the corporate news turns out to be better than was expected, the price of its stock is likely to go up.

If the investing public and institutions appear to ignore favorable news concerning a specific company or the economy at large, it may be assumed that the reported development was expected and accordingly already factored into the market price. If the news, when it is released, fails to live up to those expectations, the specific stock or the market in general has nowhere to go but down.

Two enterprising *Wall Street Journal* reporters in the early 1970s undertook an investigation of the connection between front-page news items in their widely read and respected paper and that day's behavior of stock prices as measured by the performance of the Dow Jones Industrial Average. Among their findings, as published in their book *News and the Market,* was the conclusion that when the news has a favorable or unfavorable slant, there is an 80 percent likelihood that the stock market will respond in a like manner.

The two newsmongers further observed that:

> . . . After each peak or valley had been reached, the news and the market moved in the same direction, indicating that stocks can't continue to fall in the face of a sustained dose of good news, nor continue to rise when the news is decisively bad.
>
> Equally important is what the findings didn't show—that it is not always possible to pick a market top or bottom, except in retrospect, by examining the news.[17]

How Well Does It Work?

With this background, the question that remains to be answered is: How effective has technical analysis been in calling the turns in stock index futures prices? The jury was still out by the fall of 1982, given the market's brief history up to that time.

The chart in Figure 8.10 of the December 1982 Value Line contract does offer some tentative impressions, however. During the initial six-month history of that contract, from late February through August, there were six trends of consequence, ranging from 23 points (the decline from 136.00 on April 26 to 113.00 on June 21) to about 11 points (the ensuing rally to 124.00 on July 16 and 21). In terms of their duration, the trends lasted from about two weeks (from the contract's debut on February 24 to March 12, and again the sharp rally from August 17 to August 25) to the aforementioned eight-week decline from April 26 to June 21. In terms of Dow theory, all of these trends would be classified as secondary movements.

Following the March 22 breakaway gap, when the December 1982 Value Line contract opened over a point above the March 19 settlement price and closed the day over four points higher, the ensuing five-week uptrend traced a fairly regular trend channel. Then, the April 29 violation of the trendline and the subsequent two weeks of lateral movement between 132.50 and 134.00 gave more than sufficient warning of the plunge that was to follow and afforded traders ample time to establish between 133.00 and 134.00 what turned out to be a highly profitable short position.

Another breakaway gap ended that particular decline on June 10, but the rally failed to follow through, the major downtrend resuming for another week before reaching its low at 113.00 on June 21. The overall decline traced a steeper trendline and narrower channel than the preceding March–April uptrend. By a long stretch of the imagination, it is barely possible to discern an inverted head-and-shoulders formation at the culmination of the May–June decline. But even if it were not a mirage, the formation did not unfold as technical theory says it should. After penetrating the ostensible neckline of the inverted head-and-shoulders at 122.00, the contract moved laterally between 121.00 and 124.00 for two weeks and, instead of rallying, plunged to its life-of-contract low of 110.00 on August 9.

But what of the incredible eruption that followed, the wildest and wooliest advance in stock market history? How did the technicians fare during the last two weeks of August while the December Value Line contract catapulted from 110.00 to 127.00, covering more ground in seven days than it did in five weeks in April and May, and again in June and July?

Sad to say, the technicians struck out. They never even got the bat off their shoulders— or head-and-shoulders, if you will.

Why? Because they were lulled by their own selling-climax theory, which holds that a prolonged price decline must culminate in a final, precipitous drop on extremely high volume to clear the way for the advance to follow. This time, the tide turned without a selling climax to mark the low point.

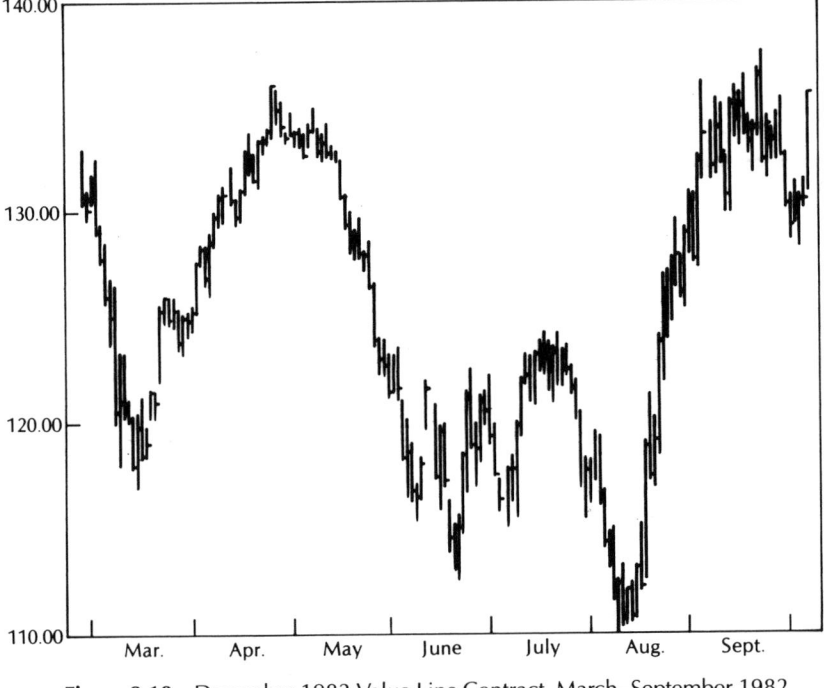

Figure 8.10 December 1982 Value Line Contract, March–September 1982

The irony of the situation, as well as a great source of mortification, was that this may have been the technicians' big chance to prove themselves in the eyes of a Wall Street establishment that had long regarded them as being somewhat suspect. They were interesting to listen to, the traditionalists—fundamentalists nearly to a man (and woman)—thought, but one shouldn't take them too seriously.

But the longer the stock market declined during the spring and into the late summer of 1982, the more talk there was about a selling climax being in the offing. Even straight-laced—not to be confused with straight-arrow—portfolio managers were overheard muttering about what the sentiment indicators portended. Those indicators told them that the market had further to fall. The proportion of cash held in institutional stock portfolios hadn't yet reached the levels attained at previous market bottoms. The bearish sentiment expressed by stock advisory services was still appreciably less than it customarily is just prior to a turnaround.[18]

The mid-August rally was supposedly triggered by a long-awaited decline in interest rates. But then, technicians don't deign to pay attention to such matters as interest rates, money supply growth, and Federal Reserve policy. The effect of all those things is supposed to be revealed to them in their trend channels, triangles, and what have you.

Yes, it was truly a replay of "Casey at the Bat." It was the bottom of the ninth inning, with two out and the bases loaded. The count is three and two. The pitcher scuffs the mound, peers at his catcher's signal, goes into his windup, and lets fly. Called strike three!

As Howard Cosell would say—and probably did—there was no joy in Mudville that night. What did the technicians do? They went back to their drawing boards, of course.

PART 3

The Professionals

CHAPTER 9

The Floor Trader and the Portfolio Manager

Readers who have persevered this far deserve to be commended. The theories, statistics, charts, and tables that comprise the first pages of this book don't make for light reading. If there had been an easier way, rest assured that I would have taken it eagerly. But then, no one ever said—to me, at any rate—that making money is easy. Losing it, perhaps. Making it, no.

In the final analysis—fundamental, technical, or any other kind you'd care to consider—markets aren't made by theories, statistics, charts, and tables; markets are made by people. Their roles, appearance, and attitudes may differ, but they are all trying to make money—for themselves, their firms, or their customers.

The charts and tables may provide some insights as to how the various market participants—floor traders, portfolio managers, brokers, or specialists of one sort or another—go about doing what they do. But the bottom line, to dust off that well-worn expression one last time, is achievement.

Therefore, a fitting way to conclude this book is to turn the spotlight on four of the individuals who, along with thousands of others, make up the stock index futures market and let them tell how they accomplish their jobs.

This is the payoff for staying the course. Listen carefully. These are among the best there are.

Lew Horowitz, Stock Specialist/Index Futures Trader

"If there's a given in this business, it's that you've got to feel good about yourself."

Lew Horowitz looks like a man who feels good about himself. Smartly turned out in a gray, pin-striped suit, pale blue shirt, maroon necktie, and silver collar pin, he appears out of place among the disheveled, mess-jacketed floor traders crowded around the semicircular ring at the New York Futures Exchange. A bystander would take him not for a commodity trader but for an upper-echelon banker or, what he was for twenty-three years, a specialist on the floor of the New York Stock Exchange.

Horowitz also stands out on account of his age. At forty-eight he is something of a father figure on the NYFE floor. Most of the other members are contemporaries of his son, a student in law school. Yet there he is, calling out bids and offers and gesticulating as vigorously as any of them.

What would make a man walk from one of the most prestigious jobs on Wall Street—the two exchanges are scarcely a stone's throw apart—into a melee of men and women half his age who are struggling to launch their careers in a new enterprise, the success of which is by no means assured? Would you call it some sort of commercial noblesse oblige or a form of enlightened self-interest?

When asked, Horowitz cites the challenge of helping the new venture get started and talks of the "ego trip" involved in contributing to NYFE's success. Then he pauses and glances at the luminescent quotations on the video screens overhead.

"Change is a difficult thing for anyone to digest, young or old. The New York Stock Exchange was my home for twenty-three years. Sure, the big institutions will always be buying shares of the IBMs and the General Motors. But I expect that within three years' time, a large proportion of the investor population will be buying and selling stocks via the futures market. Change is coming in front of our eyes in this business. I, the stock exchange, we want to be in on that change."

How is he doing at the new game? I asked. "You can hit one into the stands and then go 0-for-22. That's not at all uncommon down here. You'll have a good morning and a bad afternoon or vice versa. Four months isn't a long enough time to find the magic formula, if there is one. Like any other business, the real secret is staying power, psychologically as well as financially. That's what I mean about feeling good about yourself. Anyone who doesn't have that had better stay away."

A Friend of Trends

Horowitz talked about the different trading styles he's observed around the futures ring. It's the same cast of characters that was encountered in chapter 3 of this book. The scalpers are there, trying to make their "nickels"—that is, the .05-point minimum price fluctuations. The day traders hustle to "even up" their long and short positions by the close of each trading session. And the position traders, appearing less frantic than the others, stand a few steps apart from the fray, content to carry their contracts for a somewhat longer duration.

In which of these categories does he place himself? Horowitz has affixed to his floor member's badge a button that proclaims, "The Trend Is Your Friend." "I'm going to have more of these made up and pass them out around here. It sounds corny, I know, but that's my trading philosophy. After all," he asks rhetorically, "how many times can you be right in a 6 1/2-hour trading day? I'm not going to pooh-pooh anyone's style. As long as it works for him, that's fine. But to make five hundred dollars in the morning and then give three hundred dollars of it back in the afternoon strikes me as a tough way to make a day's pay."

Horowitz speaks of trends within trends. They are the minor fluctuations the scalpers and day traders are intent on capturing. These minitrends can change direction as frequently as seven or eight times during a single trading session. The expression "Go with the flow" is a corollary to "The trend is your friend." According to Horowitz, the futures market may flow in one direction for as little as three "ticks," or minimum fluctuations, and then flow back in the opposite direction. Or the flow may persist in one direction for as long as several days. When it does, he is happy to flow along with it for as long as he can. Mixing his metaphors ever so slightly, he says, "This market is slippery when wet. All you need is music, and you can ice-skate."

Ice-skating or trading, Horowitz's idea of a good day's work is to capture two fifty-point moves with five "lots," or contracts. Without paying brokerage commissions because he is an exchange member, that works out to a daily "wage" of $2,500. Let him enjoy two such days back-to-back, and he promises, "We'll go out to lunch." Day in and day out, he'd be satisfied with making three successful trades a day, each for twenty points on five contracts. That would give him a succession of $1,500 paydays, a level of earnings that could easily absorb the frequent replacement of pin-striped suits frayed by the constant jostling around the trading ring and punctured by the display of "The Trend Is Your Friend" buttons.

To repeat another of Horowitz's favored aphorisms, this type of trading is like eating peanuts—once you start, it's hard to stop. Two successful trades lure you back to the ring for a third attempt. That third try may be the time you give back the morning's profits and something more to boot. How many times can you be right in one day?

The big thing is to exercise discipline. Successful traders know when to stop eating peanuts. When they slip on the ice—and they all do—they know how to cushion the fall to avoid a multiple fracture. Horowitz calls it not tripping over your own ego. (That could be a destructive kind of "ego trip.") There's a fine line, he admits, between having the courage of your convictions while the minitrends are moving against you and refusing to admit that the basic trend that drew you into the market is no longer your friend—that is, it's no longer on your side.

Discipline to Horowitz—as it is to all successful traders—is the ability to acknowledge and to realize a loss before it becomes financially debilitating. A common way of maintaining trading discipline is through the use of mental stops. If, for example, he decided to go long five lots at 99.25 and the contract price subsequently started to fall, Horowitz would be prepared to exercise his mental stop at, say, 98.75. That would produce a $1,250 loss on the five contracts. If that happened to be his first trade of the day, he would then need to put three successful trades back-to-back to realize a $2,500 payday. But the next three trades could turn out to be losing propositions as well. It's a hard way of making a living however you look at it, and a person does indeed need to feel good about himself or herself to succeed at it.

Spotting a Trend

How does a trader determine which trend is his or her friend to begin with? There are a number of techniques, each one as good as the profits a trader can derive by using it. Some rely on a two-hundred-day moving-average crossover signal, similar to the method described in chapter 8.[1] When the moving average crosses from below the last price to above it, it is taken as a signal to assume a long position. When the average crosses from above to below, it's a signal to go short.

Other traders take their cues from the interest rate futures market. We established in chapter 7 that stock prices and interest rates are inversely related. When interest rates drop, stock prices are likely to rally, and when rates rise, stocks will at some point fall off in price. Since bond and Treasury-bill prices also move in inverse relation to yield, traders on the NYFE floor keep a close watch on the activity in those contracts in Chicago, reasoning that a move there one way or the other will spark a similar move in stock index futures.

NYFE traders also follow the trend of index futures prices in Kansas City and Chicago. It is to be expected that the forces that drive the Value Line and S&P 500 contracts up and down will have the same effects on the NYSE Composite contract. If prices in Chicago and Kansas City suddenly start moving up, NYFE traders begin bidding for long positions, thereby pushing their contract up in price. If they see S&P 500s and Value Lines moving down, they offer NYSE contracts for sale. The floor traders at the other two exchanges are watching their counterparts as well, so that the process begins to resemble a game of transcontinental musical chairs.

Lew Horowitz describes himself as a "tick-watcher." If the NYSE Composite contract moves down three ticks—that is, 0.15 points—he is alert to the possibility of a downtrend developing and is primed to offer contracts as a short-seller. If he sees the market move up three ticks, he is poised to go long, on the supposition that there may be an uptrend in the making. He thinks that his three-tick rule will allow him to avoid being buffeted by the "nickel" moves that the scalpers trading next to him are attempting to capture.

He and his fellow traders are still climbing the learning curve on stock index futures, Horowitz freely admits. At the same time, they're trying to avoid taking more spills on the ice than they can help. It's still early in the game for index futures, and from his perspective of twenty-three years on the stock exchange floor, Horowitz is prepared to take the long view.

"Four or five months is too soon to unearth any formulas," he repeats, "but just as the bond futures market tells a story about the [cash] bond market, it's possible that stock futures will in the not-too-distant future tell a story about the stock market itself. That has yet to be ascertained, but it's certainly a possibility."

Subindex Futures and Options

Horowitz also has great expectations for subindex futures contracts and for options on index contracts. He believes that this second and third generation of stock index contracts will open up "a tremendous new world" for both the investing public and professional traders.

In September 1982, approximately four months following the initiation of trading in the NYSE Composite contract, the Commodity Futures Trading Commission approved NYFE's application to trade additional contracts on the stock exchange's industrial, utility, and financial group indexes. Those components of the composite index consisted respectively of the 1,076 industrial, 176 utility, and 222 financial issues listed on the NYSE at that time.[2]

The new subindex contracts would be closer to the Value Line and S&P 500 contracts than to the NYSE Composite in terms of their underlying stock value because the dollar multiplier for the industrial and financial subindex contracts was $1,000, and for the lower utility subindex it was $2,000, substantially higher than the $500 multiple applied to the original composite index contracts.[3]

It was expected that the more specialized subgroup contracts would appeal to portfolio managers and stock specialists because of the better fit they would offer in hedging a particular stock position or portfolio. Public investors and speculators with an interest in a specific industry or stock group would also be attracted to these contracts to a greater extent than they would be to the broader composite indexes.

At about the same time that the regulatory commission gave the green light to the NYFE's subindex contract proposals, the Chicago Mercantile Exchange filed its own application to trade contracts based on the S&P Financial, Utility, and Transportation group indexes. Going one step further toward specialization, the CME and Standard & Poor's Corporation began collaborating in the preparation of contracts based on groups of high-technology, energy, and consumer durable goods stocks.

So as not to be shut out of the running altogether, the Chicago Board of Trade modified its earlier program to propose a new, unaligned fifty-stock index contract even as it appealed the court rulings that had blocked it from introducing a contract based on the Dow Jones Industrial Average. As a fall-back position, the Chicago Board entered into discussions with the Kansas City Board of Trade with a view toward the two exchanges' trading the Value Line Composite Average jointly.

The Chicago Board finally announced in August 1983 that it had reached a licensing agreement with the American Stock Exchange, whereby the board would conduct trading of contracts based on the Market Value Index, consisting of all Amex-listed securities, and on the Major Market Index of twenty blue-chip stocks.

Lew Horowitz is of the opinion that this proliferation of index contracts, much like the proliferation of interest rate contracts five years earlier, is a positive development that will prove beneficial to the financial community and to investors at large. He believes that the introduction of group and specific industry index contracts enhances what he calls "the single selection process." Many stock traders, he points out, act on the basis of their judgment concerning certain industry groups they believe will outperform the stock market as a whole. Only when they've developed an opinion regarding a particular industry—say, airlines—will they address the question of whether to buy (or sell short) Pan Am, Delta, American, TWA, and so forth. To make an informed choice, a diligent trader must perform numerous investigations similar to the General Electric analysis outlined in chapter 6.[4]

The single selection process eliminates the need to conduct such an extensive company-by-company analysis. If, according to Horowitz, an investor favors a particular group or industry, he or she will be better served buying the appropriate specialized futures contract than devoting additional time and effort to picking the cream of the crop. Conversely, if the investor holds a bearish view of a specific industry and there is an applicable industry group contract, why not simply sell that rather than rooting out what he or she believes to be the worst of a supposedly bad lot?

The same line of reasoning applies to portfolio managers who are concerned about a particular industry segment of their overall list. They might sell the relevant group contract to neutralize the market risk of that segment. If they have a bullish view of the prospects for a certain industry, they might buy futures contracts as alternatives to investing in specific stocks.

Limiting Exposure

Limited exposure is Horowitz's key phrase for the new options on indexes and on index futures. In the case of a stock index contract, as with all futures contracts, a trader puts up initial margin to establish a long or short position. Once that margin is paid into his or her account and the position is taken, the trader is fully exposed to the price swings of that contract, be they favorable or adverse. The only way in which that exposure can be eliminated or reduced is by liquidating the contract(s) through an offsetting trade.

Instead of making a margin deposit, a buyer of a put or call option pays a premium for that option. As the word *option* denotes, the buyer has a choice—to exercise the option or not.[5] And, as Horowitz suggests by his use of the term *limited exposure*, the buyer's financial risk is limited to the value of the premium. A trader or investor will in most instances exercise an option only when it's profitable for him or her to do so. Should he or she not choose to exercise, no more is lost than the premium.

As an example, if a trader went long one NYSE Composite Index contract at, say, 90.00, and the contract price then fell to 85.00, he or she would have to liquidate the contract to avoid further loss. If the contract were bought in at 85.00, the trader would realize a $2,500 loss. He or she might instead have decided to take a chance that the market would turn around and to deposit additional margin rather than liquidating. If in that event the contract price dipped further to 80.00, the trader has lost an additional $2,500, for a total loss of $5,000. As Lew Horowitz says, these contracts are slippery when wet, and an unwary trader could very easily slip right down the drain with them.

On the other hand, if the trader bought a call option on the NYSE Composite Index at a strike price of 90.00 for a premium of one point, or $500, he or she would simply allow the option to expire if the index dropped to 85.00 and the total loss would in that case be the $500 premium plus transaction costs. But if, wonder of wonders, the index instead soared to 100.00, the resulting profit of ten points, or $5,000—roughly a 900 percent gain less the premium and transaction costs—goes entirely to the owner of the call. In brief, an option trader gives up part of his or her prospective profit in return for limiting the potential loss to the amount of the premium.

A combination of the two instruments is an option on a futures contract. With this even more esoteric vehicle, a trader might pay a premium for a call option to buy an index futures contract at a particular level or a put option to sell that contract at the same or another level. Again, the appeal of an option on a futures contract is the limitation of risk to the amount of the option premium. The drawback is that while futures traders risk losing a major portion of their initial margin deposit and subsequent maintenance margin deposits, option traders face the certain loss of the entire option premium if the market moves against them and they are unable to exercise the option profitably. That risk is all the greater in the case of options on futures because of their higher degree of volatility.

By the end of 1982, all of the exchanges involved with index futures had applied to the SEC and CFTC for permission to begin trading in associated options as well. The Chicago Board Options Exchange was the first to debut, in March 1983, with options based on its "CBOE 100" index, subsequently renamed the S&P 100. The American Stock Exchange launched trading of its Major Market Index options a month later, and in July added options on the Amex Market Value Index based on the more than eight hundred issues listed there.

The volume of trading in the CBOE's S&P 100 option, soon to be joined by another option contract based on the S&P 500 index, forged ahead of those options offered on the several futures exchanges, in part because the CBOE instruments could be traded by stockbrokers and investors without their having to obtain a separate commodity clearance.

At the close of 1982, the SEC and the CFTC had before them applications by the New York Stock Exchange to trade options on the NYSE Composite spot index and the four subindexes and by the New York Futures Exchange for options on the NYSE Composite futures contract. The Kansas City Board and the Chicago Mercantile Exchange had also filed for approval to trade options on their respective futures contracts. Not to be left out, the American Stock Exchange and the National Association of Securities Dealers requested authorization to introduce options on their respective composite and subindexes.

Specialist Versus Trader

Which is the tougher job, physically and psychologically, maintaining a specialist's book on the stock exchange floor or trading index futures at the NYFE ring? Lew Horowitz thinks that trading futures is more enervating, both physically and emotionally. That's why it's crucial, he says, to "feel good about yourself."

Trading stock under the specialist system involves a certain degree of orchestration. Prospective buyers and sellers on the stock exchange floor generally make their intentions known, and it is the job of the specialist to act as "concert master" in pairing them off.

There is no concert master in the futures ring. There, it's every man and woman for him- or herself. While the stock specialist usually has a moment to pause and think, and to negotiate, there are no such pauses at the trading ring. In that sort of continuous open-outcry market, private negotiations between individual traders are *verboten*. There is no way of telling who the buyers and sellers are, or to what extent, until they call out their bids or offers.

A specialist or any other stock trader can probe the market for temporary price tops and bottoms. Specialists can move against the prevailing trend to some extent—indeed, that is an important part of their obligation to maintain an orderly market—because they have a general sense of where existing buy or sell orders will exert a contrary force. If a specialist thinks that a particular stock will find its temporary bottom around 85, he or she might be moved to buy one hundred shares at 85 1/2 and another one hundred at 85 1/4. If the specialist is wrong and the stock keeps dropping to 84 1/2, he or she has incurred a paper loss of around $175. That's no catastrophe.

But that sort of probing for tops and bottoms can be far more costly in the futures market. If Horowitz is right in stressing that "the trend is your friend"— and most traders would agree with him—those who trade against the trend must be their own worst enemies.

Applying the foregoing prices to a series of futures trades, if an index trader bought two lots at successive prices of 85.50 and 85.25 and then saw the price drop to 84.50, his or her loss would be $875, five times the loss on two hundred shares of stock at those prices. Even at that, futures have the potential of falling still more and at a faster rate than most stocks.

Does he ever wish he were back across the street, serving as concert master at his old post and trading stocks at a more relaxed pace instead of jousting with a crowd of energetic and hungry youngsters in a game that he concedes belongs to them?

Lew Horowitz thinks that forty-eight isn't so old. Besides, a man who feels good about himself should have the imagination and vitality to confront change head on and move with it.[6]

Mark England-Markun, Pension Fund Manager

Mark England-Markun is about the same age as Lew Horowitz's son in law school. But like the elder Horowitz, he dresses like a banker. That should be in no way surprising, inasmuch as England-Markun is a banker. In fact, he is a vice-president of Boston's prestigious State Street Bank and Trust Company. He is also the first pension fund manager in the country to have used stock index futures.

Although England-Markun's hyphenated name suggests that he is descended from British nobility, his roots are in Minnesota. As unhyphenated and untitled Mark England, instructor of economics at the University of Minnesota, he met and was captivated by Ms. Meredith Markun, a graduate student there. Having soon decided to merge their lives in matrimony, the couple elected to merge their names as well. Who said that the Age of Romance is over?

Following a tour at the University of California at Berkeley, the England-Markuns moved to Boston, where the male half of the combined enterprise joined the investment-management department of State Street Bank. The bank had a few years earlier embarked on a major expansion of its institutional investment–management operation with an eye toward securing a share of the rapidly growing pension fund–management business. England-Markun, who had decided to put his theoretical training to practical use, was one of the bright young stars recruited to spearhead this expansion effort.

State Street Bank had long been a major custodian of securities for pension and mutual funds and for other institutional investors. It was a natural step to move from this role to one of master trustee under the Employee Retirement Income Security Act (ERISA) and from there to manager of pension fund portfolios. The bank soon established as a basic investment philosophy the belief that portfolio performance is determined in large part by the allocation of assets held in those portfolios. Asset allocation sets a portfolio's ratio of common stock to bonds or places a relative emphasis on small, emerging companies rather than on large, heavily capitalized corporations. The portfolio managers at State Street Bank have from the outset acted on the premise that such determinations affect investment performance to a greater extent than individual stock selection or market timing.

Matching the Market

As contrasted with the judgmental and stock-selection approach followed by many investment managers, the managers at State Street believe that attempts to call precise turns in the stock and bond markets add little if anything to investment performance. If the best that a portfolio manager can hope to accomplish over an extended period is to match the overall performance of the stock market, it would save a lot of wear and tear on everyone concerned to simply assemble a portfolio that duplicates the stocks included in one of the broadly based market indexes.

In line with this philosophy, the first investment-management product the bank offered to prospective national institutional clients was a commingled or pooled fund made up of virtually all the stocks contained in the S&P 500 Composite Index. The stocks in the fund would be weighted by their capitalization in the same manner as the index itself.[7] By duplicating for all practical purposes the S&P 500, the State Street managers were assured of matching the behavior of the stock market as measured by that indicator.

The index fund concept was well received by institutional investors, and State Street Bank's client list and assets under management grew rapidly from the time of the fund's introduction. By the end of 1982, the bank had been selected by a number of *Fortune* 500 corporations throughout the country to manage over $2 1/2 billion in pension assets invested in stock and bond portfolios, plus an approximately equal amount placed in the bank's Short-Term Investment Fund, or STIF, a money market fund for institutional investors. Following the creation of its S&P 500 index fund, the bank offered its clients a broader fund comprised of virtually the entire five-thousand-stock universe in the U.S. stock market.

In addition to being actively involved in the management of State Street's domestic stock portfolios, England-Markun is the head of the bank's foreign investment department and as such is responsible for managing $250 million invested in foreign stocks. The index approach to investment is followed in the foreign sector as well. The department created a national stock index for each of nine major non–North American countries, plus one for each of four regions in the Pacific Basin.

In the foreign equity area, England-Markun and his department take both passive and active approaches to portfolio management. While most of the money under their supervision is invested in all of the stocks that comprise a particular national index, some portfolios have the latitude to change the asset allocation within and between the thirteen national and regional markets.

Using Index Futures

With their heavy involvement in portfolio indexing in both the domestic and foreign sectors, it was natural that the State Street investment managers would be very much aware of the new stock index futures contracts from the outset, especially the one based on the S&P 500 index. As soon as trading in these contracts was initiated, England-Markun and his associates moved to create vehicles and implement strategies with which the bank could enhance its management performance and thus capture an even larger share of the pension fund–management business.

As a master trustee of corporate pension funds, State Street Bank maintains custody of several billion dollars in pension assets, a portion of which is held in the bank's institutional money market fund. This fund contains cash-equivalent investments that the fund managers and the sponsor companies have determined should comprise the liquid reserve of a stock or bond portfolio. The fund also serves as a temporary depository for new pension contributions awaiting investment. To earn some income on these liquid assets, they are invested in such "cash equivalents" as U.S. Treasury bills and certificates of deposit.

Up to a third of these reserve funds—over $800 million—is earmarked for reinvestment in common stock at what is deemed by the managers to be an opportune time. To provide outside fund managers and their clients ongoing exposure to the stock market even while these assets are "parked" in short-term money market instruments, England-Markun and Tom Cooper, an associate, conceived the idea of creating a commingled fund that holds stock index futures as proxies for actual securities. The bank's top management concluded that their proposal had merit and authorized them to proceed.

After the necessary legal and operational groundwork was laid—including clearance from the IRS because of the nontaxable status of pension funds— State Street Bank's Stock Performance Index Futures Fund (or SPIFF, for short) opened for business on September 30, 1982.

SPIFF's managers decided to restrict the futures segment of the fund to S&P 500 contracts, their objective being to provide fund participants with daily exposure to the stock market as represented by the S&P 500 Composite Index. As was the case with the bank's money market fund, a major share of the futures fund's assets, including money earmarked for posting initial margin and any daily variation margin required on the futures contracts, would be invested in Treasury bills and certificates of deposit.

As with the original S&P 500 index fund, the goal of the new fund's managers was to match the performance of that index, with the distinction that futures contracts would be employed as surrogates for the S&P 500 stocks. Owing to the constant shifting of the index futures price structure from premium to discount and back to premium vis-à-vis the actual index, the fund's holders would obtain a better or worse return than the S&P 500 over short periods of time.

Stock-Futures Swap Strategy

A second approach developed by the State Street managers was to capitalize on recurring premium-to-discount moves by periodically shifting from an S&P 500 stock portfolio to futures or vice versa if their respective price levels offered an advantage to being invested in one medium as opposed to the other. For example, soon after this more active approach was undertaken, contracts were purchased at about a 2 percent discount from the actual index.

During the ensuing week, one in which the stock market advanced sharply, the contract price rose to a 2 percent premium. Therefore, over the course of a single week, the fund "outperformed" the S&P 500 spot index by 4 percent, certainly an auspicious beginning. But the managers were aware that the futures component was just as likely to perform relatively worse than the actual index during the succeeding weeks. England-Markun and his associates anticipated that over an extended period, the swings from discount to premium and back would cancel out, leaving the fund the duplicate of the general stock market return.

This swap strategy would dictate the purchase of futures when they are at a discount to the spot index and a switch to stock when futures move to a premium. At a minimum, such a strategy should match the return of the S&P 500 index. With judicious swapping if and when opportunities are presented, there is a possibility of achieving a somewhat higher return.[8]

Such an approach requires some fast and fancy footwork. A stock-futures swap will only be made when there is a clear advantage to be gained. With the volatility of futures prices being what it is, that advantage may disappear during the process of accumulating or disposing of five hundred different stocks. For the swap strategy to work, there must be a virtual guarantee that the entire portfolio of S&P 500 stocks can be liquidated at an aggregate price level higher than what the fund will pay for the equivalent futures contracts or can be bought at a level less than the futures sale price.

State Street Bank handles the problem of simultaneous trading by securing from its brokers guaranteed prices for all the shares it plans to buy or sell before executing the futures side of the transaction. The price guarantees are good for a set period, which may range from 1/2 to 1 1/2 hours. During that time the fund managers strive to obtain the desired futures price levels by placing through the brokers stop or limit orders.

England-Markun refers to this swap strategy as "one-sided arbitrage." A so-called pure arbitrage is one in which the same asset is simultaneously bought and sold in different markets for an assured and immediate profit.[9] There is always some price risk when shares or contracts are carried in an open position. But if the bench mark for performance is the S&P 500 index, profits and losses are determined by whether futures can be bought for relatively less and sold for relatively more than the spot index. England-Markun holds that this can be achieved with a high degree of consistency if the stock-futures swaps can be accomplished at the desired levels.

The chief source of uncertainty in applying the swap strategy arises from the variation or maintenance margin calls that must be met in the event of adverse futures price movement. The withdrawal of cash to meet such calls reduces the interest income earned on the money market segment of the fund. The managers seek to reduce that uncertainty by allotting 10 percent of the liquid portion of the fund for the purpose of making maintenance margin payments and by matching the maturities of the certificates of deposit carried in the fund with the expiration dates of the futures contracts.

Employing statistical techniques developed at the bank, the managers claim a 95 percent level of confidence that the differential they seek to capture by their swap operations will in fact enhance the fund's return. For example, if futures are either purchased or sold to secure for the fund a return 2.5 percent greater than that offered by the stock market as reflected by the S&P 500 index, there is a 95 percent probability that the fund will realize an advantage from its swap operations ranging from 2.3 percent to 2.7 percent. The usual problem with these sophisticated swapping games is that as more players become involved, especially big ones like State Street Bank, the sought-after price differences between the two markets become narrower and ultimately disappear.

England-Markun admits that neither he nor anyone else can know with certainty whether there will continue to be times when owning contracts is more attractive than owning stocks. He is inclined to believe, however, that large institutions like State Street Bank will not immediately eliminate the price differentials between stocks and related futures contracts. Even if that should occur, he is confident that such contracts will continue to play a useful role in investment management. That applies even at what he calls "neutral price levels," which means the absence of any premiums or discounts. If nothing else, there is an advantage to owning futures at neutral levels and thereby avoiding the operational routine of buying and selling five hundred stocks, collecting dividends, and monitoring the corporate activities of that many companies.

Fine-Tuning and Other Uses

Beyond the daily market exposure and stock-futures swap strategies he has already implemented, England-Markun has considered other uses for stock index futures. Since general stock market exposure is an integral part of State Street's investment philosophy, he does not think that what he calls "pure" hedging of individual stock selections will be frequently employed at the bank, though other managers might make more extensive use of that type of hedging.

As their swap strategy indicates, the State Street managers are inclined to apply stock index futures more imaginatively than merely for hedging away market risk. They believe, for example, that futures may be profitably employed to fine-tune a portfolio's market exposure. As England-Markun explains the concept, he may be managing an equity portfolio that has a target market exposure of 1.0 as measured by a beta value of that amount. Yet as a result of individual stock selection, the portfolio may have an aggregate beta value of, say, 1.1, or a 10 percent greater market exposure than his or the pension fund sponsor's established policy for that portfolio. A possible response is to alleviate the excess market exposure by selling index futures contracts short.[10]

The reverse situation may also arise. If, because of a security-by-security selection process, a portfolio falls short of its targeted market exposure, additional exposure may be built into it by means of going long futures contracts.

There should be further opportunities to fine-tune stock portfolios if and when futures contracts on particular market sectors or subsectors become extensively traded. The same sort of one-sided arbitrage that is performed in relation to the S&P 500 index may be conducted with a smaller group of stocks that comprise a specific industry group.

Subsector index contracts may also be used to neutralize what England-Markun calls "unintended industry bets." As part of its investment-management research effort, State Street Bank ranks monthly up to seven hundred stocks on the basis of its own in-house research and information obtained from outside sources. In placing the highest-ranked stocks into various portfolios, the managers may inadvertently obtain a concentration in one or more industry groups that they did not plan on having.

Where managers do not feel that an overweighting or underweighting in particular industry groups is warranted, they may restore the desired balance by going short or long the appropriate subsector or industry-specific futures contracts. In his offhand jargon, England-Markun says the subsector contracts would allow managers to place bets on the companies they like, when they like, while at the same time keeping their industry bets neutral. "Pure stock pickers," he points out, are good at making relatively narrow judgments within very narrow groups—that is, they see the trees but not the forest. Yet most of the returns on managed portfolios are not the result of those judgments but are instead due to the fact that the consequent industry group exposure differs accidently from the bench mark to which it is compared. Subsector contracts allow managers to keep their industry exposure intentional.

Expanding Exposure—and Leverage

Index contracts also allow a manager to create a portfolio that has a greater than 1.0 exposure to the stock market. If a hypothetical equity portfolio were valued at, say, $10 million and the manager buys enough index futures contracts to bring the portfolio's underlying equity value up to $12 million, he or she has created a 1.2 exposure to the stock market.

Such a strategy would be helpful to managers (and to individual traders) who have confidence in their own market-timing abilities. The way in which portfolio managers have traditionally implemented their timing decisions has been by switching their portfolios out of stocks and into cash or bonds. It can under certain circumstances be more efficient to move from, say, a 1.2 exposure to minus 1.0 by selling short futures contracts with an underlying market value approximately twice the value of the portfolio. By adjusting the futures position, managers may implement any reasonable range of market bets—pro- or antimarket—that fits their timing considerations.

Pension fund sponsors—that is, the corporations themselves—are becoming increasingly explicit in directing their managers to adhere to a predetermined market exposure and are often inclined to select managers who have been successful in maintaining the desired type of exposure in the past. Stock index futures are one means by which portfolio managers may quickly and economically implement asset allocation decisions.

England-Markun cites another advantage to holding futures contracts in lieu of stocks in some portion of the portfolio. If a manager fine-tunes a portfolio to achieve a 1.5 exposure to the stock market by going long index contracts, he or she is in effect financing one-third of the portfolio—created by the 0.5 futures component—at the so-called risk-free borrowing rate. In other words, the manager is obtaining low-cost leverage to provide a higher return on each dollar invested in the fund.

Leverage is difficult for pension funds to obtain, since they are precluded by law from borrowing. They must resort to indirect methods, such as investing in the shares of corporations that have leverage. But by holding a portion of their portfolios in the form of futures contracts, funds are in effect borrowing at the risk-free rate and are thereby accorded access to an additional source of leverage.

For example, instead of being 60 percent invested in stock and 40 percent in bonds, a portfolio might achieve a higher return through leverage by owning 59 percent stock, 39 percent bonds, and having the remaining 2 percent invested in a fund that contains futures contracts with a greater than 1.0 market exposure.

Such an approach is preferable, England-Markun believes, to reaching for greater market exposure through the purchase of high-beta-value stocks. Once a portfolio rises above the 1.25-beta range, the number of qualified stocks with beta values at that level declines to a relative handful. Therefore, as a portfolio moves higher up the market-exposure curve, a greater proportion of the portfolio's risk consists of specific company risk, and a steadily smaller share is the market risk that the manager is seeking to increase by raising the portfolio's beta value. Resort to the futures market affords the manager the undiluted market risk that he or she wants to build into the portfolio.

In addition to the theoretical and operational wrinkles that remain to be ironed out in the institutional use of stock index futures, there remain some formidable legal and regulatory obstacles. For example, regulations governing the investment of pension money make it difficult for pension funds to open margin accounts with brokers. The objection is that by maintaining a margin account, the fund's trustee is surrendering some control over the fund's assets.

Since all futures transactions are conducted on a margin basis, pension funds until recently have been blocked from directly engaging in the types of portfolio management strategies outlined above.[11]

By creating a commingled fund that invests in futures in part, State Street Bank offered pension funds a means of participating in a portfolio that does what they could not for legal reasons do for and by themselves.

From the fund manager's viewpoint, it is a good deal easier to carry out the relatively sophisticated and complex strategies index futures entail in a single commingled fund vehicle than to try accomplishing the same results for a substantial number of separate accounts.

Mark England-Markun was tired. The stock and futures markets were due to open shortly, and he had a great deal of preparation before the opening bell sounded. The day before had been Columbus Day, a state holiday in Massachusetts. The bank was closed, and he should have been at home enjoying the day with his wife.

But the markets opened as usual, both in the United States and abroad, and a pension client called him at home to say that he wanted to invest $20 million as quickly as possible. It takes time to invest that much money. England-Markun came to the office and remained until 2:00 A.M., putting the $20 million to work in markets around the globe. Now, scarcely seven hours later, the New York and Chicago markets were about to open again.

What's that old saying about keeping bankers' hours?

CHAPTER 10

The Entrepreneur and the CEO

Marty Koenig no longer keeps bankers' hours. Marty Koenig, Jr., probably wishes that he did. Marty, Jr., is seven years old, and since the founding of F. Martin Koenig & Company, his father very often doesn't get home early enough to read him a bedtime story.

For fourteen years, as a research analyst and portfolio manager with New York's Chase Manhattan Bank, Marty Koenig's investment credo was: "One of the best ways to make money is to avoid losing it; and one of the best ways to lose money is to take too much risk." That's an apt philosophy for a professional arbitrageur. And it's one that Koenig took with him when he left the bank in 1982 to launch his own investment counseling firm.

It was not a coincidence that Koenig & Company opened its doors scarcely a month following the advent of stock index futures. To some extent, the start-up of the Value Line contract in Kansas City was confirmation for the Chase portfolio manager that the world at large was about to embrace the sophisticated type of investing he had been doing for the bank's clients for more than six years.

But where State Street Bank's Mark England-Markun came to use stock index futures by way of his bank's sponsorship of an S&P 500 index fund, Marty Koenig approached them via the market for listed puts and calls. So it was that while England-Markun was the first pension fund manager to employ stock index futures in 1982, Koenig a half dozen years before was one of the first managers to use options in pension fund portfolios.

There was no listed option market when Koenig joined Chase in 1968. The Chicago Board Options Exchange was established five years later, and another five years would elapse before pension funds and other institutional investors would begin to regard option-related investment strategies as being a conservative, and therefore acceptable, means of increasing their rates of return. Chase Investors Management Corp., the investment arm of Chase, was among the first of the major institutions to develop an interest in the new medium, and in 1975 Koenig was assigned the task of determining whether and how options might be employed to improve the performance of portfolios under the bank's management. He was shortly thereafter named head of the Option Investments Division at Chase Investors and over the ensuing six years built the division's business to the point of managing about $260 million using options and related investments.

Buyers and sellers of futures contracts are at risk for the entire price movement of the assets underlying the contracts. The holder of a long contract gains dollar-for-dollar as the contract price rises above his or her purchase price and loses dollar-for-dollar as the market price drops below. Conversely, the holder of a short contract gains dollar-for-dollar when the market price falls below the sale price and loses in like amount as the price moves above it.

While gains and losses on put and call options are tied to the price movement of their underlying stocks, it is not always a dollar-for-dollar relationship. Moreover, option buyers and sellers have unequal exposure to upward and downward movements in stock price. Buyers of call options participate fully in upward price movement less the cost of the call or the premium, but they are only at risk for the amount of the premium if the stock should drop in price. Sellers or writers of calls are fully exposed to the downward movement in the stock less the amount of the premium, and profit by no more than the value of the premium when the stock rises.[1] The reverse relationships apply in the case of put options.

Because of the differences in market exposure, and hence in profit potential and risk, options and futures on the same underlying assets have different price characteristics. That in itself presents profit opportunities for astute traders. The proposed introduction of put and call options on both stock index futures contracts and the actual indexes holds out the prospect of an added dimension of profit potential for experts who can recognize and are able to exploit the price differences between these related but dissimilar instruments.

A New Firm Bows

Marty Koenig was prepared to do precisely that. Koenig established his firm to manage large institutional portfolios on a discretionary basis, meaning that he and his associates would be fully responsible for deciding what securities should be bought and sold for the portfolios and when those purchases and sales should be made. Having started in business with $40 million under management as a result of the connections, experience, and reputation he gained during his years at Chase Manhattan Bank, Koenig regarded the assortment of index instruments and options on individual stocks as likely vehicles to improve portfolio performance at relatively low levels of risk. In the highly competitive—and lucrative—pension fund management business, superior performance brings new clients with millions of dollars to invest knocking on the office door. Koenig & Company was counting on its expertise in these derivative instruments to be its winning edge in bringing a fair share of these pension assets through its door. That, appropriately enough, was at 50 Broadway, just around the corner from the NYSE and the NYFE.

The Koenig firm—consisting of three portfolio managers and support staff in addition to Koenig himself—performs both fundamental and technical analysis and relies heavily on computerized models in arriving at individual stock selections and in making portfolio timing decisions. The firm's unique character and primary strength lie in the ability of the managers to increase a portfolio's return without raising its risk component proportionately. They are able to achieve this desirable result by combining traditional stock-selection and timing techniques with a variety of investment strategies involving options, stock index futures, and the full spectrum of related hybrid instruments.

A series of computer models are employed to screen a universe of some nine-hundred-odd stocks for their intrinsic value à la Graham and Dodd. Two such fundamental valuation models scan the nine hundred companies for their earnings momentum and cash-flow plowback qualities. The earnings estimates that are developed for a particular company by security analysts tend to follow a protracted trend. It is often possible to anticipate from that trend the direction of estimated earnings revisions and, accordingly, the likely direction of future stock price movement. Stocks on the screening list that display an upward trend of earnings estimate revisions are from that standpoint considered attractive for investment. Stocks with consistently downward revisions are generally avoided.

The cash-flow plowback model measures relative value in terms of a company's cash flow (earnings plus depreciation charges), dividends, assets, liabilities, and stock price. It is a three-part mathematical model, of which the first part calculates the "plowback percentage," or cash flow retained after dividend payments as a percentage of total invested assets. The second part determines a stock's "plowback multiple" by dividing its price/cash-flow multiple by the plowback percentage. The third and final part of this model computes the stock's "relative plowback multiple" by dividing its plowback multiple by the average plowback multiple of the nine hundred stocks under review. The relative plowback multiple is a measure of a company's relative cost of internal growth. The lower its relative plowback multiple, the more attractive its stock is deemed to be.

The Koenig firm's other fundamental models evaluate the list of nine hundred stocks according to each company's anticipated stream of dividends discounted to present value, price/earnings ratio, dividend yield, earnings retention, earnings uncertainty, sales growth, and profit margin trend.

As Graham and Dodd noted fifty years ago, a considerable period of time may elapse before the market recognizes a stock's intrinsic value. Investors who buy or sell stocks strictly according to fundamentals must therefore be prepared to exercise patience and fortitude until the rest of the investment world comes around to their way of thinking.

To buy stocks closer to the time when they're "discovered" by the market at large, and thereby achieve a higher rate of return on clients' invested capital, Koenig & Company complements its fundamental research with a set of technical tools, which it calls market sponsorship models. Some of these models are derived from the firm's quantitative work in option pricing. Others track such factors as trend deviation, order flow, and the trading volume for individual stocks.

Each stock on the research list is assigned a one-to-nine ranking on the basis of its fundamental and technical computer screening. Stocks that are ranked one through three are considered attractive for purchase. Those ranked seven through nine are sale candidates, and those that fall in the middle ground from four through six are regarded as adequately priced holdings.

An Esoteric Art . . . Or a Science?

As was noted above, Koenig & Company combines its stock-selection and timing discipline with related investment strategies involving put and call options. As they try to do with the underlying stocks, the managers seek to buy puts and calls they consider to be undervalued and to sell those that they believe to be overvalued.

The art and/or science of option valuation is an esoteric one that ventures into the realm of higher mathematics. The so-called strike price at which an option may be exercised and its term to expiration are two major determinants of premium values. Another pair of determinants are the volatility of an option's underlying stock and the option's theoretical return—that is, the interest difference between the dividend yield on the underlying stock and the Treasury-bill or risk-free interest rate.

All things being equal, and assuming no special information regarding the expected return for individual stocks, the volatility of the underlying stock is treated as a proxy for the stock's potential rate of return. An option buyer will usually be willing to pay more for a put or call option on a stock that has the potential of going up or down twenty points than for an option on a stock that he or she thinks will rise or fall only ten points in the same time period. The wider price movement offers the buyer a better chance of exercising the option to buy or sell at a profit.

An option buyer doesn't receive the dividend he or she would be paid had the actual stock been bought. On the other hand, having put up only the amount of the premium, the buyer is free to invest the balance of what he or she would otherwise have paid for the stock in some money market instrument. The difference between the dividend rate on the underlying stock and the money market rate is the yield benefit of owning the option in lieu of the stock.

When money market rates exceed dividend yields by a substantial margin—dividends yielding 6 percent versus certificates of deposit at 17 1/2 percent, for example—call options will generally be priced at approximately twice the time premium of puts on the same underlying stock with an identical strike price and expiration. On the other hand, when money market rates are approximately equal to dividend yields, the time premiums of puts and calls on the same stock with the same strike price and expiration should be approximately equal to each other.

But like stocks, puts and calls rarely sell at their fair or intrinsic values for any extended period. A portfolio manager who can consistently recognize under- and overvalued options, buy the undervalued, and sell the overvalued can build a winning edge into a portfolio's overall performance.

Koenig's Strategy

Koenig & Company did well for its clients employing these specialized techniques during the firm's first half-year in business. Strangely, it did so by being long stock as the market was going down and then reversing its position and going short when the market rallied. That is precisely the opposite of what one would think is the proper way to make money in the stock market. But upon closer examination it was not so strange, considering the fact that the stock position was but one component of a stock-options "package" that was carefully designed to give a portfolio favorable market exposure with considerably less than comparable market risk.

The strategy unfolded somewhat like this: from June through the first week of August 1982, Koenig's basic position was a combination of long puts and long stock at a greater than 1:1 ratio to the related stock. A put is an option to sell one hundred shares of a particular stock at a specified price. As the market price of the stock declines, the value of the put rises because it becomes increasingly profitable to buy shares at the prevailing market price and deliver them upon exercising the put at a higher strike price.

Puts that are one strike price–interval "out of the money"—that is, those with a strike price below the stock's market price—will generally have a statistically determined hedge ratio of about 0.33. That means that over brief periods of time and for small fluctuations in a stock's price, the put will move up or down in the same direction about 1/3 point for each point that the underlying stock moves. For larger moves, the hedge ratio changes. If, for example, the market price of a stock is 100 and the strike price of a put on that stock is 90, within a price-fluctuation range of approximately 99 to 101, the 0.33 ratio will apply even though the put is 10 points out of the money (100 − 90) and will not become profitable to exercise until such time as the stock may drop below 90.

Employing a 0.33 hedge ratio, Koenig's client portfolios held three long puts for each one hundred shares of the underlying stock. So long as the stock price remained around the 99–101 range, therefore, the portfolio was neutrally hedged, with the aggregate value of the three puts rising or falling dollar-for-dollar with the stock but in the opposite direction. "At the money options"— where the option strike price and the market price of the stock are approximately equal—typically have a hedge ratio of 0.50 to 0.60. Thus, a neutral hedge "at the money" would entail two options for every one hundred shares of stock.

The key feature of this long-stock and ratioed-long-put position is that the more the stock drops below 100, the greater the hedge ratio becomes, resulting in a proportionately greater gain on the three puts than the offsetting loss in the stock. When the puts move into the money as the stock drops below 90, the hedge ratio approaches 1:1, and the three puts are compiling gains at a rate three times the growing loss on the stock.

Conversely, if the price of the stock climbs to 110, where the puts are 20 points out of the money, the hedge ratio would drop to a very small figure— say, 0.15 or less. From that point, the stock would be appreciating at a faster rate than the puts are falling in value.

For small movements in the stock price, then, the long-stock-and-ratioed-long-put position is neutrally hedged. But for substantial price moves in either direction, the portfolios are positioned to register substantial gains. Profits, whether the market moves up or down, sound too good to be true—the fabled free lunch traders are eternally dreaming about. But we've already ascertained that there is no such thing as a free lunch, and so there must be a hitch somewhere in this dazzling scheme.

The hitch is that puts are wasting assets. As such, they have no value past their expiration date. If the puts are bought at an overvalued level and drop to their fair value or become undervalued, the ratioed position incurs a loss due to a decline in the put premium. If the puts can be purchased at an undervalued level, as Koenig managed to do in June 1982, and little time elapses, the ratio strategy entails very little risk.

Two Examples

One example involves our old friend from chapter 6, General Electric. Koenig bought 2,000 shares of GE on August 5 at 63 5/8 and the same day went long 40 GE puts at 3 3/8 for a hedge ratio of 2:1 (40 puts equals 4,000 shares). By August 12, GE stock had fallen 5/8 point to 63, while the puts had appreciated 1 3/8 to 4 3/4. The total market value of the combined stock-put position on August 12 was $145,000, versus a combined cost on August 5 of $140,687. Although the stock declined slightly in that one-week period, because the position was short twice as much GE in the form of puts as it was long in shares and because of a big expansion in the put premium, the combined position scored a gain of $4,313.

By the second week of August, puts had become greatly overpriced relative to calls as interest rates continued their rapid descent. Stocks had meanwhile also declined sharply. At that point, Koenig reversed his market exposure by moving from a long to a short stock position, selling the overpriced puts and buying calls at a 2:1 or 3:1 ratio. His expectation was that as the stock market rallied, the long calls would appreciate at a much faster rate than the short stock incurred a loss. That is in fact what happened. On the other hand, he knew that if the market moved down again, the calls would only drop by a finite amount—the premium itself—while the short stock position became increasingly profitable. Moreover, the short sale of stock created a credit in the brokerage account that could be invested in the money market to raise the level of return.

Typical of this position, between August 24 and 27 Koenig bought 150 American Express calls with a strike price of 45 at prices ranging from 1 1/4 to 1 3/4 for an average price of 1.42. During the same four-day period, he sold short 8,000 shares of American Express stock at an average price of about 45 to establish a hedge ratio of nearly 2:1.

By August 31 the short stock had moved up in price to 46 1/4 for a net loss of $10,437. The call premiums meanwhile rose to 3 3/8 for a gain of $29,375. The position had therefore scored a net gain of $18,938 in a one-week period on a net outlay of minus $338,000, meaning that the short sale proceeds exceeded the cost of the calls by that amount. Including the interest earned on the short sale proceeds would have increased the rate of return on the transaction.

Transactions of this sort are beyond the experience of most investors, even institutions. But buying and selling options was what Koenig had been doing at Chase Investors for six years. To him, it was simply a case of buying a relatively cheaper asset (a put) and, when it became in his opinion overpriced, selling it and buying another relatively cheaper asset (a call). With the advent of stock index futures, options on index futures, and options on actual indexes, the added permutations and combinations would give him an even wider range of price relationships with which to fine-tune his portfolios' net market exposure, enhancing their rates of return while maintaining risk at a relatively modest level.

Some Stock Futures Strategies

How, then, do stock index futures and their related option instruments lend themselves to this kind of trading or investing? Koenig sees the same types of transactions as those described above being made more efficiently and at less cost with index futures and options on index futures than with puts and calls on individual securities.

Describing a strategy similar to Mark England-Markun's swap program at State Street Bank in Boston, Koenig outlines a sequence of going long the stock index and short the related futures contract when the latter is believed to be overpriced relative to money market rates of return and the reverse—going short the index and long the futures contract when the contract is considered underpriced relative to money market rates.

There is also the strategy of putting together hybrid hedges that seek to take advantage of a manager's stock-selection ability. Such a strategy would involve using either puts and calls or underlying stock against futures contracts.

Hedging is defined as the process of taking an equal and opposite position in a derivative market as a substitute for a later transaction in a related cash market. Table 4.9 in chapter 4 depicts a situation in which the gain on a short futures position matches the decrease in a portfolio's aggregate value plus the cash-futures basis.[2]

As an alternative to hedging with futures contracts, a portfolio manager may elect to employ a so-called *delta* or *combination* hedge using put and call options. Tables 10.1 and 10.2 show the comparable results obtained by hedging a $10-million portfolio with index futures and options. It is assumed in both cases that the hypothetical portfolio is sufficiently diversified so that changes in the portfolio match the movements in the stock index on which the futures and options are based. That is to say, there is no substantial basis risk. In reality, this is usually an unrealistic assumption for broad-based stock indexes.

Selling or writing the number of calls that equal the reciprocal of the options hedge ratio—that is, the delta—effectively hedges small changes in the stock index and the aggregate value of the portfolio. But as Koenig demonstrated in his long-stock-and-long-put and short-stock-and-long-call ratio-hedge strategies, an option's hedge ratio changes markedly with substantial changes in the stock or index price. Changes in hedge ratios caused by price

Table 10.1 Common Stock Portfolio Hedge with Futures

Common Stock Portfolio	Stock Index Futures
Establish Hedge	
Diversified common stock portfolio with current market value of $10 million when S&P 500 index is 150.00	Sell 130 S&P 500 futures contracts at 154.60 valued at $10.05 million
Terminate Hedge	
Portfolio is worth $9.25 million when S&P 500 index is 140.00	Buy 130 S&P 500 futures contracts at 142.40 valued at $9.256 million
Hedge Results	
Market loss on stock portfolio is $750,000	Gain on futures position is $794,000
Net gain on hedged portfolio is $44,000	

SOURCE: Adapted from a similar hedge example in Eugene Moriarty, Susan Phillips, and Paula Tosini, "A Comparison of Options and Futures in the Management of Portfolio Risk," *Financial Analyst's Journal*, January–February 1981, 65.

movements require repeated adjustments in the number of written options to preclude the stock portfolio's becoming overhedged or underhedged.

Because of price volatility and changing hedge ratios, delta hedging of a stock portfolio with options over a protracted period involves significant transaction and other friction costs. Such a strategy, moreover, would entail assuming simultaneous positions in three separate markets at equilibrium price levels. Futures contracts are usually more efficient hedging instruments under such circumstances because a single futures position will generally suffice to neutralize the market exposure of the stock portfolio.

Another application of options is the purchase of calls to hedge the value of securities held in a portfolio. While affording some protection against a decline, the calls allow participation in any upward movement in price. There is no comparable risk-limiting instrument available in the futures market, although a similar result may in some instances be obtained by the use of stop-loss orders entered above short futures positions, when such short positions are maintained against long positions in the underlying portfolio of stocks.

One detailed analysis of the similarities and differences between futures and options concluded that, while in theory futures and options on the same underlying asset may be considered as similar, in practice, substitution is likely

Table 10.2 Common Stock Portfolio Hedge with Options

Common Stock Portfolio	Stock Index Options
Establish Hedge	
Diversified common stock portfolio with current market value of $10 million when S&P 500 index is 150.00	Sell 130 S&P 500 150 calls for $550,000 and buy 130 S&P 500 150 puts for $440,000
Terminate Hedge	
Portfolio is worth $9.25 million when S&P 500 index is 140.00	Calls have no intrinsic value; sell puts for $650,000
Hedge Results	
Market loss on stock portfolio is $750,000	Retain $550,000 premium on calls; gain on puts is $210,000
Net gain on hedged portfolio is $10,000	

SOURCE: Adapted from a similar hedge example in Eugene Moriarty, Susan Phillips, and Paula Tosini, "A Comparison of Options and Futures in the Management of Portfolio Risk," *Financial Analyst's Journal,* January–February 1981, 65.

to be limited. In addition to the considerable cost involved in simulating a futures position with options, the study maintained that futures and options are each best suited to different risk-management objectives and that, "futures are better employed as hedging instruments and options as risk-limiting or income-generating instruments."[3]

From his unique vantage point, Marty Koenig believes otherwise. Koenig thinks that in some instances, put and call combinations may be used as substitutes for stock index futures or for the indexes themselves, and vice versa. Moreover, rather than considering that one instrument is liable to crowd out the other, he believes that stock index options and options on stock index futures are necessary to allow the index futures market to realize its full potential.

"Synthetic Contracts"

By way of making his point, Koenig cites an instance where an arbitrageur creates a "synthetic stock" by buying an undervalued call and selling an overvalued put. The long call gives the arbitrageur upmarket exposure, and the short put gives him or her downmarket risk, with the proceeds from the sale of the put serving to finance all or part of the purchase of the call. So far as Koenig is concerned, that combination is often better than owning the actual stock, in that the investor has established a market position by putting up very little if any of his or her own money.

Koenig anticipates the same type of opportunities arising with stock index futures and options. Now that trading has started in the companion option instruments, he believes that it is possible to buy undervalued calls and sell overvalued puts on an index futures contract in lieu of buying the contract itself. To Koenig's way of thinking, such "synthetic contracts" will enable traders to own futures much more efficiently. As an added benefit, the money that would normally be allotted to buying stock or index contracts outright may be invested in the money market, thereby increasing the total return of this synthetic investment.

By selling an overvalued call and buying an undervalued put, using the proceeds from the former to finance all or part of the latter, a trader may create a synthetic short position in a stock or some other underlying security. Again, the same type of exposure may be created by selling calls and buying puts on stock index futures contracts.

One feature of the stock index futures market that has impeded two-way arbitrage and has therefore restricted the development of liquidity in the market is the absence of any satisfactory means by which index futures contracts may be arbitraged against their related indexes. Although it is possible to buy shares of an index mutual fund and sell an equivalent number of index futures contracts, the inability to sell open-end mutual fund shares short makes it difficult to carry out the reverse transaction. While one-sided arbitrage can narrow the gap if the futures price moves too far above the actual index, there is accordingly no way at present by which arbitrageurs can act to restore cash-futures equilibrium when the futures price falls too far below the index.

But with options available on the actual indexes and on the related futures contracts, two-sided arbitrage is possible by creating the actual index synthetically with puts and calls in the manner described above. When the actual index and the related futures price move too far apart, dealers can bring the prices back into line by selling the more expensive instrument and buying the less expensive one. When this two-sided arbitrage occurs, the stock index futures market more closely resembles a traditional carrying charge market rather than being markedly influenced by trader expectations, as it was during the first half-year of its existence.

This type of arbitrage is almost exclusively the province of the broker-dealer community. Institutions and private traders who pay brokerage commissions and do not have access to high leverage normally would not find the margin of potential profit sufficient to attract their involvement in this type of trading.

They would be beneficiaries, however, because arbitrage invests the market with the depth and liquidity large institutions require before undertaking the various types of hedging strategies the futures exchanges are eagerly promoting.

The futures and related option markets also offer institutions access to a permissible new source of leverage, allowing them to achieve attractive rates of return at reduced risk on very low equity. While the margin buyer of stock is required to put up 50 percent of the stock's purchase price, nonhedgers deposit a 10 percent performance bond or initial margin to trade futures, and bona fide hedgers pay even less. By being able to buy and sell individual stocks and entire portfolios "synthetically" by means of stock index futures and options, adept portfolio managers may obtain increased leverage at the same time that they secure a low-risk position.

Working Harder and Longer

With all of these vistas opening, and given Marty Koenig's special brand of expertise, it would be hard to imagine F. Martin Koenig & Company *not* opening its doors in the spring of 1982. Considering the fact that becoming his own boss was a lifetime aspiration, the decision to go out on his own was probably well-nigh inevitable.

"If I had done this three or four years ago, I'd have had a hard time," he ruminates, "because the market wasn't ready for our product. Today, with stock index futures and the other new products coming on, the market is definitely ready for what we're doing."

Like most new entrepreneurs—at least those who are determined to be successful—Koenig finds himself working harder and not getting paid as much as his former earnings at the bank. But he is convinced that the potential rewards are great and feels that the psychic income from running his own business is far more gratifying.

Does he ever have any trouble sleeping? No, says Koenig. All of his firm's portfolio positions are hedged, and he has no cause to worry on that account. When he finds himself under the pressure of deadlines, he'll occasionally work through the night to complete a job so that he won't have to worry about it. But when he does sleep, he sleeps very well.

Wall Street is a very competitive place. Those who set their sights high, as Marty Koenig clearly has, must expect to work through the night once in a while.

Marty, Jr., doesn't know what an entrepreneur is yet and wishes that his dad still kept bankers' hours. His dad's competitors probably wish the same thing.

Walt Vernon, Innovative Underdog

"This thing is too big for Kansas City. We should give it to New York or Chicago."

That remark was allegedly made by a high official of the Commodity Futures Trading Commission, the agency charged by law with considering the disposition of the several stock index contract proposals submitted to it by the various commodity exchanges. Walt Vernon would like to think that it's sheer hearsay. But, then, you never know.

We were introduced to Walter N. Vernon III earlier in this book. As executive vice-president, secretary, and chief executive officer of the Kansas City Board of Trade, he and his associates had struggled for over four years against regulatory, political, and competitive opposition to win approval to trade the Value Line stock index contract.[4] But to Vernon the victory was less than sweet. He wonders if it may have come too late. Perhaps the regulator was right.

Maybe the Kansas City wheat traders had overreached themselves. After all, what did they know about securities, let alone the complexities of index trading? But in 1982 what did anyone know about that? And, to be sure, the Chicago crowd were wheat people also, even if they traded a different kind of wheat.

There are five commercial varieties of wheat grown in the United States: soft red winter, hard red winter, hard red spring, winter and spring white, and Durham. Spring wheat is so named because it is planted in the spring and harvested in late summer. The winter varieties are planted in the fall. They lie dormant over the winter, grow rapidly during the spring, and are harvested in early summer. Winter wheat is generally planted in areas that experience moderate winters and usually provides a higher-yielding crop than does the spring variety. Durham wheat is the primary ingredient for pasta.

Hard red winter wheat is grown primarily in the central and southern sectors of the Great Plains region of the United States, specifically Kansas, Nebraska, Oklahoma, Montana, Texas, and Colorado. Soft red winter is grown to the east, principally in Illinois, Missouri, Ohio, and Indiana. Hard winter wheat requires less moisture and has a higher protein content than soft wheat.

Differences in soil and climatic conditions determine the geographic distribution of the various varieties. That distribution is the reason different wheat contracts are traded in Kansas City and Chicago. The Kansas City contract specifies the delivery of hard winter wheat. The larger Chicago market basically trades a soft wheat contract.

Soft wheat was the principal variety grown in the United States until the mid–nineteenth century, when a type of hard winter wheat known as Turkey red was introduced. The Mennonites, a fundamentalist Christian sect, migrated from western Europe into czarist Russia in the late eighteenth century, fleeing military conscription and what were to them other forms of religious persecution. Less than a century later, and for much the same reasons, the group migrated again, this time to the United States. The migrants brought with them the Turkey red strain, which had yielded them good crops during their sojourn in the Ukraine.

Ironically, it was the crop failures in that very region during the early 1970s that impelled the Soviet Union to purchase from the United States the same variety of hard winter wheat that was taken out by the Mennonite emigrants in the 1870s. It was these huge export orders that rejuvenated the Kansas City Board of Trade and prompted its members to consider the development of new contracts. Apart from the cyclical nature of the world wheat markets, the board's directors realized the need to diversify beyond a single, specialized contract.

A "Stock Market Contract"

In search of ideas, the new contract committee of the exchange retained Dr. Roger Gray, a faculty member at Stanford University's Food Research Institute and a nationally recognized commodity scholar. Even though it had no immediate connection with food, the Stanford consultant took the opportunity to suggest that the committee consider his pet notion of a stock market contract. He reasoned that as "commodities," stocks meet the two primary conditions for a successful futures contract: stocks are widely held, and they are subject to wide price changes.

The concept of a stock futures contract was not original. The Chicago Board of Trade reportedly had floated the idea before the Securities and Exchange Commission in the late 1960s and was told in no uncertain terms by the SEC to stick to wheat and corn. An attempt was made to establish some sort of index contract in Europe several years later, but the project never got off the ground. A more successful "market" consisted of the bets that London bookmakers— or, as they prefer to be called, "turf accountants"—were accepting on movements in the Dow Jones Industrial Average.

The idea appealed to the people in Kansas City. It had not escaped their notice that neither the Chicago Board of Trade nor the Chicago Mercantile Exchange had stuck to their traditional contracts; they had instead moved to launch highly successful new markets in listed equity options and financial futures. The KCBT's new contract committee became convinced that common stocks were the last great untapped market for innovative futures contracts and made the decision to proceed. The committee anticipated that the newly created Commodity Futures Trading Commission would be more amenable to its proposal than the SEC had been to the Chicago Board's earlier effort. Its expectation was not met.

Walt Vernon's Role

As chief executive officer, it fell to Walt Vernon to see the proposed contract to fruition. Though not himself a futures trader, Vernon was well steeped in the grain business. After taking degrees in business administration and law at Southern Methodist University, he had joined the Dallas-based Campbell-Taggart Baking Company as associate corporate counsel. With his background in law as well as in the grain trade, Vernon was equipped to guide the contract application through the regulatory labyrinth.

Fearing that similar plans were afoot at the other exchanges, Vernon and the new contract committee rushed to complete their application and file it with the CFTC in October 1977. Their haste may have proved to be their undoing, however. Although it was not explicitly stated, the "index of thirty stocks" on which the proposed contract was based could have been nothing other than the Dow Jones Industrial Average.

The use of such a vague label was intended to mollify Dow Jones & Company. That company was, to say the least, unhappy with what it considered an infringement of its property rights, even if the average was not identified by name. Vernon admits that he and his committee did not seriously believe that the association with Dow Jones wouldn't be made. "Obviously," he says, "as a small exchange, we were hoping to capitalize on that."

But Dow Jones wasn't willing to be capitalized upon. Vernon maintains that the company consented to "a sort of gentlemen's agreement"—though nothing of the kind was ever committed to writing—not to oppose the proposal so long as its name was not "involved." If that were the case, both sides seem to have engaged in wishful thinking. Precisely what did "involvement" amount to? The issue was soon resolved in the company's mind as financial journalists, including those at its own *Wall Street Journal,* began writing about the "Dow Jones futures contract."

That was involvement in anyone's book. A lawyer representing Dow Jones telephoned Vernon the day before the CFTC was due to hold public hearings on the anonymous "thirty-stock index" application in 1978 and promised that, "if you proceed, we'll sue you and/or quit publishing the index or worse, if we can figure out worse."

Vernon protested that KCBT was blameless and asked the learned counsel at least to refrain from torpedoing the hearings while he went in search of another index. The Dow Jones lawyer agreed to stay his hand. Says Vernon with little enthusiasm, "I'll have to commend them for being gentlemen enough to understand our problem."

A Long Pipeline

The hearings were held on schedule, with the testimony overwhelmingly in favor of the Kansas City proposal. With his alleged gentlemen's agreement with Dow Jones now a dead letter, Vernon engaged in a brief courtship with Standard & Poor's Corporation on behalf of the S&P 500 Composite Index. However, that company opted for another suitor—the Chicago Mercantile Exchange—and Kansas City finally came to terms with Arnold Bernhard & Company to base a revised contract proposal on the Value Line Composite Average. It had been a bumpy beginning, but the application was in the regulatory pipeline.

It was a very long pipeline—four years long. With scarcely concealed irony, Vernon "credits" the SEC for the inordinate delay in securing the contract's approval. The Securities and Exchange Commission is charged by the Securities Acts of 1933 and 1934 with affording investors protection against assorted nefarious practices engaged in by issuers of, and dealers in, securities. A primary means of providing investor protection is the requirement for full disclosure. The theory behind full disclosure is that if all the pertinent data regarding a particular investment are made available to interested parties—usually in the form of a prospectus—they should be able to arrive at an informed decision.

Vernon makes a distinction between that sort of "regulatory protection" and what he calls "economic protection"—the ability to hedge price risk. Without putting it into so many words, he is saying that while the SEC fretted over whether investors would be sufficiently apprised of the risks associated with trading index futures, those same investors lost in aggregate billions of dollars in market value because they lacked a means of hedging during the protracted stock market decline of 1981–82.

That may be a specious argument. It is problematic how many private investors see themselves as needing or wishing to use stock index futures as hedging instruments. Just as firms such as Pillsbury, General Mills, and Campbell-Taggart Baking are the customary hedgers in the wheat market, whether in Kansas City or Chicago, the large institutional investors are the most likely hedgers in the stock index futures market. The SEC and other regulatory agencies have a cause for concern, however, that traders might turn to index futures as an efficient way to participate in the stock market without realizing that they are assuming a risk that is entirely different and in most cases of a much greater magnitude.

Even so, Vernon does have a point in questioning whether a prospectus or a risk-disclosure statement is adequate protection against the risk of ignorance. He supports the requirement that brokerage firm representatives that deal with the public—and with institutional investors, for that matter—educate their clients about the risk of using futures and obtain information about their customers in determining which investors should trade stock index futures as a speculation or as a hedge and which ones are better off not becoming involved in any way.

Vernon also harbors something less than warm feelings for his industry's regulatory agency, the Commodity Futures Trading Commission. Critical of the commission for dragging its collective feet on the Value Line contract proposal for so long, he wonders to what extent this languor was the result of legitimate concerns of commissioners and staff for investors' protection and how much was simply fear of tackling a thorny issue while the commission's own mandate was before Congress for reconsideration and renewal.

"I try to avoid being paranoid about it," Vernon asserts. "I would not like to think that our application was held up for four years so that the other exchanges could catch up. But in fact they did.

"The CFTC said in 1982 that it wouldn't allow Kansas City a one-year exclusive pilot program because these are free and open competitive markets. The facts are, of course, that if these really are free and open markets, we would have been trading our contract in 1977. They are not free due to the entry barrier of CFTC approval."

Vernon is referring to the Kansas City Board's abortive lawsuit to delay the entry of competing exchanges into the index futures market until it could establish significant trading volume and recoup its start-up costs on the Value Line contract. He claims that Kansas City's motives in bringing the action were misunderstood. What incentive does a small exchange have to develop a new contract, he asks rhetorically, when competitors are free to copy its idea with impunity? His contention—not entirely selfless, to be sure—is that competition is best served by allowing the innovating exchange a grace period in which to gain a secure foothold and to reap the fruits of its efforts, much as a manufacturer is protected by a patent or a publisher by a copyright.

"We have invested more than $1 million in Value Line to date," he says. "What's the incentive to develop a new contract if it's going to be taken away from us? We think it would be in the public interest to give any exchange a year's lead time with a new contract."

Dealing with Washington

Walt Vernon had just returned from Washington. As if he did not have to contend with a sufficient number of public servants in the securities and commodity regulatory agencies, he had to deal with the Federal Reserve Board as well. The Kansas City Board's recent move to reduce the initial margin deposit required on a Value Line contract from $6,500 to $5,000 had provoked a swift and angry response by the Fed, which claimed the reduction would lure too many ordinary investors into the stock index futures market. The old bromide about that hampering efforts to raise capital in public markets was also voiced.

In a rare display of bureaucratic collegiality, the Federal Reserve prevailed upon the chairman of the CFTC to call Vernon and "convey its reservations" about the lower margin. It would afford stock index futures an unfair competitive advantage over other financial instruments and investments, he said. The board also charged that Kansas City had violated its edict that initial margin must be at least 10 percent of a contract's underlying value.[5]

"There's a mind-set among a group of people up there who have been regulating the U.S. economy for about a hundred years," Vernon avers.

"But in Kansas City we've been setting our own margins for a hundred years. We maintain that the stock index contract is a commodity contract and that the Fed's got nothing to do with it.

"They talk about their concern for competing markets, that they want to have equality.

"I didn't say to them, 'baloney.' What I did say was, 'Hey, wait a minute. We don't read the law as establishing that the Fed can eliminate competition between markets.' "

And then there are the congressional committees that in turn regulate the regulators. The House Commerce Committee oversees the SEC, and the House Agriculture Committee performs the same role vis-à-vis the CFTC. Both committees have a stake in the regulatory turf battle.

"I testified before the House Commerce Committee," Vernon recalls, "and in effect, this is what the chairman said to me:

" 'We didn't pay any attention to you people [at the futures exchanges] until you got big and important. Now you've been telling the world how big and important you are, and that's fine.

" 'But let me tell you, Mr. Vernon, we're big and important, too. And what's really important, we regulate. That being the case, now you've got to deal with the Commerce Committee.'

"There are problems galore," concludes Vernon. "There are political problems, power problems, problems with the congressional staff, and SEC problems."

The major problem at present is the strong competition put forth by the larger exchanges. Will he and the Kansas City Board surmount those problems and remain a factor in the stock index futures marketplace? To date, they are maintaining a position and have attracted some national firms to join their market. Or was Kansas City's being the first merely a fluke and deserving only of a paragraph, or perhaps a footnote, when the history of the market is written?

Dry soil and scant rainfall make hard winter wheat grow and give it a high protein content. The grain nourishes itself, and so, one suspects, do the people who trade it in Kansas City.

This book has in its own way been a tale of two cities—New York, the origin and still the center of the national securities market, and Chicago, the seat of the principal commodity markets. As these markets coalesce, it is perhaps not surprising that the impetus should have come from a third city.

Kansas City will probably never rival New York or Chicago as a financial center. But if determination, pluck, and perseverance receive their just deserts, the Kansas City Board of Trade and Value Line stock index futures will be heard from for a long time to come.

NOTES

PART 1

Chapter 1

1. Margaret G. Meyers, *A Financial History of the United States* (New York: Columbia University Press, 1970), 120.

2. Robert Sobel, *Inside Wall Street: Continuity and Change in the Financial District*, (New York: W. W. Norton & Company, 1977), 24.

3. George W. Bishop, Jr., *Charles H. Dow and the Dow Theory*, (New York: Appleton-Century-Crofts, 1960), 38.

4. From 1885 to 1890 Dow was a member and active floor trader of the New York Stock Exchange and consequently knew at first hand whereof he wrote.

5. Quoted by Bishop, *Charles H. Dow*, 111.

6. The original list included:

Chicago & North Western	Northern Pacific Pfd.
D.L.&W.	Pacific Mail
Lake Shore	St. Paul
Louisville & Nashville	Union Pacific
Missouri Pacific	Western Union
New York Central	

7. The volume figures, as reported in the *Wall Street Journal* on June 11, include transactions on the American, Midwest, Pacific, Philadelphia, Boston, and Cincinnati stock exchanges and those reported by the National Association of Securities Dealers and Instinet.

8. Wesley C. Mitchell, *The Making and Using of Index Numbers*, (Washington, D.C.: U.S. Government Printing Office, 1938), 72.

9. Meyers, *Financial History*, 225.

10. The twelve original Dow Jones industrials were:

American Cotton Oil	Laclede Gas
American Sugar	National Lead
American Tobacco	North American
Chicago Gas	Tennessee Coal & Iron
Distilling & Cattle Feeding	U.S. Leather Pfd.
General Electric	U.S. Rubber

11. Some famous corporate names from the past that have been included and were later deleted are: Victor Talking Machine (absorbed by RCA), Famous Players Lasky, Baldwin Locomotive, Hudson Motors, and Wright Aeronautical.

12. Dow Jones & Company provides the following formula to determine the appropriate change in its divisor:

$$\frac{\text{Former divisor}}{\text{Former total value}} = \frac{\text{new divisor}}{\text{new total value}}$$

Or again resorting to our simple example,

$$\frac{3}{10 + 10 + 10} = \frac{2.50}{5 + 10 + 10}$$

(The Dow Jones Averages—A Non-Professional's Guide, [Princeton, N.J.: Dow Jones Educational Services, 1974], 4.)

13. Maurice Farrell, *The Dow Jones Averages 1885–1970* (Princeton, N.J.: Dow Jones Books, 1972), 2.

14. Standard & Poor's Corporation, *Stock Market Encyclopedia of the S&P "500,"* annual reports edition, vol. 4, no. 1, 1982. This is an excellent source for readers who wish to learn more about this particular index and obtain detailed information about the 500 stocks that comprise it.

15. Ibid., iii.

16. The algebraic expression of the S&P 500 computation (and of the New York Stock Exchange Composite Stock Index) is:

$$\text{Index} = \frac{\text{(current stock price} \times \text{number of current shares)}}{f \text{ (base period average price} \times \text{number of shares)}}$$

where f is an adjustment factor to account for the effects of increased capitalization. In the case of stock splits and stock dividends, where an increase in the number of current shares is generally offset by a proportionate decrease in the per-share price, f is unity, and the base value remains unchanged. If, for example, the current total market value of all NYSE-listed stocks were $1,250 billion, and the adjusted base market value were $700 billion, $1,250 billion divided by $700 billion multiplied by the base price of 50.00 produces a current index of 89.29.

17. Standard & Poor's Corporation, *Information Bulletin, S&P 500,* May 1982, 2.

18. See 17 above.

19. New York Stock Exchange, *Common Stock Indexes,* 1980, 2.

20. Assume that a company issues 20 million additional shares of its common stock at a price of $40 a share. If the old market value was $625 billion, the new market value would be $625.8 billion. If the old base value is $500 billion, according to the formula,

$$\frac{625.8 \text{ billion}}{\text{New base value}} = \frac{\$625 \text{ billion}}{\$500 \text{ billion}}$$

New base value × $625 billion = $625.8 billion × $500 billion.
New base value = $500.64 billion. The new index figure is therefore computed as follows:

$$\frac{\$625.8 \text{ billion}}{\$500.64 \text{ billion}} \times 50 = 62.50$$

21. The formula used to compute the Value Line index is:

$$\text{Current index} = II \left(\frac{\text{current closing price}}{\text{previous day's closing price}}\right)^{1/N} \times \text{previous day's index}$$

22. Andrew Tobias, "The Decline and Fall of the Dow Jones Industrials," *New York Magazine,* November 13, 1972, 104.

Chapter 2

1. Edward J. Dies, *The Wheat Pit* (Chicago: Argyle Press, 1925), quoted by Stanley Kroll and Irwin Shishko, *The Commodity Futures Market Guide,* (New York: Harper & Row, 1973), 5.

2. Thomas A. Hieronymus, *Economics of Futures Trading for Commercial and Personal Profit*

(New York: Commodity Research Bureau, 1971), 72. This outstanding book is highly recommended for further reading on futures markets and pricing.

3. Ibid., 73.

4. Ibid., 94.

5. Ibid.

6. Margaret Laws, "Vanguard of the Futures—That's Where Leo Melamed Has Put the Chicago Merc," *Barron's*, March 29, 1982, 28–33.

7. Allan M. Loosigian, *Foreign Exchange Futures* (Homewood, Ill.: Dow Jones–Irwin, 1981), 49.

8. Matthew Winkler, "Struggling NYFE Pins Hopes of Rebound upon Big Board Stock Index Contracts," *Wall Street Journal*, February 8, 1982, 40.

9. "New Futures Contract Based on S&P's Index Is Cleared by the CFTC," *Wall Street Journal*, April 21, 1982, 7.

10. "Court Bars the Comex from Use of S&P Index for Futures Contracts," *Wall Street Journal*, May 14, 1982, 37.

11. The Amex, in turn, licensed the Chicago Board of Trade to introduce a futures contract based upon its Major Market Index. Trading in this contract commenced July 23, 1984.

12. Richard L. Hudson, "Taking a Chance on Stock Index Futures," *Wall Street Journal*, January 26, 1982, 34.

13. Ibid.

14. "Stock Index Futures Get a Robust Start in Kansas City, Mo.," *Wall Street Journal*, February 25, 1982, 38.

Chapter 3

1. See chapter 2, page 28.

2. In the case of physical commodity contracts, a premium price structure is known as contango, or a carrying-charge market. The successively higher contract prices are held to reflect the finance and storage costs of buying the actual commodity and storing it for later delivery in each of the succeeding contract months. With the cash settlement terms of the index contracts, this element of carrying charges would appear to be absent. Some analysts claim that the index contract price structure reflects an implied financing rate that determines the cost of raising investment capital.

3. The percentage would be greater in relation to the lower NYSE index.

4. It has been argued that one reason—perhaps the primary one—for the failure of the American Stock Exchange's venture into futures trading, and for the New York Futures Exchange's initial failure, was the lack of experienced and well-capitalized professional traders who might have provided the liquidity on those exchanges that the locals do on the Chicago exchanges.

5. This may be the first and only book on futures trading that fails to recite the chant "Cut your losses short and let your profits run" in the text. The author cannot see how one more repetition of this supposedly "cardinal" rule will be heeded when the hundreds that have preceded it have not. Yet he obviously cannot resist including it as a note. Writers suffer from herd mentality as much as futures traders do.

6. The ninety-day Eurodollar contract is the only other futures contract at present that contains a cash settlement provision.

7. Readers should be cautioned, however, that much of this information is too detailed to be of direct help in analyzing and forecasting the day-to-day fluctuations in the indexes that are most important in futures trading.

PART 2

Chapter 4

1. Even a target of 1,500 for the DJIA was too modest a forecast for Thomas Blamer and Richard Shulman, who gave their book the arresting title *Dow 3000—Your Chance of a Lifetime for Capital Appreciation before the Dow Jones Average Reaches 3,000 or Higher in 1989* (New York: Wyndham Books, 1982).

2. Arnold Bernhard & Company, *The Value Line Market Averages* (New York, 1982), 2.

3. "The Trouble with the Dow Jones Averages," *Fortune*, March 1972, 143.

4. It should be noted that the term "point" has a slightly different meaning relative to the stock indexes or to their associated futures contracts. In discussing the *contracts* themselves, we have adhered to the common usage of the commodity exchanges, taking one point to be 0.01. In discussing the actual stock *indexes*, however, we have adhered to the common usage of the stock markets and taken one point to be 1.00, or one hundred times a contract point.

5. For the benefit of readers who are indeed attuned to *The Joy of Statistics*, the following formula states in algebraic terms the present value theory of stock price determination. It expresses the current and future price of a stock as:

$$P_1 = d/(1 + K) + P_2/(1 + K)$$

where P_1 = the present price, P_2 = the future price, K = the current cost of capital or discount yield, and d = the current dividend yield.

6. *Basis* is here defined as the spread between a contract price and the spot index.

7. See Allan M. Loosigian, *Foreign Exchange Futures* (Homewood, Ill.: Dow Jones–Irwin, 1981), 166. Statisticians probably have equally complimentary things to say about futures traders.

8. See page 75.

9. Drawing on our brief history of the Chicago Mercantile Exchange in chapter 2, pages 29–31, we might add as a corollary to the multibasket theory, "Sell egg futures instead."

10. A cross-hedge is one in which the futures contract is not based on precisely the same commodity or instrument as the one being hedged. If it isn't analogous to hedging apples with oranges, it would be like hedging McIntosh apples with Baldwins. My grandfather also taught me about that.

Chapter 5

1. J. P. Morgan made the same point with an expression that has since become a cliché. When a reporter asked him how the stock market would react to an imminent banking crisis, Morgan replied that the market would continue to fluctuate.

2. Genesis 41:26. This Old Testament story may provide inspiration for modern-day forecasters. Pharaoh was so impressed by Joseph's perspicacity—we don't know what he thought about the young man's taste in clothes—that he appointed him economics czar of Egypt. Whether a pharaoh outranks a czar is beside the point.

3. The term *business cycle* has been defined by two prominent students of economic analysis in the following way: a type of fluctuation found in the aggregate economic activity of nations that organize their work mainly in business enterprises. A cycle consists of expansions occurring at about the same time in many economic activities, followed by similarly general recessions, contractions, and revivals, which merge into the expansion phase of the next cycle; this sequence of changes is recurrent but not periodic. (Wesley C. Mitchell and Arthur F. Burns, *Measuring Business Cycles* [New York: National Bureau of Economic Research, 1946], 3.)

4. The subject of investor expectations and their effect on stock index futures is treated in detail in chapter 8.

5. These series are updated and published monthly in the following publications: U.S. Department of Commerce, *Business Conditions Digest,* single copy price $5.50, annual subscription price $55.00 domestic, $68.75 foreign; and Council of Economic Advisers, *Economic Indicators,* single copy price $4.25, annual subscription price $25.00 domestic, $31.25 foreign. Subscriptions to both publications may be obtained by writing to: Superintendent of Documents, U.S. Government Printing Office, Washington, D.C. 20402.

6. The following points are drawn from Nathan Belfer, in his article "Economic Indicators," *Financial Analyst's Handbook* (Homewood, Ill.: Dow Jones–Irwin, 1975), 789–99.

7. The government's role and the effect of monetary policy on stock prices is treated at some length in chapter 7.

8. Readers may wish to refer back to the discussion in chapter 4, pages 69–75, of the statistical relationship between the S&P Composite and the other indexes.

9. In this case a more appropriate phrase, and a suitable legend for his family crest as well, might have been "Prepare before you plunge." Or better still, "Plunge in haste, repent at leisure."

10. Alfred L. Malabre, Jr., "Reappraising the Business Cycle," *Wall Street Journal,* July 26, 1982, 16.

Chapter 6

1. Chapter 4, pages 88–89.

2. The technicians will have their turn at bat in chapter 8.

3. Frank E. Block, "The Place of Book Value in Stock Evaluation," *Financial Analyst's Journal,* March–April 1964, 29.

4. Benjamin Graham and David L. Dodd, *Security Analysis: Principles and Prospects,* 3d. ed. (New York: McGraw Hill, 1951).

5. Perhaps I am being presumptuous. Graham and Dodd might have appreciated the opportunity to hedge the market risk of a common stock portfolio with stock index futures.

6. Graham and Dodd, *Security Analysis,* 651.

7. We exclude from this discussion "special situations," or what Wall Street calls "asset plays," where an investor group will buy control of a neglected company for the sole purpose of breaking it up and realizing a gain on the sale of its assets.

8. Most investors recognize what Graham and Dodd call the "capitalization factor" as the price/earnings ratio.

9. Graham and Dodd, *Security Analysis,* 16–17.

10. A few examples of 1929 high and 1933 low prices compared to contemporary quotations should underscore the point.

| | | | September 1, 1982, Close | | |
	1929 High	1933 Low	Actual	Adjusted for Splits	
DuPont	503	22	35⅛	421½	4 for 1 1949
					3 for 1 1979
Sears, Roebuck	197½	9⅞	22½	360	4 for 1 1945
					2 for 1 1965
U.S. Steel	261¾	21¼	19⅛	172¼	3 for 1 1949
					2 for 1 1955
					3 for 2 1976

11. See page 134 for a description of these ratios.

12. If there was in 1982 any company that might be called the "quintessential blue chip," it could very well have been General Electric. It is (literally) a household name, has a large capitalization, a highly regarded management, and is, not illogically, one of the thirty Dow Jones Industrials.

13. Financial information regarding listed corporations and many large unlisted companies is contained in Standard & Poor's *Corporation Records* and in the Value Line *Survey*. Both services are available in many public libraries.

14. In 1976 General Electric merged with Utah International, a major coal and uranium mining company. In connection with the merger, GE's outstanding shares increased from 184.4 million to 226.6 million, but net earnings from that point on included the profits of the mining operation. Seven years later, however, GE divested itself of its stake in UI.

15. This list is adapted from a similar one provided in Charles D. Kuehner, "Efficient Markets and Random Walk," *Financial Analyst's Handbook* (Homewood, Ill.: Dow Jones–Irwin, 1975), 1226–95. The statistics are drawn from the General Electric Company 1981 annual report.

16. That price level was achieved in December 1983.

17. This index is not the one with which we are directly concerned, but the close correlation between the S&P 500 Composite Index and the 400 Industrial Index makes the comparisons shown in figure 6.2 and subsequent charts instructive so far as their application to futures trading is concerned.

18. James H. Lorie and Mary T. Hamilton, *The Stock Market: Theories and Evidence* (Homewood, Ill.: Richard D. Irwin, 1973), 218.

19. This is known in academic jargon as the "efficient-market" hypothesis, which holds that everything that is to be known about a company and its stock is instantly and widely disseminated and discounted, leaving little if any time for investors to capitalize on new information. See chapter 7, page 151, for a further discussion of this hypothesis.

20. See, for example, J.G. Cragg and B. G. Malkiel, "The Consensus and Accuracy of Some Predictions of the Growth of Corporate Earnings," *Journal of Finance,* March 1968, 67–84.

21. As with our earlier illustration involving the S&P 400 Industrial Index, the correlation between that index and the S&P 500 Composite is sufficiently close to make the present value/dividend analysis of value in appraising the outlook for S&P 500 and other index futures. For a more detailed discussion of the determination of present value, see Jerome B. Cohen, Edward D. Zinbarg, and Arthur Zeikel, *Investment Analysis and Portfolio Management* (Homewood, Ill.: Richard D. Irwin, 1977), 230.

22. Readers may refer back to table 6.2 and note how these figures compare with the high and low P/E ratios for General Electric during those years.

23. Graham and Dodd, *Security Analysis,* 415.

Chapter 7

1. Adam Smith, *An Inquiry into the Nature and Causes of the Wealth of Nations: Representative Selections* (Indianapolis: Bobbs-Merrill, 1961). Originally published in London, 1776.

2. In view of his resounding electoral victory in 1984, most Americans apparently believed the President had made good on his campaign promises.

3. Charles Maurice de Talleyrand (1754–1838) is reputed to have said, "War is much too serious a thing to be left to military men." Clemenceau attributed a similar statement to himself and was quoted to that effect by the New York Times, July 14, 1944. From *The Quotation Dictionary* (New York: Collier Books, 1967).

4. Article I, Section 8.

5. "You shall not press down upon the brow of labor this crown of thorns, you shall not

crucify mankind upon a cross of gold." Speech at the Democratic National Convention," Chicago, 1896.

6. John Maynard Keynes, *The General Theory of Employment, Interest, and Money* (New York: Harcourt, Brace and Company, 1936).

7. This is the usage that will be observed through the remainder of this chapter.

8. The eleven other district Federal Reserve Banks are situated in Boston, Philadelphia, Cleveland, Richmond, Atlanta, Chicago, St. Louis, Minneapolis, Kansas City, Dallas, and San Francisco. There are in addition twenty-four district branch banks that serve outlying areas within some districts.

9. For the sake of simplicity and clarity, the following sketches include only the expansion measures taken by the Federal Reserve to counter recession. A similar calendar may be drawn of restraining moves.

10. Readers may refer back to pages 104–105.

11. Money supply figures are reported by the Federal Reserve each Thursday after the close of the securities markets and are published in the following day's newspapers. Monthly statistics are published in the *Federal Reserve Bulletin*.

12. Beryl W. Sprinkel, "Monetary Policy and Financial Markets," *Financial Analyst's Handbook*, vol. 1, *Portfolio Management*, Sumner N. Levine, ed. in chief (Homewood, Ill.: Dow Jones–Irwin, 1975), 811–12.

13. Michael W. Keran, "Expectations, Money and the Stock Market," Federal Reserve Bank of St. Louis *Review*, January 1971, 16.

14. See, for example, Kenneth E. Homa and Dwight M. Jaffe, "The Supply of Money and Common Stock Prices," *Journal of Finance*, December 1971, 1056–66.

15. Since 1974 the board has announced publicly the limits within which it will endeavor to maintain money supply growth. Although the board is not always successful in keeping money growth within the stated limits, particularly on a month-to-month basis, the announced limits at least offer Fed watchers a rough indication of the board's probable intentions.

16. Michael S. Rozeff, "The Money Supply and the Stock Market—The Demise of a Leading Indicator," *Financial Analyst's Journal*, September–October 1975, 18–26.

17. Readers are reminded of the Phil Plunger episode that concluded chapter 5, pages 107–110.

18. If the nominal money supply is growing at, say, an annual rate of 4 percent but the general price level is rising at a 6 percent annual rate, the money supply in real terms is contracting at a rate of 2 percent a year.

19. For this reason interest rates, like M_1 and other economic variables, are measured in both nominal and inflation-adjusted, or "real," terms.

20. Since the bulk of member bank reserves takes the form of deposits held by the district Federal Reserve Banks, the borrowing and lending of federal funds among member banks is done by means of book entries noting the addition to or deduction from reserve accounts.

21. "Washington Whispers," *U.S. News & World Report,* August 2, 1982, 16.

22. Ibid., August 30, 1982, 11.

Chapter 8

1. One such editorial was "Watching the Tide," quoted in part on page 7.

2. William P. Hamilton, *The Stock Market Barometer* (New York: Harper & Brothers, 1921).

3. Robert Rhea, *The Dow Theory* (New York: Barron's, 1932). Dow Jones and Company no longer has any relationship, formal or otherwise, with the Dow theory.

4. But the railroads during their heyday also carried large passenger loads.

5. On June 30, 1966, the Dow Jones Industrial Average was 870.10. On June 30, 1978, it was 818.95, a net decline of 51.15 points, or 5.9 percent.

6. Readers may refer back to figures 7.2 and 7.3 on pages 150 and 155.

7. Because they are more familiar to investors and traders, bar charts will be used exclusively in the examples in this and in following chapters.

8. Writers have their problems, just as analysts and traders do. Although we've noted more than once that an index number is not in the strict sense a price, it is awkward to have to point this out every time the term is used. I therefore ask that readers tolerate my occasional use of the term *index price*, even though there is no such thing.

9. Two that are very good are Robert D. Edwards and John Magee, *Technical Analysis of Stock Trends*, 4th ed. (Springfield, Mass.: John Magee, 1958), and Martin J. Pring, *Technical Analysis Explained: An Illustrated Guide for the Investor* (New York: McGraw-Hill, 1980).

10. Stanley Kroll and Irwin Shishko, *The Commodity Futures Market Guide* (New York: Harper & Row, 1973), 143.

11. Ibid., 144.

12. A moving average is computed by taking an average of the most recent specified period and repeating the process daily, dropping the first number of the series and adding the latest one. For example, the ten-day average of the December 1982 NYSE Composite futures contract on September 1, 1982, was 66.60. On September 15 it stood at 69.85, and on September 30 at 70.45.

13. This index is reported monthly, along with the other economic indicators discussed in chapter 5, in the U.S. Department of Commerce publication *Business Conditions Digest*.

14. George Katona, *Psychological Economics* (New York: Elsevier, 1975), 266.

15. Katona, *Psychological Economics*, 267.

16. Katona, *Psychological Economics*, 270.

17. Frederick C. Klein and John A. Prestbo, *News and the Market* (Chicago: Henry Regnery Company, 1974), 108.

18. John W. Schulz, "Messing Up the Tea Leaves: Where Technical Analysis Went Wrong," *Barron's*, September 13, 1982, 15–19.

PART 3

Chapter 9

1. See page 178.

2. NYFE planned to introduce a contract based on the forty-six stock transportation subindex at a later date.

3. At the time the three subindex contracts were approved, the NYSE Industrial index was about 80.00, the Financial index about 71.00, and the Utility index about 40.00, making those contracts worth about $80,000, $71,000, and $80,000, respectively.

4. See pages 115–122.

5. A call is the right to buy one hundred shares of a particular stock at a stated price ("strike price") for a specified period of time. The value of a call increases as the market price of the stock rises. A put is the right to sell one hundred shares of stock at a stated price for a specified period of time. The value of a put increases as the market price of the stock declines.

6. On January 5, 1983, the New York Futures Exchange announced the election of Lew Horowitz as its president. He is still moving.

7. The State Street managers employ quantitative tests that "filter" out of the fund any stocks that comprise potential bankruptcy risks. That may at any time amount to five to twenty stocks out of the five hundred contained in the S&P Composite list.

8. See chapter 4, pages 75–77, for a discussion of the movement of futures prices between premiums and discounts relative to the spot index.

9. An example of this type of arbitrage is selling General Motors shares on the New York Stock Exchange at 48 while at the same time buying them on the Pacific Coast Exchange for 47 1/2. With the introduction of the consolidated stock ticker including prices on all exchanges, this sort of price disparity has become increasingly infrequent.

10. See chapter 4, pages 86–89, for an explanation of beta values.

11. The U.S. Department of Labor ruled at the close of 1982 that margin accounts will under certain circumstances be acceptable for pension funds, thereby opening the door for the use of futures in individual pension accounts.

Chapter 10

1. That is true when the call writer is covered, or owns the underlying stock. The profit potential–risk relationship is drastically different when the call writer is "naked," which means he or she doesn't own the shares against which the call was written.

2. See page 90.

3. Eugene Moriarty, Susan Phillips, and Paula Tosini, "A Comparison of Options and Futures in the Management of Portfolio Risk," *Financial Analyst's Journal*, January–February 1981, 61–67. The hedge examples depicted in tables 10.1 and 10.2 were adapted from similar examples in this article.

4. Walter Vernon is now president of Bartlett Futures in Kansas City.

5. "Kansas Board Raises Stock Index Margin, Bowing to Regulators," *Wall Street Journal*, October 25, 1982, 46.

INDEX

Page numbers in bold refer to figures.
Page numbers in italics refer to tables.

and General Electric average Price/
  Earnings multiples, *132*
  history, *7, 10*
  method of determining, 11–14
  relative volatility, *87*
  twelve month unit earnings figure,
    130
  30 Industrials, *13*
    eleven-year highs and lows, *68*
    price ranking at 1982 lows and
      highs, *67*
  Transportation Average, 11–12, **12**
  Utility Average, 11–12, **12**
Dow theory, 159–62, 169–70, 182
  basic principles, 160
  The Dow Theory, 159
Downtrend, 169, 171, 177

Earnings. *See also* Price/earnings ratio
  after tax, ratio to current-dollar GNP
    growth, *125*
  company's, 113
  eclectic method of projecting, 119–22
  forecasting, 119–33
  momentum, 207
  per share, 116, 119, 121
    and P/E ratios, 1981 and estimated
      1982 DJIA, *129*
  scientific method of projecting, 119–22
Eclectic method of projecting future
    earnings, 119–22
*The Economic Consequences of the
    Peace,* 141
Economic indicators, 91–92, 101–7
Efficient-market theory, 151–52
Eggs, 29
Eisenhower, Dwight D., 140
England-Markun, Mark, 195–205
Equity, 58–60
  cost of capital, 76–77, 84
Eurodollar time deposits, 32
Excess, 60
Exchange(s). *See also* specific exchanges
  commodity, 23–24
  futures, 50–51
  members, 49–50
  stock, 50
  traders, 51–53, 187–95
Exhaustion gap, 176

Expectations, 46–47
Exposure, 193, 201, 209, 214–16

F. Martin Koenig & Company, 205–16
Federal funds rate, 153–54
Federal Home Loan Mortgage
    Corporation, 32
Federal Open Market Committee, 146–49
Federal Reserve
  Bank of New York, 144–46
  Banks, 144–49
  Board (of Governors), 38, 49, 102,
    145, 148–49, 156, 222
  Index of Industrial Production, 96
  Index versus S&P 500, **97**
  easing measures versus S&P 500,
    1960–82, **150**
  policy, 147–56, 183
  System, 144–50, *145*
Financial Analysts Journal, 62
Financial data, selected, General
    Electric Company, *118*
Financial ratios, 121
Floor trading, 187–95. *See also* Traders;
    Trading
Forecasting
  earnings, 119–22, 124–33
  sales, 124–33
Forward contracting, 26–28
Friedman, Milton, 31
Full Employment Act of 1946, 144
Fundamental analysis, 111–13, 207–8
  primary elements of stock value,
    113–14
Futures. *See also* Contracts; Stock index
    futures
  commodity, 30. *See also* Forward
    contracting
  exchanges. *See also* Exchange(s);
    specific exchanges
  commodity, 23–24
  organization, 50–51
  foreign currencies, 30–31
  interest rate, 31–32
  margins, 48–49
  options, 193–94, 205–16
  subindex, 191–93, 201
  traders, 51–53, 187–95

News and stock prices, 181
NYFE. *See* New York Futures Exchange
NYSE. *See* New York Stock Exchange

Odd-lot transactions, 163–64
One-sided arbitrage, 199
One-year Treasury bills, 32
Open interest, 176–77
Open market purchases and sales, 147, 149
Open order, 55
Option(s), 193–94, 205–16
  premium, 193
Orders
  good till cancelled, 55
  open, 55
  placement and execution of, **54**
  stop, 55–56
  types of, 53–56
Outlook, 15
Output per labor hour worked, matrix of estimated changes in, corporate profits, real GNP, and general price levels, *124*
Outside paper, 51

Paine Webber, 51
Pension fund, 197–98, 202–3, 205–7
Point-and-figure. *See also* Chart(s)
  chart for December 1982 NYSE Composite, **170**
  system, 166–68
Poor's Directory of American Officials, 15
Poor's Financial Services, 15
Poor's Manual, 15
Poor, Henry Varnum, 15
Portfolio hedging. *See* Hedging, 214
Portfolio, hedged, quarterly summary, *90*
Position traders, 53, 189
Premium, 193
Premium price structure, 47
Price
  charts, 165–72. *See also* Chart(s)
  /earnings ratio(s), 117, 122, 126, 130–33, 135–37, 154, 208
  and earnings per share, 1981 and estimated 1982 DJIA, *129*
  S&P 500 Index, 1950–75, *136*
  Standard & Poor's 500 Index, 1964–81, *136*

levels, general, matrix, of estimated changes in, corporate profits, real GNP, and output per labor hour worked, *124*
structure
  discount, 47
  premium, 47
Primary trends, 160, *161*
Projecting future earnings, 119–22. *See also* Forecasting
Protracted trend, 207
Prudential-Bache, 51
Psychology, 179–81
Purchase and sale statement, 58
Put options. *See* Options

Rail averages, 160
Railroad stocks, 10
Reagan, Ronald, 140, 156
Reaganomics, 140, 155–56
Recession, 94, 96, 98, 147–50
Regression analysis, 85–86
Reserve requirements, 146–49
Resistance, 172–73
Rhea, Robert, 159–60
Risk(s), 88–90
  company-related, 111
  component, 207
  downmarket, 215
  market-related, 111, 209
  premiums, 28
Round turn, 49
Runaway gap, 175–76, **176**
Runners, 50

Sales, forecasting, 124–33. *See also* Forecasting
S&P. *See* Standard & Poor's
Scalpers, 52, 188
Scientific method of projecting future earnings, 119–22
Secondary trends, 160, *161*
Securities Acts of 1933 and 1934, 220
Security analysis, 111–37, 207
Security Analysis, 112
Securities and Exchange Commission, 37, 38–39, 218–20, 222
Selling-climax theory, 182–83
Share prices, determining, *127*
Shearson Lehman Brothers, 51

Stock value, fundamentalists primary
    elements, 113–14
Stock volatility, 208
Stocks, most active, *8*
Stop limit price, 56
Stop orders, 55–56. *See also* Orders
Strike price, 209–10
Subindex futures, 191–93, 201
Support, 172–73
Survey of Current Business, 98
Synthetic contracts, 214–16

T-bill. *See* U.S. Treasury bills
Technical
    analysis, 111–13, 159, 207–8
    evaluating, 181–84
    indicators, 162–65
Trade confirmation, 58, **59**
Traders, 51–53
    day, 52–53, 188–89
    floor, 187–95
    position, 53, 189
    scalpers, 52, 189
Trading, volume, 176–77, 208
Treasury bonds, 32
Treasury Department, 38, 145
Trend(s), 160, *161*
    channel(s), 172, 182
    December 1982 Value Line, **171**
    deviation, 208
    down, 169, 171, 177
    -line, 169–72, 182
    primary, 160, *161*
    protracted, 207
    reversal, 173–79
    secondary, 160, *161*
    spotting, 190–91
    up, 169–71, 177
Triangle formation, 175, **175**. *See also*
    Chart(s)
Trust, 10
Twelve month earnings figure, 130

U.S. Department of Commerce, 98, 102
U.S. Treasury bills, 32
U.S. Treasury Department, 38, 145
Unemployment, 154
Unemployment insurance, average
    weekly initial claims, *103,* 104

University of California Center for Real
    Estate and Urban Economics, 32
University of Michigan, 180–81
Unsystematic risk, 88–90
Up- and downtrend channels, December
    1982 Value Line, **171**
Uptrend, 169–71

Value Line (Average) Composite Index
    (VLA) (VLI), 35, 42, 62, 220
    about, 18–21
    beta value versus S&P 500 Index, *88*
    compared with other indexes, 69–75,
        71
    correlation coefficients with DJIA, S&P
        500, 1971–82, *86*
    (KCBT) futures contracts, 42–44, 78,
        183, 221. *See also* Kansas City
        Board of Trade; Stock index futures
    prices, *78, 80*
    relative volatility, *87*
    versus S&P 500 Index, **72, 74, 75**
    versus Value Line Index (KCBT)
        futures contract, *81*
Vendor performance, *103,* 104
Vernon, Walter N., III, 34, 217, 219–22
VLA or VLI. *See* Value Line (Average)
    Composite Index
Volatility, 122, 208
Volcker, Paul, 31

Wall Street, history, 3–7
Wall Street Journal, 37, 60, 181, 219
    history, 6–7
Watching the Tide, 6–7, 169
The Wealth of Nations, 139
Weighting, 9–10
    capitalization-, 16
    Dow Jones Averages, 14
    New York Stock Exchange Composite
        Index, 16–17
    Standard & Poor's 500 Index, 16
    ten most heavily weighted groups,
        17
Western Union, 4–5
Wheat, 25–27
    and corn prices at Chicago, *26*
Workweek, average, *103,* 104